Published by

ATLANTIC

PUBLISHERS & DISTRIBUTORS (P) LTD

7/22, Ansari Road, Darya Ganj, New Delhi-110002
Phones : +91-11-40775252, 40775214, 23273880, 23275880
Fax: +91-11-23285873
Web: www.atlanticbooks.com
E-mail: orders@atlanticbooks.com

Printed & bound in India by Atlantic Print Services

DEDICATION TO

The sweet memories of my dear father,

SUDHIR CHANDRA SARKER,

and my loving mother,

NILIMA SARKER,

I dedicate this labour of my old age.

Preface

Shakespeare has hugely been critically dealt with layer by layer and shred in volumes after volumes (remember the catalogue of the Folger Shakespeare Library, NY) and yet Thomas Carlyle's "second God" remains not fully explored. His biographical donnes have been poorly related to his plays; the reflections of his personal values have been scantily identified in his plays; his philosophy has not been definitely figured out in his works; in his collaborative plays his own contributions have not been indubitably earmarked; his borrowings from classical and contemporary dramatists have not as yet been fully explored; etcetera and etcetera. And to add to all these dark corners, some other very vital components of his dramatic oeuvres regrettably remain incognito till today. One such essential component in his plays is *dramatic embellishing* and this has largely been ignored by Shakespearean scholars. By *dramatic embellishing* I mean the special devices with which the dramatist enhances the moment or valuc of his plays. The contribution of these dramatic devices on the plays on the stage is enormous. But, unfortunately, these familiar phenomena in the plays of the bard are overlooked by Shakespearean scholars.

Therefore, there remains a huge hiatus in the Shakespearean scholarship, and my endeavour in this book has been to demonstrate how Shakespeare has immensely enriched his plays with his dramatic devices for embellishing his plays and how, defying Aristotle's dictum against commingling the tragic and the comedic in drama, he has prudently employed *dramatic embellishments* in all his 37 plays but only three—*Henry VI*, *Comedy of Errors,* and *King John*—as special effects, for effectual dramatic enrichments.

As a minor amateur actor in Bengali *Jatras* (theatres 'in the round') for some years, I have, perhaps, gained a little knowledge of the true nature of the theatre and the contributions of the dramatic *embellishing devices* in theatrical performances, and have, here in this book, strived to demonstrate how and to what extent the *dramatic embellishments* can enhance the effect of the plays on the audience.

I claim here no originality, whatsoever, but invite Shakespearean scholars to critically explore Shakespeare's use of his *dramatic embellishments* in his plays.

My wife, Manju, has typed out the whole manuscript of this book, I thank her. I am grateful to Atlantic Publishers and Distributors (P) Ltd., New Delhi, and, specially, to Shri Harjeet Singh Ji of that firm for getting the book published rather quickly even during the Covid-19 pandemic.

Sunil Kumar Sarker

Contents

1
Introduction

The best homage to Shakespeare was fashioned by Ben Jonson in his poem "To the memory of my beloved, the author, Mr. William Shakespeare and what he hath left us", in which Jonson gave the bard two most appropriate and insuperable encomiums "Soul of our age!", and a few lines down, "He was not of an age, but for all time." The first encomium is of course nestled in the second. The veracity of the first Jonson himself saw with own eyes; that of the second we are observing, as those who will be coming after us will continue to observe even in the distant future. For over four hundred years now, Shakespeare is not only alive but vibrant. How can this be? During these four hundred years, mother earth has produced, say, not less than four thousand dramatists all over the world. Why then none other than Shakespeare can claim immortality? During these four thousand years, there have been thousands social, cultural, philosophical, scientific, historical, political, religious and aesthetic changes in our human history. But Shakespeare has been shining all the while like the load star. Could we now go back to the hoary Elizabethan age boarding a time machine, we could see it as a somewhat strange, outlandish, bizarre age. Nothing would we see there like ours: neither the language, nor the habit, nor the habitation, nor the humour, nor the hobby, nor the whim, nor the hope, nor the hoop-la. Strange it is that Shakespeare created his plays just in that Elizabethan time and in that human space and still they do not seem to us distant. The mystery?

The mystery is that Shakespeare learnt the secret of the dramatic art not from any black-and-white book but from the open book of the world—from the book of life, that is, his instinct was to observe human behaviour; his drive was toward drama. Luckily—and perhaps luckily for us more than for him—early in his life he was exposed to be a spectator in a few theatrical performances in and around Stratford-on-Avon, and what was written from there on a youth's *tabula rasa* was naturally un-erasable. Shakespeare's early exposure to the world of drama fired his most powerful imagination. Maybe, he then imagined himself on the "wooden O" or resting his head on one of his hand with a pen in the other. God destined him to be a poet and a dramatist, and so his Muse contrived a compelling situation for him to go into self-exile in London, the city then vibrant with dramatic performances in the post-meridian solar glow. Let us see what plot did the Muse invent for him to tether him in the world of drama.

Sometime around 1582 at the age of about 18 years, Shakespeare, as luck would have it, fell into the trap of sensuality with Ann Hathaway, a woman eight years older than himself, and in that very year was forced to marry her because she was five months pregnant. Ann delivered a girl, Susanna, five months afterwards. Two years later on, Ann gave birth to a twin: Hamnet and Judith. Shakespeare's father, once a bailiff and moderately flourishing gloves and/or wool trader, earlier had became financially extremely straightened due to the dwindling of his business when Shakespeare was around 14 years old. John Shakespeare, his father, was forced by his impecuniosity to discontinue William's (our Shakespeare's) education in the Grammar school. His father could hardly sustain his big family of ten members. This is attested by Charles Knight: "In 1578, John Shakespeare mortgaged his property of Asbies, acquired by marriage. Four years before this he purchased two freehold houses in Stratford, which he always retained. In 1578, therefore, he wanted capital. In 1579, he sold an interest in some property at Snitterfield. But then, in 1580, he tendered the mortgage money to the mortgagee of the Asbies' estate, which was illegally refused, on the pretence that other money was owing. A Chancery suit was the consequence, which was undetermined in 1597. In an action for debt in the bailiff's court in 1586, the return of the sergeant-at-mace upon a warrant of distress against John Shakespeare is, that he had nothing to distrain upon. It is held, therefore, that all the household gear was then gone" (Charles Knight, 287). Shakespeare, now about 21, with a desperate view to save his family, one day, *solus*, suddenly rode a horse of his teacher and raced to an unknown destination with an unknown future. He rode to London, about 83 miles (134 kilometres) away.

This impetuosity (was it so?) of the young Shakespeare some critics explain very simply thus. Shakespeare did not see any financial succour in the village of Stratford and imagined it to be there in the city of London. But this cannot explain the whole of Shakespeare's self-exile. To an unknown destination with an unknown future—was there in him only a single motive or double? Was he only after coins, or also after creations? No; not only coins. The native poetic genius of Shakespeare was seeking something else as well—an opportunity of bursting forth. The spectacles of the theatrical performances that he viewed in Stratford in his young days were nagging after him like spectres. Great genius enkindles itself, sometimes desperately, hardly showing prudence. Perhaps his imagination around the stage got the upper hand rather than his seeking of source of financial succour, though, of course the two lucres showed insinuations all at the same time. Let us elaborate a little.

The Roman emperor Julius Caesar invaded England twice—in 55 B.C. and again in 54 B.C.—and went away plundering huge amounts of gold, silver and other materials. And after 89 years, the Roman Emperor Claudius, not being interested in plundering, occupied the land in 43 A.D. The colonial England was forced to adopt Roman law and culture as its own. Latin became the official language of the land. Roman missionaries poured into England and Christianity subplanted the prevailing druidism. Roman entertainments, such as chariot race, gladiatorial shows, etc. came into England and amphitheatres were built for the purpose. The Romans brought into their colony their own popular dramatic entertainments, which developed under the influence of the Greeks since before the birth of Christ. So, when they came into England the Grecian dramatic devices, such as masks, mimes, puppet shows, clowning, etc. followed them.

The Romans withdrew from England in 410 A.D., after 367 years of their overlordship, leaving behind their dramatic entertainments. The autochthonous mystery (or miracle) and morality pageants, which survived the Roman acculturation, continued to influence the nascent native dramatic endeavours. Additionally, there were medieval interludes, mummers' plays, mimes and even puppet shows—all that gradually came to England from other parts of Europe in the wake of the Roman invasion.

It is very possible that when these species of dramatic performances were flourishing in England, Shakespeare, who was in his teens, must have had spectating experiences of some of them and thereby was influenced by them at least to some extent because Stratford (in Warwick) was not very far from London—the central place of the country where these entertainments were galore—from where companies of performers of these species of entertainments would sometimes visit the countryside around London, including Stratford. Naturally, then, to repeat, as a young adult, Shakespeare might have witnessed some of these performances, particularly when Shakespeare's father was the bailiff of Stratford. And at one point of time, in Stratford itself there were at least three theatrical companies whose performances, we may, presume, Shakespeare must have witnessed in his young years. Here Charles Knight in his *William Shakespeare: A Biography,* has more: "It thus appears that there had been three sets of players at Stratford within a short distance of the time when William Shakspere [Shakespeare] was sixteen years of age. We shall here endeavour to present a general view of the state of the stage at this point of its history; with reference to the impressions which theatrical performances would then make upon him who would be the chief instrument in building up upon these rude foundations a noble and poetical drama" (Charles Knight, 122).

In Stratford, it was the tradition that any willing theatrical company would first show their performance before the bailiff and his men in order to get licence for performances in that town. As we have said, Shakespeare's father was for a term the bailiff of Stratford when Shakespeare was a boy. So, it is very probable that Shakespeare had opportunities of watching performances of some those theatrical companies. Charles Knight very interestingly further writes: "The first performance of each company in this town [Stratford] was the bailiff's, or chief magistrate's, play; and thus, when the father of William Shakespere [Shakespeare] was bailiff; the boy might have stood 'between the legs as he [father of Shakespeare] sat upon one of the benches'. It would appear from Willis's [R. Willis's] description that 'The Cradle of Security' [a dramatic performance] was for the most part dumb show. It is probable that he [Shakespeare] was present at its performance at Glouchester when he was six or seven years of age;..." (Charles Knight, 123). We know that in Shakespeare's young years at least three theatrical companies performed in Stratford: the Queen's Players, the Earl of Worcester's Players, and the Earl of Leicester's Players.

Charles Knight's presumption that Shakespeare in his young days witnessed theatrical performances in Stratford itself is attested also by Edgar I. Fripp in his two-volume *Shakespeare: Man and Artist*. In this book, Fripp seems to asseverate that when Shakespeare 'was at least sixteen', he witnessed at least one play, *The Harrowing of Hell*. And Fripp supports his affirmation by producing evidence: "That Shakespeare witnessed it is a natural inference from his allusions to the swaggering *Herod*, *Death Mouth*, and *Porter of Hell*, and his repeated introduction of 'morality' elements in his drama. He had not merely read Matthew ii, 16-18, but seen the story in drama to write such lines as:

> Your naked infants spitted upon spikes
> Whiles the mad mothers, with their howls confus'd
> Do break the clouds, as did the wives of Jewry
> At Herod's bloody-hunting *slaughtermen*;

or, 'I would have such a fellow whipped for o'erdoing Termagant; it out-herods *Herod*'" (*italics mine*) (Fripp, 56-57). Fripp has given five references to the above quotation thus: (1) 'Herod' in *Merry Wives*, II, i, 20; (2) 'Death Mouth' in *K. John*, II, i, 455; (3) 'Poter of Hell' in *Macb*, II, iii, 2; (4) 'slaughtermen' in

Hen. V, III, iii 38-41; and (5) 'out-herod Herod' in *Haml.* III, ii, 15f. (*ibid.*).

Following the above, we cannot agree with what Adolphus William Ward writes in his *A History of English Dramatic Literature* that we cannot be certain about why Shakespeare chose to associate himself with the dramatic circle in London rather than sought some other source of earning for his family in Stratford: "The motives which determined this choice [of Shakespeare] *are unknown...*" (*italics mine*) (Ward, vol. I, 490). We rather say that Shakespeare deliberately made this choice. The reason is not far to seek. The small town of Stratford and elsewhere around it, travelling dramatic companies from London not very rarely frequented for performances, where theatrical performances were in demand. "Everywhere there was amateur acting, and it was good—traditional and trained. We hear of May day performances at Shrewsbury in 1549 and Gloucester in 1553."—writes Fripp (Fripp, vol. I, 57). As the theatre was inchingly coming away from the church, the 'vagabonds' and 'rogues'—as earlier the players were considered as—grew in prestige and were regarded as 'gentlemen'. Our young Shakespeare must have got his native poetic imagination fired by the acting of the local and travelling companies and, additionally, was attracted by the prestige and economic value of the profession. Therefore, perhaps it did not take much time for Shakespeare to decide his future course of life, to choose his dream profession—that of the dramaturge.

Shakespeare did not go to London with a mind blank of all the memories of several theatrical devices that he happened to witness in the mystery plays, morality plays, pageants, comedia dell'arte, and perhaps even in the ancient English puppet theatres in Stratford. When sometime around 1585, at about 21 years of age, he rode towards London he did not forget all the cherished things of all the dramatic performances that he watched—the fiery dialogues, the physical movements, the laughs and weeping, the songs, and the dramatic embellishments, such as ghosts, witches, heaven, hell, angels, masques, music, songs, dances, etc., as we may understand from the above-mentioned information from Fripp (p. 3). And all these things he has accommodated in his plays, because he had seen that these things the people enjoyed much. Shakespeare did not write plays to show himself as a great dramatic artist but to entertain the mixed theatregoers, the high and the low—those of the purple sphere and those of the lowest rung of the society—so he could shore up greater amount of money. His enterprise was not literary but rather commercial. All the same, he could not hold back his poetic fury and dramatic impulse that, of necessity, tried to burst forth in his creations, which naturally he surely enjoyed, because, as we have said, he must have dreamt of acting like the actors that he saw in his young days in Stratford, and, more than that, of composing plays like those, or better than those, he saw being performed there.

This fact critics fail to notice. Shakespeare was a born poet. One popular story about him is that to help his father who, to supplement his meagre income took up the business of butchery, he would at times slaughter bulls, and before doing this exercise he would sometimes recite some extempore poetry in high pitched voice. This is merely an anecdote, but people do not create an anecdote without even a faint rhyme or reason. We may not believe the anecdote at its face value, but it perhaps suggests the young Shakespeare's poetic bent of mind. This acorn of a poet was only waiting for earth and water, which it found in London, and burst forth into an oak. Shakespeare, the acorn, went to London with the memories of the theatres in Stratford and his native poetic genius. Here we may profitably quote at some length what Sir Walter Raleigh, a very close contemporary of Shakespeare, writes in his book *Shakespeare*: "The dramatic opportunities of Stratford counted for something in his [Shakespeare's] history. Primitive drama flourishes everywhere in children's games. The rural communities of Elizabethan England did not leave the drama to children, but enlivened the festivals of the year with ancient plays and pastimes, which served to break the dull round of country life. The Morris dance was a kind of drama; Shakespeare knew it well, and alludes to Maid Marian and the hobby-horse. The rustic play of St. George has lasted in quiet districts down to our day; Shakespeare had often been entertained by this uncouth kind of acting, and preserves memories of it in *A Midsummer Night's Dream*, or, better, in *Love's Labour's Lost*. The Pageant of the Nine Worthies, presented by the schoolmaster, the curate, the unlettered Costered, and the refined traveler from Spain, is a fair specimen of the dramatic art as it was practised in villages [like Stratford]" (Raleigh, 95).

So while going to London, let us repeat, Shakespeare took in his mind the remembrances of the dramatic performances he saw in Stratford, including the wonder-works of the dramatic devises in those performances. He perhaps wondered how the people in the audience suspended their disbelief and imagined the 'Nathaniels' to be 'Alisanders' (*Love's Labour's Lost*); how a "man, with lime and rough-cast, doth present/ Wall, that vile wall" and a "man, with lanthorn, dog, and bush of thorn,/ Presenteth Moonshine" (*A Midsummer Night's Dream*); and how dances make peoples' heart dance and songs humanize them. He learned the many other things of the devices of the theatre—prologue, epilogue, chorus, clown, dumb show, masque, ghost, witch, and especially of the most influential components of the theatre—music. And of course what he learned about dialogue and its delivery; emotion and its expression; plot and its development; etc. He learnt not less; though his knowledge was rudimentary, his genius was nonpareil. Can we not then say that Shakespeare learnt the secrets of the theatre first in his birthplace Stratford? His embryonic knowledge of drama he improved while acting in the theatres in London and when he was tasked to alter and adapt existing plays for performances. His knowledge was not bookish, he got it through his wondering insight into the theatrical performances both in Stratford and in London.

A glance of Shakespeare's deep and wide wisdom about the theatre we may have from Hamlet's instructions to the 'Players'. But here, we will scoop out just a phrase from his long speech there—"mirror up to nature". This phrase is nearly the open sesame to all of Shakespeare's plays. And here lies the unconcealment of the mystery of Shakespeare's greatness: Shakespeare is the "Soul of the age!/ The applause, delight, the wonder of our stage!" and "He was not of an age but for all time!" The secret of Shakespeare is that his plays truly and adequately reflect the reality as no other dramatist's. Greek tragedies we admire all right, but they are not absolutely true to reality. They are abstract, in the sense that they are pure tragedy void of even inklings of lighter moods. The world is never absolutely tragic and never exclusively comedic; it is ever a blend of the two, in different ratios at various moments and at sundry places. Aristotle, the connoisseur of Greek tragedies, failed to see that reality is a mixed show of both tragic and comic events. Shakespeare, we may say, rightly corrected him. It is for this reason that in Shakespeare's tragedies there are comical veins as in his comedies the are tragical events. People want to see on the stage a concentrated mirror image of the reality that they inhabit, unsifted and unreformed. Shakespeare shows us this reality in its true perspective. This is why he is ubiquitous and immortal.

But how has he represented the reality on the stage—the reality of human life? Shakespeare could penetrate the core of the nature of human beings and he knew how to show human beings' true nature on the "wooden O". Human nature is ubiquitous and perennial, whatever surface changes man may betray in divers' spatiotemporal co-ordinates. Universality is the signature of core human nature. Shakespeare held fast on to this universal human nature on the stage. But to do this he designed several contrivances. Firstly, his plays are built up on universal and perennial themes of humankind—themes that are tied to man's inalienable instincts (and accompanying passions), such as love, hate, jealousy, pride, ambition, lust, vengeance, etc. as well as man's deep-seated sense of justice. Secondly, he has created many an appropriate character through which to disclose these hard-core instinctual properties of human beings—characters such as Romeo, Juliet, Macbeth, Othello, Julius Caesar, Coriolanus, Tamora, Lear, Prospero, etc. Thirdly, to make the dramatic illusion on the stage seem but real, Shakespeare has appealed to the audience to see not with their physical eyes but with their imaginative eyes. Fourthly, Shakespeare has resorted to the device of what is known in oratory as *ad captandum*, i.e., appealing to the audience's emotion. Shakespeare does this through poetic verve, through the intoxicating rhythms of his poetry.

But these are not all with which Shakespeare could make dramas life-like. Life has much more than all these. Had there been only all these, Shakespeare's theatre would be what the celebrated theatre-director Peter Brook calls "Deadly Theatre". In his *The Empty Space*, Brook speaks of four kinds of theatre: "The Deadly Theatre", "The Holy Theatre", "The Rough Theatre" and "The Immediate Theatre". The Deadly Theatre is the worst of the four. It is dull, repetitive, boring; it presents no truth or beauty or any transcendental experience. It is commercial theatre, meant only for money. Peter Brook writes about the Holy Theatre: "I am calling it the Holy Theatre for short, but it could be called The Theatre of the Invisible-Made-Visible: the notion that the stage is a place where the invisible can appear has *deep hold on our thoughts*. We are all aware that most of life escapes our senses: a most powerful explanation of the various arts is that they talk of *patterns* which we can only begin to recognize when they *manifest themselves as rhythms or shapes*" (*italics mine*) (Brook, 49). According to Brook, presentation of these patterns should be the end of all theatres. The theatre's one objective—and a very crucial one at that—is to tethering the attention of the audience onto the stage. And here the Rough Theatre shows the way. The Rough Theatre is 'rough' because it has no 'style' and no high level of civility or demeanour. And it is appropriate, because the theatre is a democratic space where *demos* of every ilk is expected. Brook writes about the Rough theatre: "The Rough Theatre doesn't pick and choose; if the audience is restive, then it is obviously more important to holler at the trouble makers—or improvise a gag—then to try to preserve the unity of style of the scene. In the luxury of the high-class theatre, everything can be all of a piece: in a rough theatre a bucket will be banged for a battle, flour used to show faces white with fear. The arsenal is limitless: the aside, the placard, the topical reference, the local jokes, the exploiting of accidents, the songs, the dances, the tempo, the noise, the relying on contrasts, the shorthand of exaggeration, the false noses, the stock types, the stuffed bellies.

The popular theatre, freed of unity of style, actually speaks a very sophisticated and stylish language: a popular audience usually has no difficulty in accepting inconsistencies of accent and dress, or in darting between mime and dialogue, realism and suggestion. They follow the line of story, unaware in fact that somewhere there is a set of standards which are being broken" (Brook, 80).

This our Shakespeare knew only too well. And this prompted him to set aside the dictum of Aristotle: tragedy from end to end, no comic halting. He held the "mirror up to nature"—nature (the world or life) where chaosmos rules, not cosmos. This is a revolutionary discovery of Shakespeare. What we will discuss in this book under the rubric of dramatic "embellishments" are, but devices wrought by him to make his plays akin to what Peter Brook calls the Rough Theatre, or, better, the Immediate Theatre.

Peter Brook's fourth category is the Immediate Theatre. Simply, it is a combination of the Holy Theatre and the Rough Theatre. The techniques of the Rough Theatre forces the audience's darting consciousness stay through-put on to the stage, free from the humdrum of the day, when the techniques of the Holy Theatre presents kaleidoscopically before it the higher values of humanity, which the audience's modified consciousness recognizes sub-consciously or viscerally. The audience are thus reformed.

Peter Brook's Immediate Theatre may be a cue to understanding Shakespeare's blending of the tragic and the comedic and his use of what is known as "dramatic embellishments", such as (only those we are going to discuss in this book) clown, music, dance, song, dumb show, play-within-play, ghost, apparition, witch, fairy, fiend, spirit, vision, masque, and pageant. We have divided these dramatic devices into two groups: devices that are non-embellishing, and devices that are embellishing. The embellishing devices serve two purposes: one, they provide entertainments to the audience; and two, they give fillip to the movement of the plot. In the non-embellishing devices, we will discuss Prologues, Epilogues, Inductions, and Choruses. In the embellishing devices, we will deal with Clowns (including Fools and Jesters), Dance, Music, Songs, Dumb Shows (including Plays-within-Plays), Ghosts (including Apparitions), Masques (including Pageants), and Witches (including Fairies, Fiends, Spirits, and Visions). Efforts will be made to quantify the embellishing devices, with a view to ascertain the frequencies of their presences in the plays, genre-wise and chronologically, to see their contribution to the popularity of the plays, and to see how Shakespeare employed these embellishments in the different periods of his creative life.

2
Prologue, Induction, and Epilogue

I

For reasons not yet discerned, Shakespeare's prologues, inductions and epilogues have not had even moderate critical attention. Perhaps critics have overlooked them or have only cast a casual glance at them, surmising that these are rather not part of the plays, that they can be detached easily from the texts of the main plays. But we should not forget that the great genius of Shakespeare was such that whatever stuff he touched upon Midas-like it transformed into gold. So, they deserve our attention. In most part of them, though, Shakespeare employed them customarily, but in some cases his genius loaded them with profundities, philosophical and theatrical.

The prologue was not an Elizabethan invention; it was borrowed from the Senecan (Roman) tradition, which owed to the Grecian. The term came from the Greek *Prologos* which means before or towards speech (*pro* = forward or towards, and *logos* = speech), and it means more than one things: 'the part before the entry of the chorus'; 'a speech before a play'; 'an introduction to a poem, etc.' Prologue also denotes the person or character who speaks the prologue.

Stanley Wells and Lena Cowen Orlin, in their *Shakespeare: An Oxford Guide*, write that the prologue and epilogue (*infra*) are "framing devices" and that (in the Elizabethan age) "such devices were considered to be separate from the play they framed and might even be recycled for use with several plays. It is possible that prologues and epilogues, which frequently ask for the audience's indulgence, were spoken only at the first performance or first revival, and not on subsequent occasions" (Wells and Orlin, 26-27). However, it is not always true to say that the epilogue—and, for that matter the prologue as well—is detachable from the body of the play, for, and here for only a single instance, the Epilogue of G.B. Shaw's *Saint Joan* is integral to the play itself. In any case, the prologue introduces a play briefly hinting to the action of it to come, and thus prepares the audience to follow it appropriately.

Ideally, the prologue is outside the cast and is an allegorical figure with his distinctive black velvet cloak. In the classical period, Euripides (c. 480-407 B.C.) is supposed to be the first ever dramatist to use the prologue. The prologue generally speaks in verse, and sometimes in prose, to introduce the play. Rarely, there may be more than one prologue in a play. This happens when there is a play-within-play in a play and the play-within-play is introduced by its own prologue, as in Shakespeare's *A Midsummer Night's Dream*, *Hamlet* and *The Two Noble Kinsmen*. The customs of the main (or beginning) prologue apply to the prologue of the play-within-play, only the speech of the second prologue is shorter. The most famous prologue in English literature is the over 800 lines Prologue to *The Canterbury Tales* by the first English poet Geoffrey Chaucer (c. 1340-1400), though it does not introduce a play but a dynamic and lively cast of characters to undertake the two or three days' journey to Canterbury.

In Shakespeare's time, the prologue was not so much in vogue, and Shakespeare was one of the few dramatists of the Elizabethan era who gave it a somewhat currency. *The Oxford Companion to the Theatre* tells us about the history of the English prologue: "Together with the epilogue, which closed the action, the prologue was extensively used during the Restoration period, and survived well into the eighteenth century. It disappeared with the crowded bills of the nineteenth century, and is now used only on special occasions. At their best the prologue and epilogue were witty and sometimes scurrilous commentaries on the politics and social conditions of the day, written by outstanding men of the theatre, of whom Dryden and

Garrick were the greatest, and spoken by the finest actors of the day" (Hartnoll, 766). In the Elizabethan age, that preceded the Restoration, the allegorical character that spoke the speech of the prologue was called chorus who, when the beginning of the play was announced by three soundings of a trumpet, immediately presented himself on the stage in the customary black velvet cloak. Since the 17th century, the prologue, for unidentified reasons began to go out of the custom.

The following is an inventory of Prologues, Inductions and Epilogues in Shakespeare's 37 Plays

Comedies

		Prologue	Epilogue
1.	*The Tempest*	no	yes
2.	*The Two Gentlemen of Verona*	no	no
3.	*The Merry Wives of Windsor*	no	no
4.	*Measure for Measure*	no	no
5.	*Comedy of Errors*	no	no
6.	*Much Ado About Nothing*	no	no
7.	*Love's Labour's Lost*	no	no
8.	*Midsummer's Night's Dream*	no	Epilogue (by Puck)
9.	*The Merchant of Venice*	no	no
10.	*As You Like It*	no	Epilogue (by Rosalind)
11.	*The Taming of the Shrew*	(2 scenes)	no
12.	*All's Well That Ends Well*	no	Epilogue (by King of France)
13.	*Twelfth Night*	no	Virtual Epilogue (clown sings a song of 20 lines)
14.	*The Winter's Tale*	no	no
15.	*Troilus and Cressida*	yes	Epilogue (by Pandarus)
16.	*Cymbeline*	no	no

17.	*Pericles*	5 Prologues	Epilogue (by Gower)

Prologue in Play-within-Play

		Prologue	Epilogue
1.	*A Midsummer's Night's Dream* (V, i)	Prologue (10+25=35 lines)	no
2.	*Hamlet* (III, ii)	Prologue (03 lines)	no

Tragedies

		Prologue/Induction	Epilogue
1.	*Coriolanus*	no	no
2.	*Titus Andronicus*	no	no
3.	*Romeo and Juliet*	yes	no
4.	*Timon of Athens*	no	no
5.	*Julius Caesar*	no	no
6.	*Macbeth*	[I, i (3 Witches = sort of Prologue]	no
7.	*Hamlet*	no	no
8.	*King Lear*	no	no
9.	*Othello*	no	no
10.	*Antony and Cleopatra*	no	no

Histories

		Prologue/ Induction	Epilogue
1.	*King John*	no	no
2.	*Richard II*	no	no
3.	*1 Henry IV*	no	no
4.	*2 Henry IV*	Induction	Virtual Epilogue (by Dancer)
5.	*Henry V*	Yes	Epilogue (by Chorus)
6.	*1 Henry VI*	no	no
7.	*2 Henry VI*	no	no
8.	*3 Henry VI*	no	no

9.	*Richard III*	no	no
10.	*Henry VIII*	Yes	Yes

Now let us compare the incidents of the prologue, induction and epilogue in the plays of Shakespeare with those in some select plays of his contemporary dramatists to see the artistic and dramatic superiority of Shakespeare's prologues, inductions, and epilogues.

1. Christopher Marlowe (1564-93): The first part of Marlowe's *Tamburlaine the Great* has a brief prologue of only eight lines, and has neither induction nor epilogue. The stoccata-like Prologue just introduces the play to the audience:

> From jigging veins rhyming mother-wits,
> And such conceits as clownage keeps in pay,
> We will lead you to the stately tent of war,
> Where you shall hear the Scythian *Tamburlaine*
> Threatening the world with high astounding terms
> And scourging kingdoms with his conquering sword.
> View but his picture in this tragic glass,
> And then applaud his fortunes as you please.

Clearly, Marlowe is here sticking to the traditional norm of the prologue: suggesting the matter of the play and inviting the attention of the audience. *Tamburlaine the Great*, Part I, entails no epilogue.

Part II of *Tamburlaine the Great* is germaine to the first part of the play as regards the matters of prologue and epilogue. It has a brief prologue of only nine lines and no epilogue. The massage of the prologue, too, is no different; its purport is to say that the present play is but the continuation of Part I of *Tamburlaine the Great*:

> The general welcomes *Tamburlaine* receiv'd.
> When he arrived last upon the stage,
> Have made our poet pen his Second Part,
> Where death cuts off the progress of his pomp,
> And murderous Fates throw all his triumphs down.
> But what became of fair Zenocrate,
> And with how many cities' sacrifice

He celebrated her sad funeral,
Himself in presence shall unfold at large.

The best remembered play of Marlowe, *Doctor Faustus* has neither prologue nor epilogue. But the first ever speech of the Chorus is prologue-like, and introduces the play in superb blank verses. Likewise, the Chorus closes it, epilogue-like, with eight wisdom-fraught blank verses. Marlowe returned to the "fashion" of the prologue and epilogue in *The Jew of Malta*, and this time elaborately. In this play, there are two Prologues (one for the Court and another for the stage) and two Epilogues (one for the Court, the other for the stage). The Prologue of 12 lines is addressed to the "Grecious and great" [Queen] and it promulgates that the play is about the "rich and famous Jew" with a Machiavellian character. And in the six lines for the Court, the Epilogue craves pardon of the "dread sovereign" should the play wrongs her patience. The Prologue to the cockpit is of 18 lines, but means not much more than there is in that at Court. The Epilogue to the cockpit desires that the play be applauded. The significant difference between the Prologue and the Epilogue to the Court and those to the stage or cockpit is that in the former two the performers (and the playwright) are, naturally, immensely apologetic and humble unlike in the other case. Marlowe's *Edward II, The Massacre at Paris* and *Dido, Queen of Carthage* have neither prologue nor epilogue.

2. **Robert Greene** (1558-92) could well vie with Marlowe in popularity with his six plays, in his own days. Greene was elaborate with prologues, in his *Alphonsus, King of Arragon*, in that he wrote one Prologue to precede each of the five Acts of the play to be spoken by Venus. And he concluded the play with an Epilogue. In this regard, *Alphonsus* is like Shakespeare's *Henry V* and *Pericles*. This not so popular—it is rather unpopular—play has a total of 133 lines for the five Prologues before the five Acts, and each one of the Prologues merely speaks about the actions ahead in uninspiring terms. The Epilogue of *Alphonsus* is also a plain speaking: at the end of the play, happily Alphonsus is going to get Iphigena as his wife, and so Venus, the Prologue, "with unwilling mind" "is forc'd to trudge to heaven again". Greene's *A Looking-Glass*

for London and England, Orlando Furioso, Friar Bacon and Friar Bungay and *George-A-Greene, the Pinner of Wakefield* have neither Prologue nor Epilogue, but his vibrant *James the Fourth* has an induction and an epilogue.

3. **Benjamin Jonson** (1572-1637), the greatest of English dramatists, except Shakespeare, has over a dozen plays, most of them comedies, in which he has generously employed the devices of the prologue, induction and epilogue. His popular *Volpone* begins with a Prologue of 36 lines (to be spoken by the Prologue) and the following epilogue (the speaker not specified):

> The seasoning of a play, is the applause.
> Now, though the Fox be punish'd by the laws,
> He yet doth hope, there is no suffering due,
> For any fact which he hath done 'gainst you;
> If there be, censure him; here he doubtful stands;
> If not, fare jovially, and clap your hands.

The above passage looks like a customary epilogue, indeed. And so seems the Prologue of the play customary. It tells that the playwright is the sole author of this "quick comedy" and that "The laws of time, place, persons he observeth". Finally, he assures the audience that—

> All gall and coppers from his ink he draineth,
> Only a little salt remaineth,
> Wherewith he'll rub your cheeks, till red, with laughter,
> They shall look fresh a week after.

Ben Jonson's *The Alchemist* and *The Devil is an Ass* each has a Prologue, but only the latter has an Epilogue. The Prologue of the earlier play is obviously fashionable; it professes that the play trades in "natural follies" and that the Prologue (who speaks the Prologue) begs of the audience "justice" for the playwright and "grace" for the performers. As has been said, *The Alchemist* has no epilogue; but the concluding speech of the character Face, to the audience may be deemed an epilogue, fit for the comedy:

> Gentlemen,
> My part a little fell in this last scene,

Yet 'twas decorum. And though I am clean
Got off from the Subtle, Surly, Mamon, Dol
Hot Ananias, Dapper, Drugger, all
With whom I traded: yet I put my self
On you, that my country and this pelf
Which I have got, if you do quit me, rests
To feast you often, and invite new guests.

The Devil is an Ass begins with a customary Prologue that begins plainly thus: "The Devil is an Ass: that is, to-day,/ The name of what you are met for, a new play." And he ends by appealing to the audience not to rashly judge that the play is a flop, but to do it after witnessing it six times:

Or, if for want of room, it must miscarry,
'T will be but justice that your censure tarry,
Till you give some: and when six times you have seen't,
If this play do not like, the Devil is in't.

The epilogue of this play does not customarily pray for the audience's applause, but hurls a hilarious joke at them:

Thus, the Projector, here, is over-thrown.
But I have now a Project of my own,
If it may pass: that no man would invite
The Poet from us, to sup forth to night,
If the play please. If it displeasant be,
We do presume, that no man will: nor we.

Ben Jonson has framed both of his comedies, *A Tale of a Tub* and *Bartholomew Fair*, with a Prologue and an Epilogue. The Prologue of the former is a plain speaking:

Not state-affairs, nor any politic club,
Pretend we in our Tale hare, of a Tub:
But acts of clowns and constables to-day
Stuff out the scenes of our ridiculous play.

The Epilogue of *A Tale of a Tub*, too, contains no conceits or needless wisdom but only repeats what the Prologue said. Interestingly, the Epilogue is spoken by the principal character of the play—Tub. Tub tells the audience:

This tale of me, the Tub of Totten Court,
A poet first invented for your sport.

The Prologue as well as the Epilogue of *Bartholomew Fair* is addressed not to the audience but to the "King's majesty", a witness to the play. The Prologue is well fashionably simple, without any errant wisdom:

Your Majesty is welcome to a Fair
. . . .
These are for your sport, without particular wrong,
Or just complaint of any private man,
Who of himself, or shall think well, or can,
The maker doth present: and hopes, to-night
To give you for a fairing, true delight.

The essential matter of the (true) prologue for the audience, that is a stoccado introduction to the play, is absent in the foregoing Prologue "To the King's Majesty", but it is plenished by the immediately succeeding Induction, presented by the Stage-Keeper, the Book-holder, and the Scrivener. However, the Epilogue of *Bartholomew* is meant for the same King's Majesty, and is fashionably traditional, though it seeks not the applause of the audience in general but only of the King:

Your Majesty hath seen the play, and you
Can best allow it from your ear and view.
. . . .
This is your power to judge, great sir, and not
The envy of a few. Which if we have got,
We value less what their dislike can bring,
If it so happy be, 't have pleased the King.

Ben Jonson's comedy, *The New Inn; or, the Light Heart*, also comprises a prologue and an epilogue, both of which are also fashionable and traditional. The Prologue begs the "acceptation" or gladness of the audience: "You are welcome, welcome all to the New Inn:/ Though the old house, we hope our cheer will win/ Your acceptation". The Epilogue is also accustomed; here the pleasure of the audience is expected:

If you expect more than you had to-night,

The maker is sick and sad. But do him right;
He meant to please you: ....

Every Man in His Humour has no epilogue. Its prologue contains the customary expectation of the poet, the delight of the audience, by showing the "image of the times" and "human follies". In *Every Man Out of His Humour* has no prologue but an epilogue. Unlike the epilogues cited above from Jonson's plays, there is in this play no appeal to the audience. The Epilogue, spoken by Macilente (a character) before Queen Elizabeth, means to say that all ill humour is now gone away from him: "All my malicious powers have lost their stings."

Jonson's *Epicene; or, the Silent Woman* has two prologues. The first one begins with the "half" truth:

Truth says, of old the art of making plays
Was to content the people; and their praise
Was to the poet money, wine, and bays.

And then persuades the audience to sit and watch the performance. The other prologue is rather a bit off the beat: it sort of edifies the audience about the stuff of a play and its general objective:

The ends of all, who for the scene do write,
Are, or should be, to profit and delight.
. . . .
Then, in this play, which we present to-night,
And make the object of your ear and sight,
On forfeit of yourselves, think nothing true:
Lest so you make the maker to judge you,
For he knows, poet never credit gain'd
By writing truths, but things (like truths) well feign'd

It is only here that, like Shakespeare, Ben Jonson, in a prologue (or epilogue), egregiously writes a commonplace truism.

Ben Jonson's comedy, *The Magnetic Lady; or, Humours Reconciled* has neither a prologue (it has an induction, though) nor an epilogue, and, likewise, his two tragedies—*Catiline* and *Sejenus*—are without any prologue or epilogue. *Epicoene; or, the Silent Woman* has two Prologues but no obvious epilogue;

however, it has a suggestion of an epilogue in the last words of the character True:

> Spectators, if you like this comedy, rise
> Cheerfully, and now Morose is gone in,
> Clap your hands. It may be, that noise
> Will cure him, at least please him. [*Exit.*]

Here, we are not taking into account Jonson's fragmentary comedy *The Sad Shepherd; or, a Tale of Robin Hood*, which has a long prologue of 66 lines, and the fragmentary tragedy *The Fall of Mortimer*, which has no prologue.

From the above, it may be clear that Ben Jonson had the wont of framing his plays with prologues and epilogues, which were customary or fashionable, in the sense that they merely appealed to the audience for their attention and appreciation.

Jonson's Plays

		Prologue	Epilogue
1.	*Volpone*	Yes	No
2.	*Alchemist*	Yes	No
3.	*The Devil is an Ass*	Yes	Yes
4.	*Tale of Tub*	Yes	Yes
5.	*Bartholomew*	Yes	Yes
6.	*New Inn/ the Light Heart*	Yes	Yes
7.	*Every Man in Humour*	Yes	No
8.	*Every Man out of Humour*	No	Yes
9.	*Epicoene / Silent Woman*	Yes (2)	Virtual Epilogue (by True)
10.	*Magnetic Lady*	Induction	No
11.	*Cateline*	No	No
12.	*Sejenus*	No	No

4. Thomas Kyd's (1558-94) most popular 4-act *The Spanish Tragedy* has no epilogue but an 85-line long Prologue, in which the Ghost of Don Andrea gives us a synoptic preview or key to the drama. He narrates how Don Andrea falls head-long in love of Bel-Imperia and thus incurs the ire of Balthazar who kills him, and how Balthazar is revenged. The Ghost begins thus:

When this eternal substance of my soul
Did live imprisoned in my wanton flesh,
Each in their function serving other's need,
My name was Don Andrea; . . . .
. . . .
In secret I possessed a worthy dame,
Which hight sweet Bel-Imperia by name.

And then narrates the story in a nut-shell.

5. Thomas Dekker (1570-1632) was prolific a writer, collaborating with many dramatists in as many as 50 plays, 20 of which have survived. But he is now remembered in good part for his masterpiece *The Shoemaker's Holiday*. His important collaborative plays are: *Northward Ho* (comedy), *Westward Ho* (comedy), *The Roaring Girl; or, Moll Cutpurse* (comedy, with Thomas Middleton or Massinger), *The Virgin-Martyr* (tragedy, with Massinger and Dekker), *The Honest Whore* (with Middleton), etc. It may be that besides *The Shoemaker's Holiday* (comedy), *Northward Ho* and *Westward Ho* are also written by Dekker singly. However, to be above any conjecture and to see Dekker's distinctive style and dramatic forms, let us deal only with his *The Shoemaker's Holiday*, as we have done in the case of Kyd, above.

Dekker's *The Shoemaker's Holiday*; or, *The Gentle Craft* has two Prologues (as well as two songs) before the play begins: one Prologue, in verse, to be spoken before the Queen's Majesty; the other, in prose, before the audience. In the Prologue before the Queen, Her Majesty's condescending indulgence and "One gracious smile" is begged on bended knees. In the Prologue to the audience, the story of the play is concisely related: "The Argument of the play I will set down in this Epistle: Sir Hugh Lacy Earl of Lincoln, had a young Gentleman of his own name, his near kinsman, that loved the Lord Mayor's daughter of London; to prevent and cross which love, the Earl caused his kinsman to be sent to Colonel of a company into France: who resigned his place to another gentleman his friend, and came disguised like a Dutch Shoemaker, to the house of Simon Eyre in Tower street, who served the Mayor and his household with shoes. The merriment that passed in Eyre's house, his coming to be Mayor of London, Lacy's getting his love, and other accidents; with two merry Three-men's songs. Take all in good worth that is well intended, for nothing is purposed but mirth, mirth lengtheneth long life; which, with all other blessings I heartily wish you."

6. Thomas Nashe (1567-1601) was basically a satirist and a pamphleteer. He collaborated with Christopher Marlowe in *The Tragedy of Dido, Queen of Carthage*. His solo dramatic productions are: *The Isle of Dogs* (now lost) and *Summer's Last Will and Testament. Summer's Last Will* has a long Prologue in prose and an elaborate Epilogue also in prose. The Prologue is spoken by the principal character himself, Will Summer, in the garb of a knave ("fool's apparel"). This Prologue is distinctive from the general fashionable Prologues of the Elizabethan era, in the sense that (i) he says nothing about the play but only that "'tis no play neither but a show"; that (ii) he casts aspersions at the author of the play; that (iii) he censors the dramatist for making "a prologue longer than his play"; that (iv) he teaches the actors of this play what to do and what not to do while they play: "Actors, you rogues, come away, clear your throats, blow your noses, and wipe your mouths ere you enter, that you may take no occasion to spit or to cough when you are non plus. And this I bar, over and besides, that none of you stroke your beards to make action, play with your cod-piece points, or stand fumbling on your buttons when you know not how to bestow your fingers. Serve God, and act cleanly;...." (cf. *Hamlet*); and, finally, that the Prologue is not at all serious, as expected, but quite jesting. The Prologue also promises to act as a chorus in the play: "I'll sit as a chorus, and flout the actors and him [the author of the play] at the end of every scene". The Epilogue of this play is cursory and customary: "Valete, spectators: pay for this sport with a plaudit, and the next time the wind blows from this corner, we will make you ten times as merry."

7. George Peele (1558-96) has five extant plays: *The Arraignment of Paris, The Battle of Alcazar, King Edward the First, The Love of King David and Fair Bathsheba* and *The Old Wives' Tale. The Arraignment of Paris* is a pastoral masque in verse, not so successful on the stage, and so is *The Love of King David and Fair Bathsheba*, a pastoral play in verse, not so fit for performance. *The Arraignment of Paris* has a Prologue of 29 lines and a scanty Epilogue of two Latin lines. The Prologue, as usual, gives in a sketchy form the story of the play: of Troy and of Priam and his "young son, the shepherd swain,/ Paris, th' unhappy organ of the Greeks." And the Prologue ends thus:

> . . . . Lordings adieu,
> Imposing silence for your task, I end,
> Till just assemblie of goddesses
> Make me begin the Tragedie of Troy.

Very exceptionally, the Epilogue of *The Arraignment of Paris* is in Latin and in just two lines, pronounced by Diana, Venus, Juno and Pallas (cf. the Prologue to the first act of Shakespeare's *Pericles*):

> *Vive diu faelix votis hominumque Deumque.*
> *Corpore, mente, libro, doctissima, candida, casta.*

Peele's *King Edward I* has neither prologue nor epilogue.

8. John Lyly (1554-1606) had at least 7 plays, most of which were played before the Queen's Majesty: *Campaspe, Sapho and Phao, Endymion: The Man in the Moon, Gallathea, Mother Bombie, The Woman in the Moon* and *Love's Metamorphosis. Campaspe* is a prose comedy that is based on the Greek mythology about Alexander, the Great; Campaspe, the most beautiful dame; and Diogenes, the stoic philosopher. It has two Prologues, one to be spoken to the Court, and the other to the audience at the Black Friars. The Prologue to the Court is a traditional one, first begging the Majesty's indulgence, and giving the Majesty a hint of the fable of the play: "...our hope is your Highness will at this time lend an era to an idle pastime. *Appion* raising *Homer* from Hell, demanded only who was his father, and calling *Alexander* from his grave, seek only who was his love...."

The Prologue then urges the audience to view the play through the prism of imagination (cf. Prologue to Shakespeare's *Pericles*, IV, iv): "But as Theseus being promised to be brought to an eagle's nest, and travelling all the day, found but a wren in a hedge, yet said, this is a bard: so we hope, if the shower of our swelling mountain seem to bring forth some elephant, perform but a mouse, you will gently say, this is a beast!" And, lastly, begs pardon for any flaw that may be in the performance:

"But however we finish our work, we crave
Pardon if we offend in matter, and patience
If we transgress in manners."

Campaspe has no epilogue.

Endymion: The Man in the Moon has both a short Prologue and a short Epilogue, and both of them in prose. The Prologue, as was the fashion simply tells the Princess what is going to happen on the stage and pleads excuse for any fault, beforehand: "Most high and happy princess, we must tell you a tale of the Man in the Moon, which if it seem ridiculous for the method, or superfluous for the matter, or for the means incredible, for three faults we can make but one excuse: it is a tale of the Man in the Moon.... We present neither comedy, nor tragedy, nor story, nor anything, but...that whosoever heareth may say this: 'Why, here is a tale of the Man in the Moon.'"

The Epilogue, too, is customary: it begs of the 'Dread sovereign' his warm favour, and pledges his submission and subservience: "A man walking abroad, the wind and the sun strove for sovereignty: the one with his blast, the other with his beams. The wind blew hard; the man wrapped his garment about him harder. It blustered more strongly; he then girt it fast to him. 'I cannot prevail', said the wind. The sun casting her crystal beams, began to warm the man; he unloosed his gown. Yet it shined brighter; he then put it off. 'I yield', said the wind, 'for if thou continue shining, he will also put off his coat'. "Dread sovereign, the malicious that seek to overthrow us with threats do but stiffen our thoughts and make them sturdier in storms. But if Your Highness vouchsafe with your favourable beams to glance upon us, we shall not only stoop, but with all humility lay both our hands and hearts at Your Majesty's feet."

Lyly's *Sapho and Phao* has two Prologues in prose and an Epilogue, also in prose—one Prologue to be delivered at the Court, the other at the Black Friars. The earlier Prologue very briefly narrates what is going to happen on the stage: "We present no conceits nor wars, but deceits and loves, wherein the truth may excuse the plainness: the necessity of the length: the poetry the bitterness.... Whatsoever we present, whether it be tedious (which we fear) or toyish (which we doubt), sweet or sour, absolute or imperfect, or whatever, in all humbleness we all, and I on knee for all, entreat that your highness *imagine yourself to be in a deep dream*, that staying the conclusion, in rising your Majesty vouchsafe but to say, *And you awaked.*" The second Prologue explains the "intent" of the author and performers of the play: "Our intent was at this time to move inward delight, not outward lightness; and to breed, if it might be, soft smiling, not loud laughing; knowing it to the wise to be as great pleasure to hear counsel mixed with wit, as to the foolish to have sport mingled with rudeness."

Gallathea, an interesting pastoral story, is framed with a Prologue and an epilogue, both in prose. The Prologue is quite obsequious to Queen Elizabeth I, begging her "judgment and favour": "Your Majesty's judgment and favour, are our sun and shadow, the one coming of your deep wisdom, the other of your wonted grace. We in all humility desire, that by the former, receiving our first breath, we may in the latter, take our last rest." Then, the Prologue does not introduce the story of the play, but merely tell her that in the play what is going to be presented is but the gold of virtue, appropriate for the gold mine of her mind. And so not even the slightest offence is intended: "...what we present your Highness, should neither offend in scene nor syllable; knowing that as in the ground where gold grows, nothing will prosper but gold; so to your Highness' mind, where nothing doth harbour but virtue, nothing can enter but virtue." In the 4-line Epilogue, Gallathea, the heroine, persuades the female members of the audience ("you, ladies") to yield to the god of love, Cupid, and yield to love: "Confess him a conqueror, whom you aught to regard, since it is impossible to resist; for this is infallible, that love conquers all things but itself, and ladies all hearts but their own." This Epilogue is a whit away from the fashionable or customary. Lyly's *Midas* opens with a Prologue, but ends not with an epilogue but with a beautiful song (cf. Shakespeare's *Twelfth Night*). The Prologue is in prose, and fashionably apologetic to the audience, whom he addresses as "Gentlemen":

> Time has confounded our minds, our minds the matter, but all comes to this pass, that what heretofore has been served [plays by Lily] in several dishes for a feast, is now minced in a charger for a Gallimaufrey. If we present a mingle-mangle, our fault is to be excused, because the whole world is become an Hodge-podge. We are jealous of your judgments, because you are wise; of our own performance, because we are imperfect; of our Author's device, because he is idle. Only this does encourage us, that presenting our studies before Gentlemen, though they receive an inward dislike, we shall not be hissed with an open disgrace.

Lyly's *Mother Bombie* has neither prologue nor epilogue but his *The Woman in the Moon* has a prologue in verse and no epilogue. The *Prologus* (Prologue) tells the audience that the play is but a dream of the playwright, and that he craves the audience's "content" or satisfaction:

> Our Poet slumbering in the Muses' laps,
> Has seen a Woman seated in the Moon,
> A point beyond the ancient Theorique:
> And as it was so he presents his dream,
> Here in the bounds of fair Utopia,
> Where lovely Nature being only Queen,
> Bestows such workmanship on earthly mould
> That Heavens themselves envy her glorious work.
> But all in vain: for (malice being spent)
> They yield themselves to follow Nature's doom;
> And fair Pandora sits in Cynthia's orb.
> This, but the shadow of our Author's dream,
> Argues the substance to be near at hand:
> At whose appearance I most humbly crave,
> That in your forehead she may read content.
> If many faults escape in her discourse,
> Remember all is but a Poet's dream,
> The first he had in Phoebus' holy bower,
> But not the last, unless the first displease.

Above, we have seen how Shakespeare's famous contemporary dramatists employed the prologue and the epilogue and for what purposes, and also have seen the literary and dramatic values of them. Let us now summarize the features of their prologues and epilogues, in general.

1. The prologues are confined with the bound of the basic objective of the prologue: to introduce, very concisely, the story. The epilogue is generally intended for applause.
2. There is no broad and sweeping philosophic comments on life, the stage, etc.
3. Sometimes there are double prologues: one for the court; another for the audience.
4. There are perhaps no play in which each act is preceded by a prologue, like Shakespeare' *Henry V.*
5. Justifiably for the dramatic reason, the literary value of the prologue and, for that matter, of epilogue, is minor, compared to that of the body of the play. This is deliberately done in order not to underrate the value of the main text.
6. Verse, particularly rhymed verse, is very rarely used either in the prologue or in the epilogue.
7. There is no prologue or epilogue in the form of the sonnet.

Now let us see how Shakespeare's extraordinary dramatic and poetic genius has devised prologues and epilogues that are, in general, distinctive and superior to those of his contemporary dramatists. Shakespeare has been generous for the prologue and the epilogue—for the prologue, particularly—in writing verses or lines for them. The following data, at a glance, may give an idea about the amount of the speeches of prologues and epilogues in Shakespeare.

1. *Henry V.* It has five Prologues: one Prologue before each of the five Acts. The Prologues are in unrhymed verses. All the Prologues are delivered by the Chorus. The number of lines of the successive Prologues are: 34, 42, 36, 54 and 45. The total number of the lines of the five Prologues are: 211.

2. Pericles, Prince of Tyre. Like *Henry V*, this play also has one Prologue before each Act, but it has two more Prologues—one in the fourth scene of the fourth Act (before the *Dumb Show*) and another in the second scene of the fifth Act. All the Prologues are in verse, mostly rhymed, and all are spoken by Gower, the Chorus.

The total number of lines of the five Prologues separately are: 42, 40, 60, 52 and 24. The total number of the lines of the five Prologues are 218. The total number of the lines of the two (extra) Prologues in IV, iv and V, ii, spoken by (also) Gower is 51 + 20 = 71. Therefore, the grand total of the number of lines/ verses of all the 7 Prologues is 289.

3. *Romeo and Juliet*. This play has two Prologues: one before Act I and the other before Act II, both the Prologues being of 14 lines of verse. So, the total number of verse lines of *Romeo and Juliet* is 14 + 14 = 28. Interestingly, both are in the sonnet form in the rhyme scheme: a b a b c d c d e f e f g g. *Romeo and Juliet* has no epilogue; it concludes with Escalus' (the prince of Verona) lamentation: "...never was a story of more woe/ Than this of Juliet and her Romeo."

4. *Troilus and Cressida*. Like *Romeo and Juliet*, this play is also devoid of an epilogue, but has got a Prologue of 31 unrhymed verses.

Therefore, in the above four plays—*Henry V, Pericles, Romeo and Juliet* and *Troilus and Cressida*—Shakespeare has 559 verses (rhymed and unrhymed) for all his Prologues. But, in addition to these Prologues, he has two more *Prologues* for his two Plays-within-plays: one in *A Midsummer Night's Dream* (V, i) and the other in *Hamlet* (III, ii). The *Prologue* of *A Midsummer Night's Dream* has 35 rhymed verses and the *Prologue* of *Hamlet* has only three rhymed verses. So, the grand total of the lines of the Prologues (including the *Prologues* in the plays-within-plays) is 597.

Shakespeare has another device or contrivance of introducing a play, which may be deemed to be sort of a surrogate Prologue—Induction. The objective of Induction is the same as that of the Prologue, but while the Prologue directly addresses the audience and rapidly gives them a glimpse of what is going to happen on the stage, the Induction creates an occasion on the stage through performance (dumb-show) that will naturally be succeeded by the main play. While the Prologue is a speech, the induction is a performance (theatrical), and while the Prologue can in no way be linked to the main performance, the Induction may be deemed to be a part of the play. Induction is the introductory scene of a play. Each of Ben Jonson's *Bartholomew Fair* and *The Magnetic Lady* has an Induction. About the Induction in *The Magnetic Lady*, the stage-direction is "The Induction; or, Chorus". It comprises some 5/6-page conversation of three characters: Mr. Probee, Mr. Damplay and a "Boy of the house". Through their conversation, the stem of the story sends a flash. The distinction between Prologue and Induction may become obvious in Ben Jonson's comedy *Bartholomew Fair* where both Prologue and Induction are present. The Prologue, as if, does not stand on a "stage" but on a "platform"; and for the Induction the stage-direction is: "The Stage. Enter the Stage-Keeper". The Prologue speaks to the King's Majesty:

> Your Majesty is welcome to a Fair;
>
> . . . .
>
> The maker doth present: and hopes, to-night
> To give you for a fairing, true delight.

The Induction is sort of a scene acted out by Stage-Keeper, Book holder and Scrivener.

Shakespeare has employed Induction in two plays: *The Taming of the Shrew* and *Henry IV, Part 2*. In the former, there are two elaborate Scenes in the Induction—the first Scene of 136 verses, which, according to the stage-direction, is "Scene I (*Before an alehouse on a heath*)". The next Scene of 141 verses is, according to stage-direction, Scene II (*A bed-chamber in the Lord's house*). In Induction, Scene I, Christopher Sly, being boozed, falls asleep in the alehouse. A local Lord, returning from hunting, plans a joke on Sly. He asks his huntsman to remove the unconscious Sly to his house and orders serving-men to dress him in luxurious garbs and treat Sly as a noble man gone insane for many years now. At this time a traveling dramatic company has arrived and the Lord asks them to perform for Sly. He also asks a page to cross-dress and act as Sly's wife. In Induction, Scene II, Sly comes out of unconsciousness and protests that he is noble man, but is duped into believing that he is behaving abnormally. And he is persuaded to enjoy a *play* about to be performed by the travelling company in no time. This *play* is the play *The Taming of the Shrew.*

The Induction of 2 *Henry IV,* spoken by the "Presenter" Rumour who is "painted full of tongues", comprises 40 verse lines. (Rumour is the personification of false news.) Rumour announces that he has put forth a false report, following King Henry IV's victory at the battle of Shrewsbury—that the King and Prince were killed and the rebels were victorious. This report, says Rumour, is now reaching Warkworth castle, home of Hotspur's father, the Earl of Northumberland.

Shakespeare has more epilogues than prologues but fewer verses and sentences (*As You Like It*), taken together, for his epilogues, than he has verses for his prologues. He has prologues in only four plays, but epilogues in 9 plays. He has both prologues and epilogues in three plays: *Henry V, Pericles* and *Troilus and Cressida.* The following table gives a summary of all these.

Sl. No.	Plays	Number of verses or clauses/sentences in the Epilogue	Epilogue Spoken by
1.	*All's Well That Ends Well*	6 rhymed verses	King of France
2.	*Henry IV*	33 clauses/sentences	A Dancer
3.	*As You Like It*	20 clauses/sentences	Rosalind
4.	*Henry V* [Also a Prologue]	14 verses (in sonnet form)	Chorus
5.	*Henry VIII*	14 verses (in sonnet form)	No direction

Sl. No.	Plays	Number of verses or clauses/sentences in the Epilogue	Epilogue Spoken by
6.	*A Midsummer Night's Dream*	16 rhymed verses	Puck
7.	*Pericles* [Also a Prologue]	18 rhymed verses	Gower, the Chorus
8.	*Troilus and Cressida* [Also a Prologue]	14 rhymed verses and 7 sentences (a peculiar Epilogue)	Pandarus
9.	*The Tempest*	20 rhymed verses	Prospero

* *Love's Labour's Lost*: instead of epilogue, two songs—one by Ver (Spring), the other by Hiems (Winter).

Shakespeare's Prologues have some distinctive features and values. Firstly, his Prologues are rather longish, compared to most of the Prologues of his contemporary dramatists. Take, for instance, Marlowe's four, out of his seven plays, which have Prologues. His *Edward II, The Massacre at Paris* and *Dido, Queen of Carthage* have no Prologue. Marlowe's *Tamburlaine*, Part I has a brief Prologue of only 8 lines, *Tamburlaine*, Part II only 9 lines, and *Faustus*—a little longer—26 lines. His *The Jew of Malta* has two Prologues: the Prologue, to be delivered "at Court" contains 12 lines and that to be spoken on the stage, or to the audience, contains 18 lines.

Secondly, Shakespeare's Prologues are all in verses and some of them are rhymed, as shown below:

Plays	Number of Verses/Clauses In the Prologue	Speaker of the Prologue
1. *Henry V*		
(a) Prologue to Act I	34 verses (unrhymed)	Chorus (It is here that the Prologue introduces himself)
(b) Prologue to Act II	42 verses (unrhymed)	Chorus
(c) Prologue to Act III	36 verses (unrhymed)	Chorus
(d) Prologue to Act IV	54 verses (unrhymed)	Chorus
(e) Prologue to Act V	45 verses (unrhymed)	Chorus
*Total verses: 211		

2. *Pericles*		
(a) Prologue to Act I	42 verses (rhymed)	Gower
(b) Prologue to Act II	40 verses (rhymed) [After 16 verses, a Dumb Show, and then 24 verses]	Gower
(c) Prologue to Act III	60 verses (rhymed)	Gower
(d) Prologue to Act IV	52 verses (rhymed)	Gower
(e) Prologue to Act V, Scene i	24 verses (alternate verses are rhymed)	Gower
(f) Prologue to Act V, Scene ii	20 verses	Gower
*Total verses: 238		
3. *Romeo and Juliet*		
(a) Prologue to Act I	14 verses (in Sonnet form)	Chorus
(b) Prologue to Act II	14 verses (in Sonnet form)	Chorus
*Total verses: 28		
*4. *A Midsummer Night's Dream* (V, i)	35 verses (alternate verses are rhymed)	Quince (a carpenter)
(Play-within-Play)	(after the 10th verse, there is a break)	
5. *Troilus and Cressida*	40 verses (unrhymed)	Prologue
*6. *Hamlet* (III, ii) (Play-within-Play)	03 verses (unrhymed)	Player *Prologue*

Thirdly, Shakespeare has used varieties of Prologue-forms: Prologue in rhymed verses, Prologue in unrhymed verses, and Prologue interrupted by a Dumb Show (cf. Prologue to Act III of *Pericles*). In the two Prologues before Act I and Act II of *Romeo and Juliet*, Shakespeare has, uniquely and appropriately for the play, two sonnets that hover over the theme of love (and, originally, sonnet was done for love), both rhyming a b a b c d c d e f e f g g (the Shakespearean form). And Shakespeare's Prologue is as long as of 60 verses (Prologue to Act III of *Pericles*) and as brief as only 3 verses (player *Prologue* of the Play within-Play in Act III, sc. ii of *Hamlet*) which, as Hamlet truly says is as brief as "the posy of a ring".

Fourthly, in the "masque" in Act I, sc. iv of *Romeo and Juliet* (vide p. 281), Romeo truly insinuates that the purpose of the prologue is an "excuse" for the performance of the play or an "apology" for the same. Indeed, one main objective of the prologue, since Seneca, has been to seek the indulgence of the audience. This is obvious from what Romeo in the above-mentioned masque asks Benvolio: should they perform the masque without a prologue?—

> What, shall this speech be spoke for our excuse?
> Or shall we on without apology?

Fifthly, the other objective of the Prologue was to give the audience a swift survey, or at least an inkling, of the legend or story of the play and ask their attention. The Elizabethan playwrights stuck to these two objectives. But Shakespeare everywhere is distinctive; he, whenever he finds an opportunity, stuffs his Prologues with important dramatic *obiter dicta*. To take just a few of the Prologues of Shakespeare's contemporaries with the view to show the speciality of Shakespeare's Prologues:

1. The Prologue of Marlowe's *Tamburlaine*, Part I, tells us that we are going to see—"the Scythian *Tamburlaine*/ Threatening the world". Also asks us—"And then applaud his fortunes as you please." Part II of *Tamburlaine* is no different, as regards the Prologue. The Prologue reminds us of the "general welcomes" that *Tamburlaine* received in the First Part, and tells us that we will see what happened to Zenocrate. The "Prologue at the Court" of *The Jew of Malta*, in effect, says only that the play is about "The story of a rich and famous Jew" and the "Prologue to the Stage" tells us that the play was written by "the best of poets" and that the part of the Jew will be played by one who could be ranked with "Proteus for shapes, and Roscius for a tongue". The Prologue of *Doctor Faustus* tells the audience: "Only this, gentlemen,—we must perform/ The form of Faustus' fortunes, good or bad:" and then he briefly describes the life-trajectory of Faustus.

2. Thomas Kyd's Prologue is no different from Marlowe's. In his *The Spanish Tragedy*, the Ghost of Don Andrea, in his 85-line (verse) Prologue, speaks of his love of his wife Bel-imperia, and his experiences of seeing many things ("I saw more sights than thousands tongues can tell"). After this, Revenge (personified) tells him:

"Then thou, Andrea, that thou arriv'd
. . . .
And serve for Chorus in this tragedy."

3. The Prologue in Thomas Dekker's *The Shoemaker's Holiday* is in prose, and it seeks the audience's indulgence in this comedy, and then succinctly summarizes the story of the play.

4. Thomas Nashe's *Summer's Last Will and Testament* also has a prose Prologue, to be delivered by the Chorus. This prologue is slightly at variance with the general run of the prologues of Elizabethan playwrights, except Shakespeare. The Prologue of *Summer's Last Will and Testament* jocosely satirizes the playwright and the actors, besides appealing to the audience for their cooperation.

These few instances of the Prologues of Shakespeare's contemporary playwrights may suffice to show us the features and characteristics of the Elizabethan Prologues, in general.

Shakespeare's Prologues may, generally, claim to be distinctive, compared with the Prologues of his contemporary dramatists. His Prologues often go beyond the *customary bound* of the Prologue. For one thing, the Prologue sometimes (emphatically) appeals to the audience's "imaginary forces" and thought, to see the "wooden O" as the wide world or at least as a vast state, or to see the "cipher" performers as kings or dignitaries, or to fly over a long gap of time or of huge water-body, and such other things. Secondly, while Shakespeare's contemporary playwrights did not make the Prologues somewhat high-falutin, or did not invest them with literary excellences, Shakespeare's Prologues often exude poetic flavor. One single instance of the Prologue to the first Act of *Henry V* may illustrate the two points (so we are quoting it entirely):

O for a Muse of fire, that would ascend
The brightest heaven of invention,
A Kingdom for a stage, princes to act
And monarchs to behold the swelling scene!
Then should the warlike Harry, like himself,
Assume the port of Mars; and at it heels,
Leash'd in the hounds, should famine, sword and fire

Crouch for employment. But pardon, gentles all,
The flat unraised spirits that have dared
On this unworthy scaffold to bring forth
So great an object: can this cockpit hold
The vastly field of France? Or may we cram
Within this wooden O the very casques
That did affright the air at Agincourt?
O pardon! Since a crooked figure may
Attest in little place a million;
And let us, ciphers to this great accompt,
On your imaginary forces work.
Suppose within the girdle of these walls
And now confined two mighty monarchies
Whose high upreared and abutting fronts
The perilous narrow ocean parts asunder:
Piece out our imperfections with your thoughts;
Into a thousand parts divide one man,
And make imaginary puissance;
Think when we talk of horses, that you see them
Printing their proud hoofs i' the receiving earth;
For 'tis your thoughts that now must deck your kings,
Carry them here and there; jumping o'er times,
Turning the accomplishment of many years
Into an hour-glass: for the which supply,
Admit me the Chorus to this history;
Who prologue-like your humble patience pray,
Gently to hear, kindly to judge, our play.

The appeal to imagination is renewed in the Prologue before Act III:

Thus with imagined wing our swift scene flies
In motion no less celerity
Than that of thought. Suppose that you have seen
The well-appointed King at Hampton pier
Embark his royalty; . . . .
. . . .
. . . . . . O, do but think
You stand upon the rivage and behold
A city on the inconstant billows dancing;

For so appears this fleet majestical
Holding due course to Harfleur. Follow, follow!
Grapple your minds to sternage of this navy, etc.

And again in the Prologue to Act V:

Behold, the English beach
Pales in the flood with men, with wives and boys,
Whose shouts and claps out-voice the deep-mouth'd sea,
Which like a mighty whiffler 'fore the king
Seems to prepare his way: so let him land,
And solemnly see him set on to London.
So swift a pace hath thought that even now
You may imagine him upon Blackheath;
Where that his lords desire him to have borne
His bruised helmet and his bended sword
Before him through the city: he forbids it,
Being free from vainness and self-glorious pride,
Giving full trophy, signal and ostent
Quite from himself to God. But now behold
In the quick forge and working-house of thought,
How London doth pour out her citizens!....

Such poetic passages are thickly strewn over the whole canon of Shakespeare, as not to be found elsewhere in the whole history of English drama. It is this poetic verve of those passages that has contributed mightily to the reason of Shakespeare being immortal.

Epilogues

Epilogues are reasonably of inferior importance, compared to prologues, because when the epilogue enters, the play is over and the audience rise to swiftly depart. So, the epilogue everywhere is generally scanty; it only expresses gratitude, apologizes for faults, or hopes to present better performances in future. But then the epilogue carries the courtesy of thanks giving; that is why epilogues are more frequent than prologues. The prologue is formal; he wears a formal robe of black cloak, but the epilogue has no special dress. The prologue is generally not spoken by any one of the cast, he may be a chorus, though.

Sometimes someone outside the cast may speak the prologue as he can the epilogue. Of course, rarely though, an actor speaks the epilogue. Sometimes, again, instead of closing a play with an epilogue, it closes with a dance (cf. *Much Ado About Nothing*) or a song or two (cf. *Love's Labour's Lost*). In earlier times most plays used to end with a lively jig.

The most plays by Shakespeare's contemporaries used to end with a short epilogue or without any epilogue, or, as in *The Knight of the Burning Pestle* of Beaumont and Fletcher, for example, the play used to end with a dialogue, in which there is an implied epilogue. Over all, the epilogues of Shakespeare's contemporary dramatists are more or less of that ilk. Shakespeare, as is his own proverb—"variety is the spice of life"—uses various devices of closing a play, though his objective was to be obsequious to the audience. However, Shakespeare concludes the following 10 plays with an epilogue: *All's Well That Ends Well, As You Like It, 2 Henry IV, Henry V, Henry VIII, A Midsummer Night's Dream, Pericles, The Tempest, Troilus and Cressida* and *Twelfth Night*. Of these, eight are in verse and two are in prose.

The epilogue of *As You Like It* (spoken by Rosalind) rightly says that "a good play needs no epilogue." The epilogue is, therefore, almost an unnecessary appendage; its only function is to tell the performers' and the poet's gratitude to the audience; and to beg pardon of the audience if the play cannot give entertainment to them. Shakespeare's epilogues well discharge these two duties, as those of his contemporaries. But Shakespeare's genius is, we repeat, always and everywhere inventive: his epilogues are not dull and perfunctory but are lively and entertaining. Further, he has invented a variety of epilogues.

Firstly, Shakespeare is perhaps the first playwright to allow a female character, Rosalind, to speak the epilogue in *As You Like It* (the female character in Shakespeare's time being played by a boy with a shrill voice). Rosalind says: "It is not the fashion to see the lady the epilogue; but it is no more unhandsome than to see the lord the prologue." Secondly, it is not the fashion that the protagonist or the main character speaks the epilogue.

Shakespeare, on the contrary, has just done this: in *The Tempest*, Prospero, the principal character, speaks the epilogue:

Now my charms are all o'er thrown,
And what strength I have's mine own,
Which is most faint.
. . . .
As you from crimes would pardon'd be,
Let your indulgence set me free.

Thirdly, the Epilogue of *Henry V* is indeed a novelty. It is well in the sonnet form, rhyming a b a b c d c d e f e f g g:

Thus far, with rough and all-unable pen,
Our bending author hath pursued the story,
In little room confining mighty men,
Mangling by stars the full course of their glory.
Small time, but in that small most greatly lived
This star of England: Fortune made his sword;
By which the world's best garden he achieved,
And of it left his son imperial lord.
Henry the Sixth, in infant bands crown'd King
Of France and England, did this King succeed;
Whose state so many had the managing,
That they lost France and made his England bleed:
Which oft our stage hath shown; and, for their sake,
In your fair minds let this acceptance take.

In three of his plays, Shakespeare has substituted three various devices in lieu of the epilogue. *Love's Labour's Lost* closes with two very famous songs: one by Ver (Spring), beginning—

When daisies pied and violets blue
And lady-smocks all silver-white
And Cuckoo-buds of yellow hue
Do paint the meadows with delight,
The cuckoo then, on every tree,
Mocks married men: . . . . etc.

The other by Hiem (Winter), beginning—

When icicles hang by the wall,
And Dick the shepherd blows his nail,

And Tom bears logs into the hall,
And milk comes frozen home in pail,
When blood is nipp'd, and ways be foul,
Then nightly sings the staring owl:
'Tu-who;
Tu-whit, Tu-who'—A merry note,
While greasy Joan doth keel the pot. Etc.

Both the songs are of 16 lines, and both are mellifluous and poetic.

Twelfth Night, on the other hand, closes with a single song (by the Clown):

When that I was and a little tiny boy,
        With hey, ho, the wind and the rain,
A foolish thing was but a toy,
        For the rain it raineth every day. Etc.

It should be noted here that the emphatic regular rhythms of this song causes an impulse to dance, though there is no stage direction for dance in the text.

And, lastly, *Much Ado About Nothing* actually closes with a dance by Benedick, a young lord of Padua.

Induction

Another device for Shakespeare to begin a play is Induction. "The induction was at first (an even) more primitive device than the dumb show. The presenter merely introduced the characters or expounded the moral, acting as an undisguised author's mouthpiece and sometimes pretending to be the author of the play. Sometimes particular personages were used to cast a "tone" over the rest of the play, to tinge it with their peculiar personality. The Witches in *Macbeth* might be considered as an induction to the play" (Bradbrook, 44). *The Wordsworth Dictionary of Shakespeare* tells us that Induction is a "Dramatic device of the 16th and 17th centuries—an introductory scene or set of scenes that frankly announce the presentation of a play...." Strictly speaking, an induction, though similar in purpose to a prologue, consists of dialogue instead of a single speech.... "An induction was generally found most appropriate in a comedy, for it emphasizes the artificiality of the presentation to follow and prepares the audience to accept the ridiculous confusions that characterise the genre. It places the audience at a distance from the main action, which effectively becomes a play within a play" (Boyce, 309).

Ben Jonson's Induction to *The Magnetic Lady* may serve as an illustration of Induction in general. The Induction of this play, which has also been called Chorus, is spoken by two Gentlemen, and a Boy who is taking care of the "Poetique Shop" (i.e. the stage). The Gentlemen have been sent by play-goers (as is implicit) to see if a good play is available for watching. The Boy says that one play is ready to start—*The Magnetic Lady; or, Humors Reconciled*, and explains that it is about a Lady: "A Lady a brave beautiful House-Keeper, and a virtuous Widow: who having a young Niece, ripe for a man and marriageable, he [the poet or author of the play] makes that his Center attractive, to draw thither a diversity of Guests, all persons of different humours to make up his *Perimiter*. And this [play] he has called *Humors reconciled*." The Boy further tells them that the poet "will not be intreated by us, to give it a Prologue." And, lastly, he requests them to take a few seats enjoying the play: "Please you take a couple of Seats".

Thomas Kyd's *The Spanish Tragedy* has a peculiar Induction. In the text, it is called Prologue, but as by definition prologue is a speech by a single person and Induction is a discourse between two or more persons, it may also be called Induction.

In the Induction of *The Spanish Tragedy*, the Ghost of Don Andrea, in his 85 unrhymed verses, gives an intimation of what is going to happen on the stage—Hieronimo's taking revenge on Balthazar. Revenge (personified) then tells Andrea (the ghost of Don Andrea):

> Then know, Andrea, that thou ariv'd
> Where thou shalt see the author of thy death,
> Don Balthazar, the prince of Portingale,
> Depriv'd of life by Bel-imperia:
> Here sit we down to see the mystery
> And serve for Chorus in this tragedy.

Shakespeare has Induction in two of his plays: *The Taming of the Shrew* and in *2 Henry IV*. The Induction of *The Taming of the Shrew* comprises two rather short scenes—one "Before an alehouse on a heath" and the other is "A bed-chamber in the Lords house." They are also called Induction I and Induction II. In Induction I, Christopher Sly, after a heavy booze, falls asleep. The local Lord returns from hunting with two huntsmen. The Lord orders that Sly be removed to his house. When Sly awakes every one treats him as a gentleman gone out of wits for many years. The Lord asks his servant, Page, to cross-dress and behave as if he is Sly's wife. Meantime, a travelling company of players arrive, whom the Lord asks to perform to entertain Sly.

In Induction II, Sly protests he is not mad, but all around him strongly persuade him to believe he actually is. Sly entreats Page, dressed as his wife, to come to Sly's bed: "Madam, undress you and come now to bed." The faking Page returns:

> For your physicians have expressly charg'd,
> In peril to incur your former malady,
> That I should yet absent me from your bed.

Just now, the Messenger announces that the players are ready to perform a "pleasant comedy". And the play *The Taming of the Shrew* begins.

It may be noted here that Act I, scene i of *Macbeth*, according to M.C. Bradbrook, may also be considered as an Induction. Bradbrook writes: "The Witches in *Macbeth* might be considered as an induction to the play" (*Bradbrook,* 44*)*. Bradbrook is right because Act I, scene i of *Macbeth*, where the Witches confer, necessarily leads to the play itself; it is not an announcement like a Prologue. The Witches also set the tone and outcome of the play. Let us see how—

Act I, scene i: *A desert place. Thunder and lightning. Enter three Witches.*

> *1 Witch.* When shall we three meet again? In thunder, lightning, or in rain?
>
> *2 Witch.* When the hurly burly's done. When the battle's lost and won.

3 Witch. That will be ere the set of sun.
1 Witch. Where the place?
2 Witch. Upon the heath.
3 Witch. There to meet with Macbeth.
1 Witch. I come, Gramalkin!
2 Witch. Paddock calls.
3 Witch. Anon.
All. Fair is foul, and foul is fair:
Hover through the fog and filthy air.
[*Witches vanish.*]

The "introduction" to *2 Henry IV* Shakespeare calls Induction and he calls Rumour, the speaker of the Induction, "the Presenter". At a glance, the Induction looks like Prologue in so far as the Induction is delivered by a single person. But Rumour, "the Presenter", is not a person outside the drama, like the prologue, but is involved in it, is integral to it. Rumour himself confesses:

. . . . my office is
To noise abroad that Harry Monmouth fell
Under the wrath of the noble Hotspur's sword,
And that the King before the Douglas's rage
Stoop'd his anointed head as low as death.
This have I rumour'd through the peasant towns
Between the royal field of Shrewsbury
And this worm-eaten hold of ragged stone,
Where Hotspur's father, old Northumberland,
Lies crafty-sick. The posts come tiring on,
And not a man of them brings other news
Than they have learnt of me. From Rumour's tongues
They bring smooth comforts false, worse than true wrongs. [*Exit.*]

Undoubtedly, even here Shakespeare is unique and inventive.

3
Chorus

Unlike in India or Britain or anywhere in the other parts of the world, say China and Russia, drama in Greece, uniquely, originated in the Grecian dithyramb—a hymn sung in honour of Bacchus or Dionysus, the god of nature and wine—accompanied by a wild and rapturous dance. This dance would be done by a chorus that contained a big group of persons. H.D.F. Kitto writes that dithyramb is "a type of hymn in honour, originally, of the Greek god Dionysus [Bacchus, in Rome], then of other deities. It was performed by a chorus of fifty and would normally relate some incident in the life of the deity to whom it was addressed. The leader of the chorus later became semi-detached, as a soloist; and in the question-and-answer that might pass between him and the rest of the chorus lies, almost certainly, the origin, or one of the origins, of drama" (Hartnoll, 242).

Robert Tracy is almost certain that the chorus was the origin of the Greek drama. According to him, the Greek chorus has had different metamorphoses in its role since ancient Greece down to the 20th century. He writes that the chorus in Greek drama was "a group of actors who stood aside from the main action of the play and commented on it. In Elizabethan phraseology, the Chorus was the speaker of the introductory prologue, as in Shakespeare's *Henry V, a* legacy from Euripides via Seneca. In the modern theatre, the word is usually taken to mean the chorus of a musical comedy, which reached its apogee in the late nineteenth century, particularly at the Gaiety Theatre [London]. It consisted of a number of beautiful young women who could sing and dance a little, stand and move gracefully, and wear lovely clothes. As their attire became scantier their activities increased, until in the 1920s they wore practically nothing at all and reached an exceedingly high standard, particularly in the clockwork precision of their dancing. The male members of the musical comedy chorus have, on the other hand, remained almost static throughout, merely acting as foils for the women, and being entirely dispensed with in some plays and in revue. Under the influence of the modern American musical play the chorus tends to have a greater share in the actual development of the plot, and to attain, in both sexes, a good standard in singing, dancing, and acting. The use of the chorus in the Greek sense has been revived in some modern poetic plays, notably in T.S. Eliot's *A Murder in the Cathedral* (Hartnoll, 176). In the ancient chorus, there was no dialogue, but only songs. In the 6th century B.C., it was Thespis who added the first actor, who would engage in dialogues with the leader of the chorus, and thus the full-fledged drama came into being. So, the great importance of the chorus in the history of drama cannot be gainsaid.

The members of the Greek chorus wore masks called *prosopon*, originally made of finely chiseled stone, and usually black costumes to hide their individual identities, so they could unanimously voice out the opinion of the public, or their idea, or their conscience in response to the action of the first actor. Before that, that is, before the induction of the first actor by Thespis, the chorus—which consisted of between 50 and 150 members—would sing about the universal ideal or conscience. (It is interesting to note that till the recent past the Bengali drama also had the tradition of the chorus of around 15 boy dancers in female dress with their ankles having jingling bells around, who would definitely perform at the beginning of a play and, sometimes, before each act, as this author had witnessed several times in his young ages.) The entrance and exit of the chorus would signify change of acts. In ancient Greece, the chorus, rarely of course, continued to be on the stage throughout the whole performance of the play. In ancient Greece, the chorus comprised not only men but also women, but the women sang and danced separately as they were deemed inferior to men. The choruses were generally identified by different appellations, such as the chorus of Aeschylus' *Agamemnon* was called "the elderly men of Argos" and the chorus of his *Prometheus Bound* was called "Oceanids" as it was composed of Oceanids (nymphs who were children of Oceanus, the god of ocean, and his wife Thetis). However, the chorus members would sing and dance in unison to emphasize the fact that they were but *one voice, one action, one ideal spectator, and one commentator*. Further, as one spectator and commentator, they also spoke in one voice when they commented upon the actions of the characters of the play.

The Greek chorus used to accomplish several vital dramatic functions. Firstly, as a built-in spectator, the chorus commented on the principal actions of the characters and the course of the drama. Secondly, the chorus would fill up the gaps between two acted-out parts of the story-line. For instance, in *The Winter's Tale* (4.1), Time, the single-person chorus, slides' over sixteen years and connects the two parts of the story which are separated by a gap of sixteen years. The chorus tells the audience:

> Now take upon me, in the name of Time,
> To use my wings. Impute it not a crime
> To me or my swift passage, that I slide
> O'er sixteen years and leave the growth untried
> Of that wide gap, since it is in my power
> To o'erthrow the law and in one self-born hour
> To plant and o'erwhelm custom.

Thus, Shakespeare very convincingly violates the classical iron order of unity of time.

Thirdly, another important function of the chorus is to accentuate the emotion already generated at a particular moment in the course of the play. In the classical drama, this was a potent tool of the playwright. For example, in Aeschylus' *Agamemnon*, the chorus (of twelve Elders of Argos) whets the empathetic sorrow of the audience at Agamemnon's sacrifice of his own daughter for the god of wind in order to help navigate his ship to Troy:

> Heedless of her tears,
> Her cries of 'Father!' and her maiden years,

Her judges valued more
Their glory and their war.
A prayer was said. Her father gave the word.
Limp in her flowing dress
The priest's attendants held her high
Above the alter, as men hold a kid.
Her father spoke again, to bid
One bring a gag, and press
Her sweet mouth tightly with a cord,
Lest Atreus' house be cursed by some ill-omened cry.

And fourthly, the chorus narrates the off-stage events; for instance, in the excerpt we just now took from *Agamemnon*. The sacrifice of Agamemnon's daughter is not shown on the stage, but is only narrated in the song of the chorus. In the classical dramas, which begin *in media res*, this function of the chorus is of great importance. Off-stage events are mostly reported by messengers or by the chorus. Fifthly, the chorus explains and explicates the complexities of the story or the actions involved therein. Sixthly, sometimes the chorus foretells the future, and thus leads the audience along the storyline with stimulated interest and suspense. And lastly, the chorus is the agent, so to say, of the author of the play: what the author cannot himself express he speaks through the mouth of the chorus. As the virtual deputy of the playwright, the chorus often performs the function of a moral educator.

As Thespis (6th c. B.C.) added the first actor (or protagonist) to the chorus—the first actor who conversed with the leader of the chorus—so Aeschylus (525-456 B.C.) added a second actor (the deuteragonist) to the *dramatis personae*, and withal reduced the number of the chorus members to less than 30. About three decades on since then Sophocles (496-506 B.C.) added the third actor (the tritagonist) and simultaneously reduced the number of chorus to about 12. And at the end of this thinning process, the chorus ultimately became a single person enterprise even in the country of its origin—Greece. The Roman drama, as regards its form, was an imitation of the Greek, and so the Roman or Latin dramatists' choruses were also a band of singers and dancers (Greek *choros* means dance). Seneca (the younger: c. 4 B.C.-A.D. 65), the model of the English tragic playwrights, also used group chorus; for instance, in *Oedipus Rex* (chorus of Theban elders), *Medea* (chorus of Corinthians), *Phaedra* (chorus of Athenian citizens), *Thyestes* (chorus of citizens of Mycenae), *Troades* (chorus of captive Trojan women), *Agamemnon* (chorus of Argive women), etc. And it is via Seneca that the Roman dramatic art reached the Elizabethan stage. Nevertheless, the chorus of a group of performers did not suit the English taste and so the Elizabethan playwrights all chose the chorus of a single person or character.

In the Elizabethan era, the chorus was not an all-forgotten phenomenon as may be apparent from the following short list of plays where there are choruses:

1. Ben Jonson, *The Magnetic Lady; or, Humours Reconciled* (1641): Chorus (Induction)
2. Christopher Marlowe, *Doctor Faustus* (c. 1589): Chorus (Prologue)
3. Thomas Kyd, *The Spanish Tragedy* (c. 1589): Chorus (of the Ghost of Andrea and Revenge after acts I, II, III and IV (the last Act)
4. Robert Greene, *James the Fourth* (c. 1591): Chorus of Bohan and Oberon (the king of the Fairies): firstly they jointly speak the Prologue; then, at the end of act I, they speak the long chorus. In acts II and III, the chorus is spoken by Bohan singly; and in act IV, the chorus is spoken by Oberon and Bohan jointly. In act V, there is no chorus.
5. Thomas Kyd, *The Tragedy of Soliman and Perseda* (1588): The chorus is present at the end of acts I, II, III, IV and V. The chorus consists of Love, Fortune and Death.
6. George Gascoigne, *The Glass of Government* (1575).

The chorus has not vanished even from modern English literature and also from modern literatures in other languages. In the modern literary world, it has occasionally surfaced—

at times in guises, though—in drama, novel and poetry, for instance, in the works of Bertolt Brecht (1898-1956), Jean Anouilh (1910-1987), Thomas Hardy (1840-1928), William Faulkner (1897-1962), Tennessee William (1911-1983) and T.S. Eliot (1888-1965). About Hardy, David Cecil writes: "There is one category among Hardy's characters...what may be called Hardy's 'chorus' characters, the groups of rustics which in his greatest works form, as it were, the chorus to the main drama: the choir led by tranter [hawker] Dewey in "Under the Greenwood Tree"; the tuft-cutters in "The Return of the Native"—Fairway, Christian, Grandfer Cantle and the rest; the collagers of Little Hintock—Wood, Cawtree, Upjohn, Crendon; the Casterbridge gossips in "The Mayor of Casterbridge"; Bathsheba's labourers in "Far From the Madding Crowd"—Joseph Poorgrass, Henry Fray, Billy Smallbury, Jan Coggan; the grave-diggers in "A Pair of Blue Eyes"; Haymoss, Blore and the rest of Lady Constantine's tenantry in "Two on a Tower". They cannot be compared with the central figures in the drama just because they are placed in the story to provide a chorus. They always appear in a group, never separately [like the members of a Greek chorus]. They are not full-length portraits [again, like the persons in a Greek chorus]. Moreover, they are drawn in a different convention. Here Hardy is in the straight tradition from Shakespeare. These minor characters are the direct descendants of Bottom and Dogberry [the former from *A Midsummer Night's Dream* and the latter from *Much Ado About Nothing*] and the rustics who gather in response to Falstaff's call to arms at the house of Justice Shallow—'character parts,' as they say on the stage, made up of a few strongly marked, deliberately caricatured personnel idiosyncrasies. They need not fear comparison with their ancestors. Rich fragments of rusticity, they are as entertaining as any of the classic comic characters of Fielding or Goldsmith. But, unlike theirs and like Shakespeare's, they can also stir serious emotion" (Cecil, 91-92). Choruses are also present in Hardy's 'unstageable' epic drama *The Dynasts* (monumental in balk, comprising 3 Parts, 19 acts and 130 scenes).

William Faulkner has also utilized the device of the chorus in his novels—in *As I Lay Dying* and *A Rose for Emily*. In the former novel, Faulkner absents himself from the course of the narrative and directs the characters to speak straight to the reader, and this creates a sort of chorus of characters. In *A Rose for Emily,* the townspeople act as a chorus when they begin to comment on Miss Emily's dating Homer Barron. The chorus is present also in Faulkner's *The Hamlet, The Mansion,* and *The Reivers.*

The French playwright Jean Anouilh, in his play *Antigone*, which is based on Sophocles' *Antigone*, has employed the chorus following the original drama, and so has done Bertolt Brecht in his *Antigone*. Brecht has also utilized the device of the chorus in his plays *The Caucasian Chalk Circle* and *Mother Courage*. In fact, in Brecht's epic theatre the device of the chorus has found a very effective role. The chorus is present also in Tennessee William's *The Glass Menagerie* and George Eliot's *Silas Marner.*

In poetry, T.S. Eliot has engaged the chorus the most in his verse plays, his chorus being modeled on the chorus of ancient Greek tragedies. Eliot, following the Greek dramatists, introduced the chorus in his poetic drama. The credit of re-introducing verse drama with chorus in it in the modern world of extremely realistic mentality must go to Eliot, and he has shown great courage and skill in this. Eliot's verse drama *Murder in the Cathedral* is heavily dependent on the chorus. Part I of the play even begins with the "Chorus of the women of Canterbury" who are apprehensive of some unknown and imminent danger (which, in fact, foreshadows the murder of Becket, the head priest of Canterbury Cathedral):

Chorus. Here let us stand, close by the cathedral.
Here let us wait.
Are you drawn by danger? Is it the knowledge of safety, that draws our feet?
Toward the cathedral?

After this, throughout the play, the chorus appears on the stage several times to help the play move on, and to comment on the characters and the actions. In Eliot's other play, *The Family*

Reunion, the chorus is not modeled on the chorus of the ancient Greek drama but on that of the Elizabethan plays, in so far as it does not participate in the dialogue but only comments on the actions of the characters. For instance, in the first scene of Part II of *The Family Reunion*, the Chorus sings:

> And whatever happens began in the past, and presses hard on the future.
>
> The agony in the curtained bedroom, whether of birth or of dying,
>
> Gathers in itself all the vices of the past, and projects them into the future.

All in all, in Eliot's dramaturgy, the chorus occupies a prominent place, indeed.

However, although in the Elizabethan era the chorus was fast petering out, Shakespeare did not hesitate to employ it in as many as 7 out of his 37 plays, in 2 of which he has used it rather abundantly, so to say, to wit, in his *Henry V*, each of its five acts is preceded by a speech of the chorus. And, likewise, in his *Pericles*, each act is preceded by a speech of Gower, the chorus. In *Romeo and Juliet*, both act I and act II are preceded by a speech of the chorus. In *The Winter's Tale*, the chorus appears only once—at the opening of act IV—and here the chorus's speech is spoken by the character Time. In *Troilus and Cressida*, *Antony and Cleopatra*, *King Lear* and *Timon of Athens*, Shakespeare has devised very skilfully sort of disguised choruses, who do not appear as overt choruses, but their functions are like those of the chorus, indeed. As choruses they hide themselves behind normal characters, with names and personal identities, but they act like the chorus—they comment on the emerging events, prognosticate about the course of events, whet the dramatically generated emotions, fill up the gaps in the narratives, if there be any, and, above all, behave as the ideal spectators. There is not a single province in the domain of the drama where Shakespeare's inventive genius has not shown its spark. During his days, the chorus, though it was going to vanish, was not all out of fashion—the spectators enjoyed and expected the chorus in the theatre. The wisdom of

Shakespeare, therefore, has kept the chorus but he has loaded it with additional protocols. Let us see how.

In *Henry V,* the chorus, acting as Prologue, introduces all the five acts. But he does not seem to confine himself within the bound of the services of the prologue; he also comments on the actions on the characters and sometimes appeals to the audience for their indulgence and imagination. The first chorus of *Henry V* principally urges the audience to press into service their imaginative faculty to behold the "swelling scene" of the play in the cribbed "cockpit" of the stage:

> O, pardon! Since a crooked figure may
> Attest in little place a million;
> And let us, ciphers to this great accompt,
> On your imaginary force work.
>
> ....
>
> Think, when we talk of horses, that you see them
> Printing their proud hoofs i' the receiving earth;
> For 'tis your thoughts that now must deck our kings,
> Carry them here and there; jumping o'er times.

Here is the addition of Shakespeare—the chorus' appeal to the viewers to use their imagination. But here the chorus has not forgotten the basic duty of the prologue: he reports that "the warlike Harry, like himself,/ Assume the port of Mars" and humbly appeals to the viewers for their patience and kindly to judge the play—"Your humble patience pray/ Gently to hear, kindly to judge, our play." The chorus also tells the viewers that he is here doing the job of the prologue.

In the next Prologue (to act II) of *Henry V,* the chorus is serving an altogether different function: he gives the audience a vision of what is happening now in the belligerent England:

> Now all the youth of England are on fire,
> And silken dalliance in the wardrobe lies:
> Now thrive the armourers, and honour's thought
> Reigns solely in the breast of every man:
> They sell the pasture now to buy the horse,

Following the mirror of all Christian kings,
With winged heels, as English Mercuries.

The Chorus is here giving the audience a daguerreotyped narrative of the present war-ready England, which is not presented on the stage, and which he urges the audience to view imaginatively. Here the chorus is helping to shrink the volume of the play. He also comments on the flawed actions of England:

O England! model to thy inward greatness,
Like little body with a mighty heart,
....
But see thy fault! France hath in thee found out
A nest of hollow bosoms, which he fills
With treacherous crowns; and three corrupted men,
One Richard Earl of Cambridge, and the second,
Henry Lord Scroop of Masham, and the third,
Sir Thomas Grey, Knight of Northumberland,
Have for the gift of France,—O guilt indeed!

Lastly, in this Prologue, the chorus leads the audience's attention to the new scene of Southampton: "But, till the King come forth, and not till then,/ Unto Southampton do we shift our scene."

The chorus in the Prologue to the third act of *Henry V* once again appeals to the imagination and fancy of the audience:

Thus with imagined wing our swift scene flies
In motion of no less celerity
Than that of thought. Suppose that you have seen
The well-appointed King at Hampden pier
Embark his royally;

This Prologue is imbued with high-falutin poetic vision. It leads the audience along the thread of the narrative, filling up the gap between this act (act II) and the previous one. And, lastly, it once again appeals to the audience to "Still be kind,/ And eke out our performance with your mind."

The fourth Prologue of the chorus, before the fourth act, also underscores the use of the audience's imagination to realize the state of the belligerent armies at Agincourt—the army of

Henry V against the army of France. The English army views its lowly defeat, and the army of France is overconfident of victory. And yet the fierce battle rages:

> Now entertain conjecture of a time
> When creeping murmur and poring dark
> Fills the wide vessel of the universe.
> ....
> Fire answers fire, and through their flames
> Each battle sees the other's umber'd face;
> Steed threatens steed, in high and boastful neighs
> Piercing the night's dull ear;..................
> ....
> Proud of their numbers and secure of souls,
> The confident and over-lusty French
> Do the low-rated English play at dice;
> ....
> The poor condemned English,
> Like sacrifices, by their watchful fires
> Sit patiently and inly ruminate
> The morning's danger, and their gesture sad
> Investing lank-lean cheeks and war-worn coats
> Presenteth them unto the gazing moon
> So many horrid ghosts.

At this most dejected hour, the presence of Henry V galvanizes the spirit of the English troops:

> O now, who will behold
> The royal captain of this ruin'd band
> Walking from watch to watch, from tent to tent,
> Let him cry "Praise and glory on his head!"
> ....
> For forth he goes and visits all his hosts,
> Bid them good morrow with a modest smile
> And call them brothers, friends and countrymen.
> ....

> That every watch, pining and pale before,
> Beholding him, plucks comfort from his looks:

And, lastly, the Chorus urges the audience to see, or, rather, imagine the real battle from its mimicry now to be presented on the stage: "Yet sit and see,/ Minding true things by what their mockeries be."

The Chorus re-iterates the importance of imagination in the Prologue to the last act of Henry V, while he is narrating Henry V's triumphant return to England. He begins his speech with the limitation of the theatre to present the "huge and proper life" of the English and French nations during the battle at Agincourt on the little "O" of the stage. The Chorus implores the audience to engage their 'winged thoughts' and to—

> Behold, the English beach
> Pales in the flood with men, with wives and boys,
> Whose shouts and claps out-voice the deep-mouth'd sea,
> Which, like a mighty whiffler 'fore the King
> Seems to prepare his way: so let him land,
> And solemnly see him set on to London.

The Chorus here fills up the gap in the story-line of the play with this narrative, and urges the audience to think ("After your thoughts") that now the scene (of the play) is not France but England. He also speaks the Epilogue of *Henry V.* Here he says that the author of this play humbly admits his weakness in portraying the history of Henry V, and says that after Henry V, his son Henry VI will be the king, as they have often shown on the stage. Thus, the Chorus with his speeches not only fills up the gaps in the story of the play but also connects the story's past, present and future.

Pericles has similarity with *Henry V,* in that in both the five acts are preceded by a chorus part, but whereas the chorus parts in *Henry V* are spoken by a chorus (without a name or any personal identity), those of *Pericles* are spoken by a named character, to wit, Gower. Gower (perhaps modeled on John Gower, the poet: 1330-1408), an old man, summarizes and moralizes the play, and bridges distant years. He appears before each act and speaks the 'prologue', and before V, ii he speaks an extra 'prologue' and closes the play with the 'epilogue'. The 'prologue' to the first act is spoken by Gower where he introduces himself and tells the audience that the story of the play is of old, and then briefly narrates it up to a point, and then, as the fashion was, asks the audience to judge his promise—"To glad your ears, and please your eyes." In the 'prologue' to the second act, Gower tells the audience that fleeing from Antioch, where the King is guilty of incest with his daughter, Pericles is now warmly received in Tarsus. But soon he receives a letter from Antioch to the effect that Thaliard, lord of Antioch, had plotted to kill him, and so he fled away from there by sea and was shipwrecked, fortunately only to be washed ashore. Gower's narrative is symbolically performed by the players of the Dumb-Show. What was heard is now seen in the Dumb-Show.

In the 'prologue' to the third act, Gower, tells the audience that Thaisa, the daughter of Simonides, the King of Pentapolis, whom Pericles had married, is now pregnant. From the intervening Dumb-Show, as it is narrated by him, the audience learn that Pericles receives another letter—this one from Helicanus—requiring Pericles to return to Tyre on an emergency. So, Pericles swiftly thither sails. Gower concludes his narrative of the event by asking the audience—

> In your imagination hold
> This stage the ship, upon whose deck
> The sea-tost Pericles appears to speak.

Here, obviously, Gower, the 'chorus', narrates the off-stage events and here again he appeals to the audience to use its imaginative faculty and see the stage as the deck of a ship tossed on the violent sea. Before the beginning of the fourth act, Gower, the 'chorus', for the fourth time, urges the audience to imagine what he narrates, but first to—

> Imagine Pericles arrived at Tyre,
> Welcomed and settled to his own desire.

And then narrates the off-stage past events and recommends the "unborn event" to the audience, which next is going to be performed by the Dumb-Show. In the fourth 'chorus', Gower speaks of the time-shift from the third act to the fourth, depending on the imagination of the audience:

> Only I carry the winged time
> Past on the lame feet of my rhyme;
> Which never could I so convey,
> Unless your thoughts went on my way.

Appeal to the imagination continues through the last act. Pericles has arrived Mytilene by sea to fetch his daughter Marina—who has escaped bawdry—and is warmly received by the people of Mytilene. Gower now entreats the audience to imagine Pericles on the coast of Mytilene: "on this coast/ Suppose him now at anchor." And he implores them to—

> In your supposing once more put your sight
> Of heavy Pericles; think this his bark:
> Where what is done in action, more, if might,
> Shall be discover'd; please you, sit and hark.

In addition to these five 'choruses', there is another 'chorus' which, as we have told, is in the second scene of the fifth act. It consists of 20 lines, and uniquely occupies the whole of the scene. Here Gower concludes the storyline and appeals to the audience to relieve him—

> Now our sands are almost run;
> More a little, and then dumb.
> This my last boon, give me,
> For such kindness must relieve me—
> That you aptly will suppose
> What pageantry, what feats, what shows,
> What minstrelsy, and pretty din,
> The regent made in Mytilene
> To greet the King. So he thrived
> That he is promis'd to be wived
> To fair Marina; but in no wise
> Till he had done his sacrifice,
> As Dian bade; where to being bound,

The interim, pray you, all confound.
In feather'd briefness sails are fill'd,
And wishes fall out as they're will'd.
At Ephesus the temple see,
Our King, and all his company.
That he can hither come so soon,
Is by your fancies' thankful doom.

It may be noted here in passing that only in the two plays of Shakespeare—*Henry V* and *Pericles*—the 'chorus' is hugely present: the chorus appears 5 times in *Henry V* and delivers 209 unrhymed verses in the 'Prologue' and 14 verse lines in the 'Epilogue'. The Chorus speaks approximately 15% of the total 3389 lines of the play. Interestingly, the 'Epilogue' is a sonnet in the Shakespearean rhyme scheme: ab ab cd cd ef ef gg (in the sonnet form). The Chorus of *Pericles* has also some unique features. He speaks the 'prologue' five times, delivering 218 verse lines that rhyme with alternate verses, and quite uniquely, he occupies the whole of the second scene of the fifth act of *Pericles* and speaks 18 rhymed verses (in the sonnet form). The total lines of *Pericles* is around 2020 lines and the chorus (Gower) speaks approximately 10% of them.

Romeo and Juliet has two quite uncommon Prologues—one before the first act and the other before the second act, both spoken by the Chorus, and both are sonnets. The earlier Prologue spoken by the chorus:

Two households, both alike in dignity,
In fair Verona, where we lay our scene,
From ancient grudge break to new mutiny,
Where civil blood makes civil hands unclean.
From forth the fatal loins of these two foes
A pair of star-cross'd lovers take their life;
Whose misadventur'd piteous overthrows
Doth their death bury their parents' strife.
The fearful passage of their death-mark'd love
And the continuance of their parents' rage,
Which, but their children's end, nought could remove,

Is now the two hours' traffic of our stage;
The which if you with patient ears attend,
What here shall miss, our toil shall strive to mend.

It may be noted that this sonnet's rhyme-scheme is: ab ab cd cd ef ef gg. Now the other sonnet that is before the second act, also spoken by the Chorus:

Now old desire doth in this death-bed lie,
And young affection gapes to be his heir;
That fair for which love groan'd for and would die,
With tender Juliet match'd, is now not fair.
Now Romeo is belov'd, and loves again,
Alike bewitched by the charm of looks;
But to his foe suppos'd he must complain,
And she steal love's sweet bait from fearful hooks.
Being held a foe, he may not have access
To breathe such vows as lovers use to swear;
And she as much in love, her means much less
To meet her new beloved any where.
But passion lends them power, time means, to meet,
Temp'ring extremities with extreme sweet.

The rhyme-scheme of this sonnet is: ab ab cd cd ef ef gg.

There is also a sonnet-like succulent conversation between Romeo and Juliet in the fifth scene of the first act of this play, whose rhyme-scheme, again, is the same:

Romeo. (to Juliet). If I profane with my unworthiest hand
This holy shrine, the gentle fine is this:
My lips, two blushing pilgrims ready stand
To smooth that rough touch with a tender kiss.

Juliet. Good pilgrim, you do wrong your hand too much,
Which mannerly devotion shows in this;
For saints have hands that pilgrims' hands do touch,

And palm to palm is holy palmers' kiss.
Romeo. Have not saints lips, and holy palmers too?
Juliet. Ay, pilgrim lips that they must use in pray'r.
Romeo. O, then, dear saint, let lips do what hands do!
They pray; grant thou, lest faith turn to despair.
Juliet. Saints do not move, though grant for prayers' sake.
Romeo. Then move not while my prayer's effect I take.

All the three sonnets' rhyme-scheme, as told before, is the same: abab cdcd efef gg, which is called Shakespearean rhyme-scheme.

The first two sonnets are verily chorus-like, for in the first one the speaker narrates the preamble of the play and concludes with an appeal to the audience to watch patiently the play which is but "two hours traffic", and in the second sonnet (prologue) the speaker tells what is going to happen next—Juliet to reciprocate Romeo's love and the fission between them over time will end "with extreme sweet".

In *The Winter's Tale*, like in *2 Henry IV*, the chorus is an embodiment of an abstraction: in *2 Henry IV*, it is Rumour, "painted full of tongues", and in *The Winter's Tale,* it is Time, with a pair of wings with which it jumps over a wide stretch of time, 16 years, to be specific—16 years between the end of the third act and the beginning of the fourth act. As the chorus in *Pericles* occupies the whole of the second scene of the fifth act, so Time occupies the whole space of the first scene of the fourth act of *The Winter's Tale*. He narrates the intervening 16 years' loneliness of King Leontes and Perdita and foretells that the audience will shortly meet Florizel, the son of King Polixenes. It may be noted that Time is here acting as both prologue and chorus, though the stage direction simply is such: "Enter Time, the Chorus."

Let us see how Time persuades the audience to assume that he has hovered over the space of sixteen years:

Now take upon me, in the name of Time
To use my wings. Impute it not a crime
To me or my swift passage, that I slide

Over sixteen years..........................
....
Your patience this allowing,
I turn my glass and give my scene such growing
As you had slept between.

Time then narrates that the grief-stricken Leontes has shut himself up, and implores the audience to imagine that he is now in Bohemia: "imagine me,/ Gentle spectators, that I now may be/ In fair Bohemia". He then briefly speaks about Florizel and Perdita and asks the audience to follow what is being performed next on the stage. It may be noted here that Time is none in the actual cast of the play—no one in the *dramatis personae*. He is outside the play. And so Shakespeare has very appropriately devised special language for him—language that is quite different from that of all of the cast. His rhyming couplets are uniquely his. Time is also, as some commentators say, the delegate of Shakespeare whose principal duty is to jump over sixteen years with the audience on his wings.

Troilus and Cressida has also an uncommon chorus—Thersites. He is not called a chorus in the cast or anywhere in the text but from his actions we can perhaps safely say that he is "almost a chorus". Shakespeare created him on the model of Homer's Thersites (in *Iliad*, Bk II) who fought in the Trojan War. In *Iliad*, Thersites is a scathing critic of Agamemnon for his inhumane act of sacrificing his daughter. In *Troilus and Cressida* also Thersites heavily censors Agamemnon. Moreover, both in the epic and in the play Thersites is physically handicapped. In the *dramatis personae* of *Troilus and Cressida*, moreover, Thersites is called "a deformed and scurrilous Greek". In the play, he appears thrice: in II, iii; V, i (soliloquizes twice) and V, iv.

In II, iii, Thersites pulls up Ajax, and then comments on Patroclus, Achilles, Agamemnon and, risibly, himself: "Agamemnon is a fool to offer to command Achilles; Achilles is a fool to be commanded of Agamemnon; Thersites is a fool to serve such a fool, and Patroclus is a fool positive." In the first scene of the fifth act, Thersites, in two soliloquies in prose, comments on Achilles, Patroclus, Agamemnon, Menelaus and Diomedes. The first soliloquy:

Thersites. With too much blood and too little brain, these two [Achilles and Patroclus] may run mad; but if with too much brain and too little blood they do, I'll be a curer of madmen. Here's Agamemnon, an honest fellow enough, and one that loves quails; but he has not so much brain as ear-wax: and the goodly transformation of Jupiter there, his brother, the bull,—the primitive statue, and oblique memorial of cuckolds; a thrifty shoeing-horn in a chain, hanging at his brother's leg,—to what form but that he is, should wit larded with malice and malice forced with wit turn him to? To an ass were nothing; he is both ass and ox; to an ox were nothing; he is both ox and ass. To be a dog, a mule, a cat, a fitchew, a toad, a lizard, an owl, a puttock, or a herring without a roe, I would not care; but to be a Menelaus! I would conspire against destiny. Ask me not what would be, if I were not Thersites; for I care not to be the louse of a lazar, so I were not Menelaus. Hoy-day! spirits and fires!

Again, Thersites in the same scene of the same act soliloquizes, chiding Diomedes, after some 20 lines below:

Thersites. That same Diomed's a false-hearted rogue, a most unjust knave; I will no more trust him when he leers than I will a serpent when he hisses. He will spend his mouth and promise, like Brabbler the hound; but when he performs, astronomers, foretell it: there will come some change; the sun borrows the moon, when Diomed keeps his word. I will rather leave to see Hector than not to dog him. They say he keeps a Trojan drab, and uses the traitor Calchas' tent. I' will after. Nothing but lechery! All incontinent varlets!

Lastly, also in the fourth scene of fifth act of *Troilus and Cressida,* Thersites carps and comments on Diomedes and others in his soliloquy, standing in the plain between Troy and the Grecian camp:

Now they are clapper-clawing one another; I'll go look on. That dissembling abominable varlet, Diomed, has

> got that same scurvy doting foolish young knave's sleeve of Troy there in his helm. I would fain see them meet, that that same young Trojan ass that loves the whore there might send that Greekish whore-masterly villain with the sleeve back to the dissembling luxurious drab of a sleeve-less errand. A th' t'other side, the policy of those crafty swearing rascals—that stale old mouse-eaten dry cheese, Nestor, that same dog-fox, Ulysses—is not prov'd worth a blackberry. They set me up, in policy, that mongrel cur, Ajax, against that dog of as bad a kind, Achilles; and now is the cur Ajax prouder than the cur Achilles, and will not arm to-day; whereupon the Grecians begin to proclaim barbarism, and policy grows into an ill opinion.

Like Thersites, Domitius Enobarbus in *Antony and Cleopatra* is also "an almost chorus" character. Enobarbus, friend to Mark Antony, is not only a soldier but he also comments on most of the principal characters of the play and, sometimes, joins in the narrative of the story, and it is in this sense that he may be counted "an almost chorus".

We meet Enobarbus in as many as ten scenes of the play: I, ii; II, ii; II, vi; II, vii; III, ii; III, v; III, vii; III, xiii; IV, ii; and IV, vi.

In the second scene of the first act, Enobarbus speaks of the wonderous beauty of Cleopatra to Antony. Fluvia, Antony's wife, has died in Rome, and the penitent Antony is anxious to break away from the spell of Cleopatra and leave Egypt the sooner for Rome:

> *Antony.* I must be gone.
>
> *Enobarbus.* Under a compelling occasion, let women die: it were pity to cast them away for nothing; though, between them and a great cause, they should be esteemed nothing. Cleopatra, catching but the least noise of this, dies instantly; I have seen her die twenty times upon her poorer moments: I do think there is mettle in death, which commits some loving act upon her, she hath such a celerity in dying.

Antony is in a double bind—he cannot bear with the loss of Fulvia and regrets being drawn to Cleopatra as well:

Antony. Would I had never seen her!

Enobarbus. O sir, you had then left unseen a wonderful piece of work, which not to have been blest withal would have discredited your travel.

In the second scene of the second act, Enobarbus makes his two famous speeches in which he draws a zeuxian portrait of the supra-mundane beauty of Cleopatra:

Enobarbus. When she first met Mark Antony, she purs'd up his heart, upon the river of Cydnus.

Agrippa. There she appear'd indeed! or my reporter devis'd well for her.

Enobarbus. I will tell you.
The barge she sat in, like a barnish'd throne,
Burn'd on the water. The poop was beaten gold;

....

For her own person,
It begger'd all description. She did lie
In her pavilion, cloth-of-gold, of tissue,
O'erpicturing that Venus where we see
The fancy out-work nature. On each side her
Stood pretty dimpled boys, like smiling Cupids,
With divers-colour'd fans, whose wind did seem
To glow the delicate cheeks which they did cool,
And what they undid did.

Next, in the sixth scene of the same second act, Enobarbus predicts—and here he is 'exactly' a chorus—that Antonio will desert Octavia and go to Cleopatra. Enobarbus tells Menas, friend to Pompey, that Octavious, whom Antony had married after Fluvia died, "is of a holy, cold, and still conversation."

Menas. Who would not have his wife so?

Enobarbus. Not he that himself is not so; which Mark Antony is. He will to his Egyptian dish again;....Antony will use his affection where it is; he married but his occasion is here.

After this, in the seventh scene of the second act, we see Enobarbus just taking part in the banquet and Baccanalian drinking spree with Antony, Menas and others on board Pompey's galley, off Misenum.

So far, Enobarbus has commented on Antony and Cleopatra. Now, in the second scene of the third act, he comments on Lepidus, one of the Triumvirs of Rome, and also on Caesar and Antony like a true chorus:

Agrippa. 'Tis a noble Lepidus.
Enobarbus. A very fine one. O, how he loves Caesar!
Agrippa. Nay, but how dearly he adores Mark Antony!
Enobarbus. Caesar? Why he is the Jupiter of men.
Agrippa. What's Antony? The god of Jupiter.
Enobarbus. Spake you of Caesar? How! the nonpareil.
Agrippa. O, Antony! O thou Arabian bird!
Enobarbus. Would you praise Caesar say 'Caesar'—go no further.
Agrippa. Indeed, he plied them both with excellent praises.
Enobarbus. But he loves Caesar best. Yet he loves Antony.
Hoo! hearts, tongues, figures, scribes, bards, poets, cannot
Think, speak, cast, write, sing, number—hoo!—
His love to Antony. But as for Caesar,
Kneel down, kneel down, and wonder.
Agrippa. Both he loves.
Enobarbus. They are his shards, and he their beetle.

In the thirteenth scene of the third act, Enobarbus once again censors Antony, and pronounces a fatal judgment on Cleopatra. In her palace in Alexandria, Cleopatra sees herself in a dangerously violent war between Caesar and Antony, and asks Enobarbus about who should be held responsible for all this:

> *Cleopatra.* Is Antony or we in fault for this?
>
> *Enobarbus.* Antony only, that would make his will
> Lord of his reason.

And, before this, in the self-same scene, Enobarbus castigated Cleopatra for her double-dealing, doom-drawing, instinct of love, pandered both to Caesar and Antony, all at the same time:

> *Cleopatra.* What shall we do, Enobarbus?
>
> *Enobarbus.* Think, and die.

Thus, we have seen Enobarbus both as a narrator and as a commentator. But besides narrating and commenting, he sometimes gives very humorous advices. For instance, in the seventh scene of the third act, when Cleopatra asks Enobarbus whether she could join the on-going war between Antony and Caesar, he crossly advises her (comments on her thinking) for refraining from the war:

> If we should serve with horse and mares together
> The horse were merely lost; the mares would bear
> A soldier and a horse.

This is a crass sexually humorous expression of Enobarbus. He has other humorous expressions also. For instance, in the second scene of the fourth, he tells Antonio:

> What you mean, sir,
> To give them this discomfort?
> Look, they weep;
> And I, an ass, am onion-ey'd.

But, then, Enobarbus is not a clown in the true sense of the term, though at times he talks light-heartedly, or, better, sardonically. He is wise, unlike the stock character of a clown or fool, and at times highly poetic. However, we see Enobarbus for the last time in the sixth scene of the fourth act. Here his jovial nature and earthly wisdom sinks too low. He switched from Antony's side to Caesar's; and now, as Caesar ceases to be the most mighty, he is penitential: "I am alone the villain of the earth,/ And feel

I am so most, O Antony,/... I will go seek/ Some ditch wherein to die; the foul'st best fits/ My later part of life."

Like Enobarbus, the Fool in *King Lear* may also be considered as a 'chorus', in so far as he comments especially on King Lear, slantingly though. In, *King Lear*, the Fool appears in five scenes: I, iv; I, v; II, iv; III, ii; III, iv and III, vi. The Fool comments on the actions of other characters as well through verses, songs, quips and retorts. Though in the *dramatis personae* of the text of the play he is called Fool, he is actually not a fool in ordinary sense of the word. "'Fool' was a common term of endearment in Shakespeare's day..." (Boyce, 199). It is in this sense that in the third scene of the fifth act of *King Lear*, Lear, holding the dead body of Cordelia grieves: "And my poor fool is hang'd." However, Fool is a "Character type often used by Shakespeare, as a sharp-tongued comic, usually a professional jester, who wittily insults other characters and comments on their actions. He often serves as a *chorus,* providing a position outside the plot with which we, the audience, can identify" (*italics mine*) (Boyce, 198).

However, in *King Lear,* the Fool is with us since the first act and throughout the third. He keeps us buoyed up with his witty jestings, and comments on characters' actions, and before the beginning of the fourth act in which the tragedy begins to intensify, he retires. In the two scenes of the first Act—I, iv and I, v—the Fool verbally castigates Lear for giving away his whole kingdom to Goneril and Regan. A great part of the fourth scene of the first act of this play is covered by Lear and the Fool in conversation. We will cite only an excerpt from that conversation to show the Fool as a clown and as a *chorus*:

Fool. Sirrah, I'll teach thee a speech.
Lear. Do.
Fool. Mark it, nuncle:
Have more than thou showest,
Speak less than thou knowest,
Lend less than thou owest,
....

Fool. Dost thou know the difference, my boy, between a bitter fool and a sweet one?

Lear. No, lad; teach me.

Fool. The lord that counsell'd thee
To give away thy land,
Come place him here by me,—
Do thou for him stand:
The sweet and bitter fool
Will presently appear;
The one in motley here,
The other found out there.

Lear. Dost thou call me fool, boy?

Fool. All thy other titles thou hast given away; that thou wast born with.

....

Lear. When were you wont to be so full of songs, sirrah?

Fool. I have us'd it, nuncle, e'er since thou mad'st thy daughters thy mothers; for when thou gav'st them the rod, and put'st down thy own breeches.

[*Sings*] Then they for sudden joy did weep,
And I for sorrow sung,
That such a king should play bo-peep
And go to the fools among.

Noble is the Fool, indeed, in commenting on his king. However, in the fifth scene of first act, the Fool catechises Lear in pragmatic relationship between a father and his daughters, thereby insinuating (and thus commenting on) Lear's foolishness in giving his all away to his daughters:

Fool. Canst tell how an oyster makes his shell?

Lear. No.

Fool. Nor I neither; but I can tell why a snail has a house.

Lear. Why?

Fool. Why, to put's head in; not to give it away to his daughters, and leave his horns without a case.

In the second scene of the third act of *King Lear*, when in the heath Lear raves against the hard wind, torrential rain, and thunder bolts, being maddened by his two daughters' damn ingratitude, the Fool verbally flagellates him, telling him that his suffering is his own making:

He that has a house to put's head in has a good head-piece.
The cod-piece that will house
Before the head has any,
The head and he shall louse;
So beggars marry many.
The man that makes his toe
What he his heart should make
Shall of a corn cry woe.
And turn his sleep to wake.

The wise Fool thus flabbergasts the woebegone Lear at every turn of the way he leads him through to whip up his sense of justice from under a thick layer of passion. And so, the Fool may be counted as a chorus.

And so also the Poet in *Timon of Athens* is a chorus-like character, in so far as he anticipates the ending of the play. "He anticipates the play's truths when he tells [in I, i] that the poem he is writing, in which Timon is shown as a favourite of the goddess Fortune, contains the warning that when Fortune changes, her exfavourites are abandoned by their seemingly loyal followers" (Boyce, 508). In the first scene of the first act of *Timon of Athens*, the Poet (a character) tells the Painter about the matter of the poem he is now composing:

Poet. ....
I have in this rough work, shap'd out a man,
Whom this beneath world doth embrace and hug
With amplest entertainment: my free drift
Halts not particularly, but moves itself

In a wide sea of tax. No levell'd malice
Infects one comma in the course I hold,
But flies an eagle flight, bold and forth on,
Leaving no tract behind.

Painter. How shall I understand you?

Poet. I will unbolt to you.
You see how all conditions, how all minds—
As well of glib and slipp'ry creatures as
Of grave and austere quality, tender down
Their services to Lord Timon. His large fortune,
Upon his good and gracious nature hanging,
Subdues and properties to his love and tendence
All sorts of hearts; yea, from the glass-fac'd flatterer
To Apemantus, that few things loves better
Than to abhor himself; even he drops down
The knee before him, and returns in peace
Most rich in Timon's nod.

....

Poet. When Fortune in her shift and change of mood
Spurns down her late beloved, all his dependants,
Which labour'd after him to the mountain's top
Even on their knees and hands, let him slip down,
Not one accompanying his declining foot.

4
Clowns, Fools, and Jesters

In his *Dictionnaire Philosophique* (1765), Voltaire shockingly calls Shakespeare a "buffoon" (Ralli, vol. I, 46), but Shakespeare's clownery (he could not altogether escape his age's dramatic convention and spectators' demand), in many cases, is not wholly buffoonery, for it has prudential and philosophic drags underneath. The term 'clown' is defined in *The Chambers Twentieth Century Dictionary* (1981) as "a rustic or country-fellow: one with the awkward manners of a countryman: an ill-bred fellow: a fool or buffoon, esp. of the harlequinade or the circus." John Russell Taylor, in *The Penguin Dictionary of the Theatre*, writes in the entry 'Clown': "Comic performer in theatre or circus. Some of the functions of the medieval and Renaissance court jester are carried over into the fools of the Elizabethan stage, such as the jesters in *Twelfth Night* and *King Lear*: These are professional humorists, as distinct from the comic butts of pastorals like *As You Like It*" (Taylor, 63).

From the above we may understand that the term 'clown' is a portmanteau word that allows two other senses: jester, fool. F.E. Halliday writes that "The word [clown] is probably connected with 'clod', a stupid, rustic fellow. The Elizabethans appear to have used 'clown' and 'fool' indiscriminately.... "The clown is a stock character in Shakespeare's plays, from Launce in *The Two Gentlemen of Verona* to Stephano in *The Tempest*, commonest of course in the Comedies: the Dromios, Grumio, Costard, the Gobbos, Bottom, Dogberry, and the delightful shepherd's son in *The Winter's Tale*; rarer in the Histories, though no doubt Mistress Quickly was played by a 'clown'; and there are few Tragedies without a clown, from the poor shadowy creature in *Titus Andronicus* to the gravediggers in *Hamlet*, the porter in *Macbeth*, and the clown who brings the asps to Cleopatra. But the broad comedy of most of these parts should be distinguished from that of the much more subtle and intellectual comedy of the professional 'fools' (apparently descended from the Vice of medieval drama), Touchstone and Feste, with their music, and the tragic jesting of Lear's Fool, parts probably played by Armin, much less of a clown than Tarlton and Kempe. The chief comedians of Shakespeare's company appear to have been Kempe, Pope, Armin, Cowley, Robinson and Shank" (Halliday, 1969, 106-07). However, as in the circus, the clown in the Elizabethan period used to wear a distinctive dress: a motley long coat and a hat adorned with a clout (for which the manner of the clown is called clouterly)—the clout being made usually of cock's feathers.

With this much as an introduction to the curiously interesting stock character of Shakespeare—the clown—let us go into some details about his dramatic functions in the bard's plays.

Shakespeare has an unprecedented long list of clowns or clownish characters (jesters, fools, irregular humorists). Here is a list of the plays and their respective clowns or clownish characters:

A. COMEDIES

1. *All's Well That Ends Well* (Lavache)
2. *As You Like It* (Touchstone, clownish fool, and Jaques, a humorous character)
3. *Love's Labour's Lost* (Costard)
4. *Twelfth Night* (Feste, a Clown)
5. *The Winter's Tale* (Old Shepherd's son, a Clown)
6. *The Two Gentlemen of Verona* (Speed, a clownish servant to Valentine)
7. *The Merchant of Venice* (Launcelot Gobbo, a Clown)
8. *Much Ado About Nothing* (Dogberry, a humorist)
9. *A Midsummer Night's Dream* (Bottom)

B. TRAGEDIES

1. *Titus Andronicus* (a Clown)
2. *Hamlet* (Grave-diggers, two Clowns)
3. *Macbeth* (Porter, a clownish character)
4. *Antony and Cleopatra* (Clown)
5. *Othello* (Clown, servant to Othello)
6. *King Lear* (Fool, a clownish but wise character)

C. HISTORY

Henry IV, Part Two (Five irregular humorists: Falstaff, Edward Poins, Bardolph, Pistol and Peto)

A. COMEDIES

1. *All's Well That Ends Well*

In this play, Monsieur Lavache (V, ii) is the name of the Clown, though in the *dramatis personae* he is introduced simply as "Clown". His appearances in the play are extraordinary, in the sense that he appears in all the five Acts: I, iii; II, ii; III, ii; IV, v; and V, ii.

In I, iii, the function of the Clown is only to provide (low) amusement to the audience through his dialogue with the Countess of Rousillon. Take a slice of their conversation, for an instance. The Clown wants to marry Isabel (a ghost character—never appears on the stage).

Clown. I do beg your good will in this case.
Countess. In what case?
Clown. In Isabel's case and mine own....
Countess. Tell me thy reason why thou wilt marry.
Clown. My poor body, madam, requires it: I am driven by the *flesh;* and he must needs go that the devil drives.

In II, ii, again, there is a risible low conversation between the Countess and the Clown. A quote from the conversation:

Countess. Marry, that's bountiful answer that fits all questions.

Clown. It is like a barber's chair that fits all *buttocks*, the pin-buttock, the quatch-buttock, the brawn buttock, or any *buttock*.

In III, ii, yet again we find a ludicrous interchange between the Countess and the Clown:

Clown. By my troth, I take my young lord [Bertram] to be a very melancholy man.

Countess. By what observance, I pray you?

Clown. Why, he will look upon his boot and sing; mend his ruff and sing; ask questions and sing; pick his tooth and sing. I know a man that had this trick of melancholy sold a good manor for a song.

In the next scene (IV, v), the Countess is replaced by Lafeu in the dialogue. A scoopful from the low dialogue between the Clown and Lafeu:

Lafeu. Whether dost thou profess thyself a knave or a fool?

Clown. A fool, sir, at a woman's service, and a knave at a man's.

Lafeu. Your distinction?

Clown. I would cozen the man of his wife and do his service.

Lafeu. So you were a knave at his service indeed.

Clown. And I would give his wife my *bauble*, sir, to do her service.

And lastly, in the beginning of the second scene of the fifth act, the Clown and Parolles engage in a jestful conversation. A specimen from that:

Parolles. Good Monsieur Lavache, give my Lord Lafeu this letter: I have ere now, sir, been better known to you, when I have held familiarity with fresher clothes; but I am now, sir, muddied in fortune's mood, and smell somewhat strong of her strong displeasure.

Clown. Truly, fortune's displeasure is but sluttish, if it smell so strongly as thou speakest of: I will henceforth eat no fish of fortune's buttering. Prithee allow the *wind*.

Parolles. Nay, you need not to stop your nose, sir, I speak but a metaphor.

Clown. Indeed, sir, if your metaphor stink, I will stop my nose; or against any man's metaphor. Prithee, get thee further. (*italics mine*)

In this play, the Clown is for the most part a jester—an entertainer. Special notice may be taken of his low and foul words and suggestions.

2. *As You Like It*

Touchstone is the *court jester* of this play. He appears in as many as seven scenes: I, ii; II, iv; III, ii; III, iii; V, i; V, iii; and V, iv. He is witty and a 'natural' fool. He is a rodomontade too, for he compares himself with Ovid (his name derives from Ovid's *Metamorphoses*). An excerpt from the second scene of the first act to show Touchstone's jesting and witticism:

Touchstone. Mistress, you must come away to your father.

Celia. Were you made the messenger?

Touchstone. No, by mine honour: but I was bid to come for you.

Rosalind. Where learned you that oath, fool?

Touchstone. Of a certain knight that swore by his honour they were good pancakes, and swore by his honour the mustard was naught. Now I'll stand to it, the pancakes were naught and the mustard was good, and yet was not the knight forsworn.

Celia. How prove you that, in the great leap of your knowledge?

Rosalind. Ay, marry, now unmuzzle your wisdom.

Touchstone. Stand you both forth now: stroke your chins and swear by your beards that I am a knave.

Celia. By our beards, if we had them, thou art.

Touchstone. By my knavery, if I had it, then I were. But if you swear by that that is not, you are not forsworn; no more was this knight, swearing by his honour, for he never had any; or if he had, he had sworn it away before ever he saw those pancakes or that mustard.

Celia. Prithee, who is't that thou mean'st?

Touchstone. One that did old Frederick, your father loves.

Celia. My father's love is enough to honour him. Enough, speak no more of him; You will be whipt for taxation one of these days.

Touchstone. The more pity that fools may not speak wisely what wise men do foolishly.

In II, iv, Touchstone, in the guise of a shepherd, is accompanying the disguised (in men's apparels) Celia (as Aliena) and Rosalind (as Ganymede), who are feeling home to arrive into the forest of Arden. As in the previous scene, here too Touchstone is making occasions for enjoyable laughter over his wittily constructed complex sentences. A specimen of Touchstone's wit-wantoning is being given bellow.

Rosalind. Alas, poor shepherd! Searching of thy wound, I have by hard adventure found my own.

Touchstone. And I mine. I remember, when I was in love, I broke my sword upon a stone, and bid him take that for coming a-night to Jane Smile; and I remember the kissing of her batler, and the cow's dugs that her pretty chopt hands had milk'd; and I remember the wooing of a peascod instead of her; from whom I took two cods, and giving her them again, said with weeping tears 'Wear these for my sake'. We that are true lovers run into strange capers; but as all is mortal in nature, so is all nature in love mortal in folly.

Rosalind. Thou speak'st wiser than thou art ware of.

Touchstone. Nay, I shall ne'er be ware of my own wit till I break my shins against it.

Rosalind. Jove, Jove! this shepherd's passion
Is much upon my fashion.

Touchstone. And mine; but grows something stale with me.

In III, ii, Touchstone has the most space for showing his métier as a jester and his linguistic jugglery. For brevity, let us have just a scoop of it. In the forest of Arden, Touchstone converses with the shepherd, Corin.

Corin. And how like you this shepherd's life Master Touchstone?

Touchstone. Truly, shepherd, in respect of itself, it is a good life; but in respect of that it is a shepherd's life, it is nought. In respect that it is solitary, I like it very well; but in respect that it is private, it is a very vile life. Now in respect it is in the fields, it pleaseth me well; but in respect it is not in the court, it is tedious. As it is a spare life, look you, it fits my humour well; but as there is no more plenty in it, it goes much against my stomach. Hast any philosophy in thee, shepherd?

Next, going further a little in the same scene, we find Touchstone parodying the couplets, Rosalind reads.

Rosalind. From the east to western Inde,
No jewel is like Rosalinde.
Her worth, being mounted on the wind,
Through all the world bears Rosalinde.
All the pictures fairest lin'd
Are but black to Rosalinde.
Let no face be kept in mind
But the fair of Rosalinde.

Touchstone. I'll rhyme you so eight years together, dinners, and suppers, and sleeping hours, excepted. It is the right butter-women's rank to market.

Rosalind. Out, fool!

Touchstone. For a taste:
If a hart do lack a hind
Let him seek out Rosalinde.
If the cat will after kind,

So be sure will Rosalinde.
Winter garments must be lin'd,
So must slender Rosalinde.
They that reap must sheaf and bind,
Then to cart with Rosalinde.
Sweetest nut hath sourest rind,
Such a nut is Rosalinde.
He that sweetest rose will find.
Must find love's prick and Rosalinde.

This is the very false gallop of verses; why do you infect yourself with them?

Rosalind. Peace, you dull fool! I found them on a tree.

In the just next scene, to wit in III, iii, Touchstone has a romantic encounter with Audrey, Jaques being the only witness.

Touchstone. Come apace, good Audrey; I will fetch up your goats, Audrey. And How, Audrey, am I the man yet? Doth my simple feature content you?

Audrey. Your features! Lord warrant us! What features?

Touchstone. I am here with thee and thy goats, as the most capricious poet, honest Ovid, was among the Goths.

Jaques. [*Aside*] O knowledge ill-inhabited, worse than Jove in a thatch'd house!

Touchstone. When a man's verses cannot be understood, nor a man's good wit seconded with the forward child understanding, it strikes a man more dead than a great reckoning in a little room. Truly, I would the gods had made thee poetical.

Audrey. I do not know what 'poetical' is. Is it honest in deed and word? Is it a true thing?

Touchstone. No, truly; for the truest poetry is the most feigning, and lovers are given to poetry; and what they swear in poetry may b said as lovers they do feign.

Audrey. Do you wish, then, that the gods had made me poetical?

....

Touchstone. Well, praised be the gods for thy foulness; sluttishness may come hereafter. But be it as it may, I will marry thee; and to that end I have been with Sir Oliver Martext, the vicar of the next village, who hath promis'd to meet me in this place of the forest, and to couple us.

Jaques. [*Aside*] I would fain see this meeting.

Audrey. Well, the gods give us joy!

Skipping over the whole of the fourth act, the jestful romance between Touchstone and Audrey is present in three of the four scenes of the fifth Act: V, i; V, iii and V, iv. First look at the very risible jokes in V, i between Touchstone and William, a country fellow, both of whom loves Audrey.

Enter William

Touchstone. It is meat and drink to me to see a clown. By my troth, we that have good wits have much to answer for: we shall be flouting; we cannot hold.

William. Good ev'n Audrey.

Audrey. God ye good ev'n, William.

William. And good ev'n to you, sir.

Touchstone. Good ev'n, gentle friend. Cover thy head, cover thy head; nay, Prith be cover'd. How old are you, friend?

William. Five and twenty, sir.

Touchstone. A ripe age. Is thy name William?

William. William, sir.

Touchstone. A fair name. Wast born i' th' forest here?

William. Ay, sir, I thank God.

Touchstone. 'Thank God'. A good answer. Art rich?

William. Faith, sir, so-so.

Touchstone. 'So-so' is good, very good, very excellent good; and yet it is not; it is but so-so. Art thou wise?

William. Ay, sir, I have a pretty wit.

Touchstone. Why, thou say'st well. I do now remember a saying: 'The fool doth think he is wise, but the wise man knows himself to be a fool.' The heathen philosopher when he had a desire to eat a grape, would open his lips when he put it into his mouth; meaning thereby that grapes were made to eat and lips to open. You do love this maid?

William. I do, sir.

Touchstone. Give me your hand. Art thou learned?

William. No, sir.

Touchstone. Then learn this of me: to have is to have; for it is a figure in rhetoric that drink being pour'd out of a cup into a glass, by filling the one doth empty the other; for all your writers do consent that ipse is he; now, you are not ipse, for I am he.

William. Which he, sir?

Touchstone. He, sir, that must marry this woman. Therefore, you clown, abandon—which is in the vulgar leave—the society—which in the boorish is company—of this female—which in the common is woman—which together is: abandon the society of this female; or clown, thou perishes; or, to thy better understanding, diest; or to wit, I kill thee, make thee away, translate thy life into death, thy liberty into bondage. I will deal in poison with thee, or in bastinado, or in steel; I will bandy with thee in faction; I will o'er-run thee with policy; I will kill thee a hundred and fifty ways; therefore tremble, and depart.

Audrey. Do, good William.

William. God rest you merry, sir.

In V, iii of *As You Like It*, Touchstone meets Audrey in the forest of Arden for a little while, and hear a song by a page of the banished Duke—"It was a lover and his lass, etc." When the singing is finished, Touchstone comments on the song:

Touchstone. Truly young gentlemen, though there was no great matter in the ditty, yet the note was very untuneable.

First Page. You are deceiv'd, sir; we kept time, we lost not our time.

Touchstone. By my troth, yes; I count it but time lost to hear such a foolish song.
God buy you; and God mend your voices. Come Audrey.

Here Touchstone's quip about the time of the song is witty, indeed.

In the next scene—V, iv—there is Touchstone's rather long jugglery of words or prattlement before the Senior Duke and Jaques. An excerpt

Touchstone. Salutation and greeting to you all!

Jaques. Good my lord, bid him welcome. This is the motely-minded gentleman that I have so often met in the forest. He hath been a courtier, he swears.

Touchstone. If any man doubt that, let him put me to my purgation. I have trod a measure; I have flatt'red a lady; I have been politic with my friend, smooth with mine enemy; I have undone three tailors; I have had four quarrels, and like to have fought one.

Jaques. And how was that ta'en up?

Touchstone. Faith, we met, and found the quarrel was upon the seventh cause.

Jaques. How seventh cause? Good my lord, like this fellow.

Duke Senior. I like him very well.

Touchstone. God 'ild you, sir, I desire you of the like. I press in here, sir, amongst the rest of the country copulatives, to swear and to forswear, according as marriage binds and blood breaks.

A poor virgin, sir, an ill-favour'd thing, sir, but mine own; a poor humour of mine, sir, to take that that no man else will. Rich honesty dwells like a miser, sir, in a poor house; as your pearl in your foul oyster.

Duke Senior. By my faith, he is very swift and sententious.

Touchstone. According to the fool's bolt, sir, and such dulcet diseases.

Jaques. But, for the seventh cause: how did you find the quarrel on the seventh cause?

Touchstone. Upon a lie seven times removed—bear your body more seeming, Audrey—as thus, sir. I did dislike the cut of a certain courtier's beard; he sent me word, if I said his beard was not cut well, he was in the mind it was. This is call'd the Retort Courteous. If I sent him word again it was not well cut, he would send me word he cut it to please himself. This is call'd the Quip Modest. If again it was not well cut, he disabled my judgment. This is call'd the reply Churlish. If again it was not well cut, he would answer I speak not true. This is call'd the Reproof Valiant. If again it was not well cut, he would say I lie. This is call'd the Countercheck Quarrelsome. And so to Lie Circumstantial and the Lie Direct.

Jaques. And how oft did you say his beard was not cut well?

Touchstone. I durst go no further than the Lie Circumstantial, nor he durst not give me the Lie Direct; and so we measur'd swords and parted.

Jaques. Can you nominate in order now the degrees of the lie?

Touchstone. O, sir, we quarrel in print by the book, as you have books for good manners. I will name you the degrees. The first, the Retort Courteous; the second, the Quip Modest; the third, the Reply Churlish; the forth, the Reproof Valiant;

the fifth, the Countercheck Quarrelsome; the sixth, the Lie with Circumstance; the seventh, the Lie Direct. All these you may avoid but the Lie Direct; and you may avoid that too with an If. I know when seven justices could not take up a quarrel; but when the parties were met themselves, one of them thought but of an If, as: 'If you said so, then I said so'. And they shook hands, and swore brothers. Your If is the only peace-maker; much virtue in If.

3. *Love's Labour's Lost*

Costard is the clown in this play. Both he and Don Armado love Jaquenetta, a country wench. As a messenger, he confuses Berowne's letter to Rosalin with Armado's letter to Jaquenetta. And at the end of the play, he plays "Pompion the Great" in the Interlude. Costard appears in III, i; IV, i; IV, ii; and V, ii. Snippets of Costard's clowning from these four scenes are given below.

In III, i, Costard converses with Don Armado and Armado's page Moth:

Moth. A wonder, master! Here's a costard broken in a shin.

Armado. Some enigma, some riddle; come, thy l'envoy; begin.

Costard. No enigma, no riddle, no l'envoy; no salve in the mail, sir. O, sir, plantain, a plain plantain; no l'envoy, no l'envoy; no salve, sir, but a plantain!

....

Armado. Come hither, come hither. How did this argument begin?

Moth. By saying that a costard was broken in a shin.
Then call'd you for the l'envoy.

Costard. True, and I for a plantain. Thus came your argument in;
Then the boy's fat l'envoy, the goose that you bought;
And he ended the market.

Armado. But tell me: how was there a costard broken in a shin?

Moth. I will tell you sensibly.

Costard. Thou hast no feeling of it, Moth; I will speak that l'envoy.

I, Costard, running out, that was safely within,
Fell over the threshold and broke my shin.

In IV, i, Costard mingles in the company of the Princess of France, Rosaline, Maria, Katherine, Boyet, Lords and attendants in "The Park" to deliver a letter of Lord Berowne to Rosaline. An excerpt:

Enter Costard

Boyet. Here comes a member of the commonwealth.

Costard. God dig-you-den all! Pray you, which is the head lady?

Princess. Thou shalt know her, fellow, by the rest that have no heads.

Costard. Which is the greatest lady, the highest?

Princess. The thickest and the tallest.

Costard. The thickest and the tallest! It is so, truth is truth.
An your waist, mistress, were as slender as my wit,
One o' these maids' girdles for your waist should be fit.
Are not you the chief woman? You are the thickest here.

Princess. What's your will, sir? What's your will?

Costard. I have a letter from Monsieur Berowne to one Lady Rosaline.

In the very next scene, i.e. in IV, ii, Costard of course appears, but he has very little of his clowning to present, the scene being heavily dominated by the wiseacre gas-bag Holofernes, the schoolmaster.

In V, ii of *Love's Labour's Lost*, Costard participates in the pageant of the Nine Worthies as "Pompion the Great" or

Pompey the Great. He parleys after swizzling with Berowne, first, and then with Berowne, Boyet, Dumain and the Princes of France. A snippet from the scene:

Berowne. Lo, he is tilting straight! Peace; I have done.

Enter Costard.

Welcome, pure wit! Thou part'st a fair fray.

Costard. O Lord, sir, they would know
Whether the three Worthies shall come in or no?

Berowne. What, are there but three?

Costard. No, sir; but it is vara fine, For every one pursents three.

Berowne. And three times three is nine.

Costard. Not, so, sir; under correction, sir,
I hope it is not so.
You cannot beg us, sir, I can assure you, sir; we know what we know;
I hope, sir, three times thrice, sir—

Berowne. Is not nine.

Costard. Under correction, sir, we know whereuntil it doth amount.

Berowne. By Jove, I always took three times threes for nine.

Costard. O Lord, sir, it were pity you should get your living by reck'ning, sir.

Berowne. How much is it?

Costard. O Lord, sir, the parties themselves, the actors, sir, will show whereuntil it doth amount. For mine own part, I am, as they say, but to perfect one man in one poor man, Pompion the Great sir.

Berowne. Art thou one of the Worthies?

Costard. It pleased them to think me worthy of Pompey the Great; for mine own part, I know not the degree of the Worthy; but I am to stand for him.

Berowne. Go bid them prepare.

Costard. We will turn it finely off, sir; we will take some care.

[*Exit Costard.*]

....

[The pageant begins]

Enter Costard, *armed for* Pompey.

Costard. *I Pompey am—*

Berowne. You lie, you are not he.

Costard. *I Pompey am—*

Boyet. With libbard's head on knee.

Berowne. Well said, old mocker; I must needs be friends with thee.

Costard. *I Pompey am, Pompey surnam'd the Big—*

Dumain. The *Great.*

Costard. It is *Great*, sir.

Pompey surnam'd the Great.

That oft in field, with targe and shield, did make my foe to sweat;

And travelling along this coast, I here am come by chance,

And lay my arms before the legs of this sweet lass of France.

If your ladyship would say "Thanks, Pompey", I had done.

Princess. Great thanks, Great Pompey.

Costard. 'Tis not so much worth; but I hope I was perfect. I made a little fault in *Great.*

Berowne. My hat to a halfpenny, Pompey proves the best Worthy.

4. *Twelfth Night*

In this play, Feste is textually designated Clown. His importance here may be figured out from the fact that he is present in as many as seven scenes: I, v; II, iii; II, iv; III, i; IV, i; IV, ii; and V, i.

In the first half of I, v, Feste, the Clown jests, first with Maria and then with Olivia. An excerpt:

Enter Maria *and* Clown.

Maria. Nay, either tell me where thou hast been, or I will not open my lips so wide as a bristle may enter in way of thy excuse; my lady will hang thee for thy absence.

Clown. Let her hang me. He that is well hang'd in this world needs to fear no colours.

Maria. Make that good.

Clown. He shall see none to fear.

....

Enter Olivia *and* Malvolio

Clown. Wit, an't be thy will, put me into good fooling! Those wits that think they have thee do very oft prove fools; and I that am sure I lack thee may pass for a wise man. For what says Quinapalus? 'Better a witty fool than a foolish wit.'
God bless thee lady!

Olivia. Take the fool away.

Clown. Do you not hear, fellows? Take away the lady.

Olivia. Go to, y're a dry fool; I'll no more of you. Besides, you grow dishonest.

Clown. Two faults, madonna, that drink and good counsel will amend; for give the dry fool drink, then is the fool not dry. Bid the dishonest man mend himself: if he mend he is no longer dishonest; if he cannot, let the botcher mend him. Anything that's mended is but patch'd; virtue that transgresses is but patch'd with sin, and sin that amends is but patch'd with virtue. If that this simple syllogism will serve, so; if it will not, what remedy? As there is no true cuckold but calamity, so beauty's a flower. The lady bade take away the fool; therefore, I say again, take her away.

Olivia. Sir, I bade them take away you.

Clown. Misprision in the highest degree! Lady, 'Cucullus non facit monachum'; that's as much to say as I wear not motley in my brain. Good madonna, give me leave to prove you a fool.

Olivia. Can you do it?

Clown. Dexteriously, good madonna.

Olivia. Make your proof.

Clown. I must catechize you for it, madonna. Good my mouse of virtue, answer me.

Olivia. Well, sir, for want of other idleness, I'll bide your proof.

Clown. Good madonna, why mourn'st thou?

Olivia. Good fool, for my brother's death.

Clown. I think his soul is in hell, madonna.

Olivia. I know his soul is in heaven, fool.

Clown. The more fool, madonna, to mourn for your brother's soul being in heaven. Take away the fool, gentlemen.

In II, iii and II, iv, we see another accomplishment of Feste besides his jesting or foolery—he can sing, moderately well. In the third scene of the second act, in Olivia's house he sings, on a demand from Sir Toby Belch, uncle to Olivia, a love song:

O mistress mine, where are you roaming?
O, stay and bear; your true love's coming,
That can sing both high and low. [...]

Then, when Sir Toby Belch sings under influence of swizzling, Feste, the Clown, sings parodying him:

Sir Toby. Farewell, dear heart, since I must needs be gone.

Maria. [*Sings*] Nay, good Sir Toby.

Clown. [*Sings*] His eyes do show his days are almost done.

Malvolio. Is't even so?

Sir Toby. [*Sings*] But I will never die. [*Falls down*.]

Malvolio. This is much credit to you.

Sir Toby. [*Sings*] Shall I bid him go?

Clown. [*Sings*] What an if you do?

Sir Toby. [*Sings*] Shall I bid him go, and spare not?

Clown. [*Sings*] O, no, no, no, no, you dare not.

In II, iv, Feste once again shows his ability to sing:

Come away, come away, death;
And in sad cypress let me be laid;
Fly away, fly away, breath,
I am slain by a fair cruel maid. [...]

In III, i, the Clown does a long jesting with Viola (in man's clothes) in Olivia's garden, the Clown having a tabor with him. An excerpt:

Viola. Save thee friend, and thy music! Dost thou live by thy tabor?

Clown. No, sir, I live by the church.

Viola. Art thou a churchman?

Clown. No such matter, sir: I do live by the church; for I do live at my house, and my house doth stand by the church.

Viola. So, thou mayst say the king lies by a beggar, if a beggar dwell near him; or the church stands by the tabor, if thy tabor stand by the church.

Clown. You have said, sir. To see this age! A sentence is but a chev'ril glove to a good wit. How quickly the wrong side may be turn'd outward!

Viola. Nay, that's certain; they that dally nicely with words may quickly make them wanton.

Clown. I would, therefore, my sister had had no name, sir.

Viola. Why, man?

Clown. Why, sir, her name's a word; and to dally with that word may make my sister wanton. But indeed words are very rascals since bonds disgrac'd them.

In IV, i of *Twelfth Night*, the Clown, Feste, has a short parrying with Sebastian whom he mistakes to be Viola-Cesario:

Clown. Will you make me believe that I am not sent for you?

Sebastian. Go to, go to, thou art a foolish fellow; let me be clear of thee.

Clown. Well held out, i' faith! No, I do not know you; nor I am not sent to you by my lady, to bid you come speak with her; nor your name is not Master Cesario; nor this is not my nose neither. Nothing that is so is so. [...]

In the immediately following scene (IV, ii), the Clown, Feste, both jests and sings. Here the Clown disguises himself, at the instance of Maria, as Sir Topas, the Curate or Master Parson, wearing a gown and a beard. An excerpt from the scene:

Enter Sir Toby *and* Maria.

Sir Toby. Jove bless thee, Master Parson.

Clown. Bonos dies, Sir Toby; for as the old hermit of Prague, that never saw pen and ink, very wittily said to a niece of King Gorboduc 'That that is is'; so I, being Master Parson, am Master Parson; for what is 'that' but that, and 'is' but is?

Next, even in the same scene, we see Malvolio incarcerated, due to his overbearing behaviour, giving out that he is mad. On the other hand, the Clown, disguised with a gown and a beard, impersonates himself as certain Sir Topas. Presently, he feels the urge to void himself.

Clown. Nay, I am for all waters.

Maria. Thou mightst have done this without thy beard and gown: he [Malvolio] sees thee not.

Malvolio's prison is drowned in darkness and so he cannot distinguish between the Clown and Sir Topas (or the distinguished Clown). To hold out his camouflage, the Clown sometimes speaks to Malvolio as Master Parson and sometimes as Sir Topas. [Here is, perhaps, Shakespeare's only instance of ventriloquism.] However, when Sir Toby Belch, uncle of Olivia is fed up with the Clown's knavery, the Clown departs, singing catches of songs, Malvolio urging him from behind for a lighted candle:

Clown. [*Sings.*] Hey, Robin, jolly Robin,
Tell me how thy lady does.

Malvolio. Fool!

Clown. [Sings.] My lady is unkind, perdy.
Malvolio. Fool!
Clown. [Sings.] Alas, why is she so?
Malvolio. Fool I say!
Clown. [Sings.] She loves another—Who calls, ha?

At the end of this scene, Malvolio spurs the Clown to go away (to fetch a candle), and the Clown departs singing:

I am gone, sir,
And anon, sir,
I'll be with you again,
In a trice, [...]

And Feste, the Clown, pervades throughout the single scene of the fifth act, jesting first with Fabian, then with Sir Toby Belch, and then with Olivia, and lastly sings the epilogistic song:

When that I was and a little tiny boy,
With hey, ho, the wind and the rain,
A foolish thing was but a toy,
For the rain it raineth every day. [...]

5. *The Winter's Tale*

In this play the Clown is the son of Old Shepherd, reputed father to Perdita. He appears four times in the play: in III, iii; IV, iii; IV, iv and V, ii. In the third scene of the third act an old shepherd discovers the left-out new born Perdita by the sea-side and meets the Clown who has just seen Antigonus devoured by a bear—two contrasting images: one of birth, the other of death.

Clown. Hilloa, loa!
Shepherd. What, art so near? If thou'lt see a thing to talk on when thou art dead and rotten, come hither. What ail'st thou, man?
Clown. I have seen two such sight, by sea and by land! But I am not to say it is a sea, for it is now the sky; betwixt the firmament and it you cannot thrust a bodkin's point.
Shepherd. Why, boy, how is it?
Clown. I would you did but see how it chafes, how it rages, how it takes up the shore! But that's

not to the point. O, the most piteous cry of the poor souls! Sometimes to see 'em, and not to see 'em; now the ship boring the moon with her main-most, and anon swallowed with yeast and froth, as you'd thrust a cork into a hogshead. And then for the land service—to see how the bear tore out his shoulder-bone; how he cried to me for help, and said his name was Antigonus, a nobleman! But to make an end of the ship—to see how the sea flap-dragon'it; but first, how the poor souls roared, and the mock'd them; and how the poor gentleman roared, and the bear mock'd him, both roaring louder than the sea or weather.

Shepherd. Name of mercy, when was this, boy?

Clown. Now, now; I have not wink'd since I saw these sights; they are not yet cold under water, nor the bear half din'd on the gentleman; he's at it now. [...]

In IV, iii, the Clown meets with the rogue Autolycus on a road in Bohemia. This is a unique scene, because here the witty Clown is over witted by the dissembling rogue Autolycus and as well robbed by him of his purse. In the next scene (IV, iv), the Clown is before the Old Shepherd's cottage, along with the Shepherd, Polixenes, Camillo (disguised), Mopsa, Dorcas and others. Here Florizel, assuming the name of Doricles, is engaged in wooing Perdita, and even here, the Clown is trying to show his love for Mopsa to Mopsa. Here is also present the rogue Autolycus, who in the immediately preceding scene cozened away all the money that the Clown had, and now shows himself as a haberdasher who also sells ballads. A scoop of the dialogue among the Clown, Mopsa, Dorcus and Autolycus:

Clown. If I were not in love with Mopsa, thou shouldst take no money of me; but being enthroll'd as I am, it will also be the bondage of certain ribbons and gloves.

Mopsa. I was promis'd them against the feast; but they come not too late now.

Dorcas. He hath promis'd you more than that, or there be liars.

Mopsa. He had paid you all he promis'd you. May be he hath paid you more, which will shame you to give him again.

Clown. Is there no manners left among maids? Will they wear their plackets [an item of female dress] where they should bear their faces? .... Clammer your tongues, and not a word more.

Mopsa. I have done. Come, you promis'd me a tawdry-lace, and a pair of sweet gloves.

Clown. Have I not told thee how I was cozen'd by the way, and lost all my money?

....

[*Exit with Dorcas and Mopsa.*]

Sometime afterwards, but in the same scene, the Clown reappears and converses with the Shepherd and Autolycus. But here in this scene, the Clown is not so much a witty prankster, as, for instance in V, ii. A snippet from V, ii follows:

Clown. You are well met, sir. You denied to fight with me this other day, because I was no gentleman born. See you these clothes? Say you see them not and think me still no gentleman born. You were best say these robes are not gentlemen born. Give me the lie, do; and try whether I am not now a gentleman born?

Autolycus. I know you are now, sir, a gentleman born.

Clown. Ay, and have been so any time these four hours.

Shepherd. And so have I, boy.

Clown. So you have; but I was a gentleman born before my father; for the King's son took me by the hand and call'd me brother; and then the two kings call'd my father brother; and then the Prince, my brother, and the Princess, my sister, call'd my father father. And so we wept; and there was the first gentleman-like tears that ever we shed.

6. *The Two Gentlemen of Verona*

In this play, Speed is the clown, and his considerable clownery is spread over the major part of the play right from the first scene of the first act through the first scene of the fourth. A snippet from the enjoyably witty conversation between Speed and Proteus in the first scene of the first act, just after Valentine has left for Milan:

Speed. Sir Proteus, save you! Saw you my master?
Proteus. But now he parted hence to embark for Milan.
Speed. Twenty to one then he is shipp'd already,
And I have play'd the sheep in losing him.
Proteus. Indeed a sheep doth very often stray,
An if the shepherd be awhile away.
Speed. You conclude that my master is a shepherd, as I a sheep?
Proteus. I do.
Speed. Why then, my horns are his horns, whether I wake or sleep.
Proteus. A silly answer, and fitting well a sheep.
Speed. This proves still a sheep.
Proteus. True; and thy master a shepherd.
Speed. Nay, that I can deny by a circumstance.
Proteus. It shall go hard but I'll prove it by another.
Speed. The shepherd seeks the sheep, and not the sheep the shepherd; but I seek my master, and my master seeks not me; therefore, I am no sheep.

Speed's facetiousness is apparent here, but he is showing his witty jocosity in tandem with wisdom in II, i. where he parries with Valentine. A scoop:

Valentine. Why, how know you that I am in love?
Speed. Marry, by these special marks: first you have learn'd, like Sir Proteus, to wreath your arms like a malcontent; to relish a love-song, like a robin redbreast; to walk alone, like one that had

the pestilence; to sigh, like a school-boy that had lost his A B C; to weep, like a young wench that had buried her grandma; to fast, like one that takes diet; to watch, like one that fears robbing; to speak puling, like a beggar at Hallowmas. You were wont, when you laughed, to crow like a cock; when you walk'd, to walk like one of the lions; when you fasted, it was presently after dinner; when you look'd sadly, it was for want of money. And now you are metamorphis'd with a mistress, that, when I look on you I can hardly think you my master.

Valentine. Are all these things perceiv'd in me?

Speed. They are all perceiv'd without ye.

Valentine. Without me? They cannot.

Speed. Without you! Nay, that's certain; for, without you were so simple, none else would: but you are so without these follies that these follies are within you, and shine through you like the water in an urinal, that not an eye that sees you but is a physician to comment on your malady.

Valentine. But tell me, dost thou know my lady Silvia?

Speed. She that you gaze on so, as she sits at supper?

....

Valentine. I have lov'd her ever since I saw her, and still I see her beautiful.

Speed. If you love her, you cannot see her?

Valentine. Why?

Speed. Because Love is blind. O that you had mine eyes; or your own eyes had the lights they were wont to have when you chid at Sir Proteus for going ungarter'd!

In the even next scene, Speed is present, but his part consists of only three short sentences which are plain and not so clownish.

Speed and Launce, the clownish servant of Proteus, occupy the whole fifth scene of the second act of *The Two Gentlemen of Verona*. A few verbal exchanges between them:

Speed. Launce! By mine honesty, welcome to Padua.

Launce. Forswear not thyself, sweet youth, for I am not welcome. I reckon this always, that a man is never undone till he be hang'd, nor never welcome to a place till some certain shot be paid, and the hostess say 'Welcome!'

Speed. Come on, you madcap; I'll to the alehouse with you presently; where, for one shot of five pence, thou shalt have five thousand welcomes. But, sirrah, how did thy master part with Madam Julia?

Launce. Marry, after they clos'd in earnest, they parted very fairly in jest.

Speed. But shall she marry him?

Launce. No.

Speed. How then? Shall he marry her?

Launce. No, neither.

Speed. What, are they broken?

Launce. No, they are both as whole as a fish.

Speed. Why then, how stands the matter with them?

Launce. Marry, thus: when it stands well with him, it stands well with her.

Speed. What an ass art thou! I understand thee not.

Launce. What a block art thou that thou canst not! My staff understands me.

Speed. What thou say'st?

Launce. Ay, and what I do too; look thee, I'll but lean, and my staff understands me.

Speed. It stands under thee, indeed.

Launce. Why, stand-under and under-stand is all one.

It is to be noticed here that Launce is betraying himself more as a clown than Speed himself. This is why in the *dramatis personae* Speed is designated as "a clownish servant to Valentine" and Launce is designated as "the like [clownish] to Proteus".

Like in II, v, in the last one third of III, i also the two clowns—Speed and Launce—converse clownishly, the latter more so than the former, with puns and other sorts of playing upon words, such as we have seen in II, v. A takeaway from their verbal exchanges in III, i:

Speed. How now, Signior Launce! What news with your mastership?
Launce. With my master's ship? Why, it is at sea.
Speed. Well, your old vice still: mistake the word. What news, then, in your paper?
Launce. The black'st news that ever thou heard'st.
Speed. Why, man? How black?
Launce. Why, as black as ink.
Speed. Let me read them.
Launce. Fie on thee, jolt-headed; thou canst not read.
Speed. Thou liest; I can.
Launce. I will try thee. Tell me this: Who begot thee?
Speed. Marry, the son of my grandfather.
Launce. O illiterate loiterer. It was the son of thy grandmother. This proves that thou canst not read.

And we see Speed on the stage for the last time in IV, i of *The Two Gentlemen of Verona* where he presents very little of clownery.

7. *The Merchant of Venice*

In this play, Launcelot Gobbo, son of Old Gobbo and servant of Shylock, is the Clown. He helps Lorenzo, against his conscience, to elope with Shylock's daughter Jessica. Launcelot Gobbo, or simply, Launcelot flourishes only in the three scenes of the second act (II, ii; II, iii; and II, v) and very briefly shows up in V, i.

In the second scene of the second act, Launcelot soliloquises on his double-think—whether to stay in the house of Shylock, the Jew and 'devil incarnation', or to run away. Launcelot then dissembles with his own sand-blind father. Let us hear only one expatiated speech of his:

Launcelot. Certainly, my conscience will serve me to run from this Jew my master. The fiend is at mine

> elbow and tempts me, saying to me 'Gobbo, Launcelot Gobbo, good Launcelot' or 'good Gobbo' or 'good Launcelot Gobbo, use your legs, take the start, run away'. My conscience says 'No; take heed, honest Launcelot, take heed, honest Gobbo' or, as aforesaid, 'honest Launcelot Gobbo, do not run; scorn running with thy heels'. Well, the most courageous friend bids me pack. 'Via!' says the friend; 'away!' says the fiend. 'For the heavens, rouse up a brave mind' says the fiend 'and run.' Well, my conscience, hanging about the neck of my heart, says very wisely to me 'My honest friend Launcelot, being an honest man's son' or rather 'an honest woman's son'; for indeed my father did something smack, something grow to, he had a kind of taste—well, my conscience says 'Launcelot, budge not'. 'Budge' says the fiend. 'Budge not' says my conscience. 'Conscience,' say I 'you counsel well.' 'Fiend,' say I 'you councel well.' To be rul'd by my conscience, I should stay with the Jew my master, who—God bless the mark!—is a kind of devil; and, to run away from the Jew, I should be ruled by the fiend, who—saving your reverence!—is the devil himself. Certainly, the Jew is the very devil incarnation; and, in my conscience, my conscience is but a kind of hard conscience to offer to counsel me to stay with the Jew. The fiend gives the more friendly counsel. I will run, fiend; my heels are at your commandment; I will run.

This humorously meandering argument of Launcelot is much facetious, indeed. However, Launcelot proceeds with his clownery further in the same scene with his father and others.

Next, Launcelot shows up in the very next scene, to wit, in the third scene of the second act. This is a very short scene and here the pervading mood is that of grief, for Jessica is mulling leaving Shylock's home for ever to become Christian and Lorenzo's wife. So, clownery from Launcelot is not to be expected here. In II, v also there happens no occasion for Launcelot to indulge in clownery, for here Shylock is sternly guarding Jessica against any Christian allurement, such as a masque in the street. And, lastly, though Launcelot appears on the stage for the last time in V, i, he stays for a trice: and talks with Lorenzo clownishly:

Launcelot. Sola, sola! wo ha, ho! sola, sola!
Lorenzo. Who calls?
Launcelot. Sola! Did you see master Lorenzo? Master Lorenzo! Sola, sola!
Lorenzo. Leave holloaing, man. Here!
Launcelot. Sola! Where, where?
Lorenzo. Here!
Launcelot. Tell him there's a post come from my master with his horn full of good news; my master will be here ere morning. [*Exit.*]

8. *Much Ado About Nothing*

Dogberry, a constable, is to be deemed a clown in this play like Nick Bottom, a weaver, in *A Midsummer Night's Dream* (Boyce, 71-72 and 158). Dogberry's clownery generates mostly from malapropism, and that is why malapropism is also known as dogberrism. Dogberry (the name derives from the wild fruit of dogwood) appears in the play four times: III, iii; III, iv; IV, ii and V, i. In the beginning half of the third scene of the third act of this play, we get an instance of Dogberry's wont to use malapropism and clownery:

Dogberry. First, who think you the most *desertless* man to be constable?
First Watch. Hugh Oatcake, sir, or George Seacoal; for they can write and read.
Dogberry. Come hither, neighbor Seacoal. God hath bless'd you with a good name. To be a well-favoured man is the gift of fortune; but to write and read comes by nature.
Second Watch. Both which, Master Constable—

Dogberry. You have; I know it would be your answer. Well, for your favour, sir, why, give God thanks, and make no boast of it; and for your writing and reading, let that appear when there is *no need of such vanity*. You are thought here to be the most *senseless* and fit man for the constable of the watch; there bear you the lantern. This is your charge: you shall *comprehend* all *vagrom* men; you are to bid any man *stand*, in the Prince's name.

Second Watch. How if a' will not *stand*?

Dogberry. Why, then, take no note of him, but let him go; and presently call the rest of the watch together, and thank God you are rid of a knave. (*italics mine*)

Dogberry's malapropism is more pronounced in the fifth scene of the third act of *Much Ado About Nothing*, where he converses with Leonato and Verges. An excerpt:

Leonato. What would you with me, honest neighbor?

Dogberry. Marry, sir, I would have some *confidence* with you that *decerns* you *nearly*.

Leonato. Brief, I pray you; for you see it is a busy time with me.

Dogberry. Marry, this it is, sir.

Verges. Yes, in truth it is, sir.

Leonato. What is it, my good friends?

Dogberry. *Goodman* Verges, sir, speaks a little off the matter—an old man, sir, and his wits are not so *blunt* as, God help, I would desire they were; but, in faith honest as the *skin between his brows*.

Verges. Yes, I thank God I am as honest as any man living that is an old man and no honester than I.

Dogberry. Comparisons are *odorous, palabras*, neighbor Verges. (*italics mine*)

A few more malapropism of Dogberry and his jesting is to be found in IV, ii and V, i of *Much Ado About Nothing*. For instance, in IV, ii, Dogberry enquires: "Is our whole *dissembly* [assembly] appear'd?" And, at the close of the same scene, Dogberry fumes at Conrade who calls him an ass:

Conrade. Away! you are an ass, you are an ass.

Dogberry. Dost thou *suspect* my place? Dost thou not *suspect* my years? O that he were here to write me down an ass! But, masters, remember that I am an ass; though it be not written down, yet forget not that I am an ass. No, thou villain, thou art full of piety, as shall be prov'd upon thee by good witness. I am a wise fellow; and, which is more, an officer; and, which is more, a householder; and, which is more, as pretty a piece of flesh as any is in Messina; and one that knows the law, go to; and a rich fellow enough, go to; and a fellow that hath had losses; and one that hath two gowns, and everything handsome about him. Bring him away. O that I had been writ down an ass!

Dogberry's buffoonery or jesting like a clown is quite conspicuous here. His last show of clowning and malapropism happen in the first scene of the last act. A snippet:

Dogberry. Your lordship speaks like a most thankful and reverend youth, and I praise God for you.

Leonato. There's for thy pains.

Dogberry. God save the *foundation*!

Leonato. Go; I discharge thee of thy prisoner, and I thank thee.

Dogberry. I leave an arrant knave with your worship; which I beseech your worship to correct yourself, for the example of others. God keep your worship well; God restore you to health! I humbly give you leave to depart; and if a merry meeting may be wish'd, God *prohibit* it! Come, neighbor. (*italics mine*)

9. *A Midsummer Night's Dream*

Nick Bottom, a weaver, is the clown in this play. He is not shown as a clown in the *dramatis personae* of the text. But his "comical ignorance and his tendency to mangle language make Bottom a typical Shakespearean clown" (Boyce, 71-72). Bottom appears on the stage in only three scenes: I, ii; III, i and IV, i. In the second scene of the first act, Bottom knows from Quince that in the *Pyramus and Thisby* play he is to act the role of Pyramus, and seems delighted; and boasts that he can play the role of Thisby too. A snippet:

Bottom. Ready. Name what part I am for, and proceed.

Quince. You, Nick Bottom, are set down for Pyramus.

Bottom. What is Pyramus? A lover, or a tyrant?

Quince. A lover, that kills himself most gallant for love.

Bottom. That will *ask some tears* in the true performing of it. If I do it, let the audience look to their eyes; I will move storms; I will condole in some measure. To the rest—yet my chief humour is for a tyrant. I could *play Ercles [Hercules] rarely*, or a part to tear a cat in, to make all split.

"The raging rocks
And shivering shocks
Shall break the locks
Of prison gates;
And Phibus' car
Shall shine from far,
And make and mar
The foolish fates."

This is lofty. Now name the rest of the players. This is Ercles' vein, a tyrant's vein: a lover is more *condoling*.

....

Bottom. An I may hide my face, let me play Thisby too. I'll speak in a *monstrous* little voice: 'Thisne, Thisne!' [*Then speaking small*] 'Ah Pyramus, my lover dear! Thy Thisby dear, and lady dear!' (*italics out of text mine*)

Bottom's ludicrous character, or his clownish manner, and his malapropisms may be surmised from the above quote.

One rare quality of Bottom as a clown, or risible character, is that he can sing. In III, i, during the rehearsal of the play *Pyramus and Thisby* in the wood, Puck plays a prank. He puts an ass's head on Bottom's head which all but Bottom can perceive. Thus, being metamorphosed, Bottom becomes a frightening object, and so all but he leaves the place. The lonely Bottom, to muster courage and suppress his fear, resorts to singing:

> The ousel cock, so black of hue,
> With orange-lawny bill,
> The throstle with his note so true
> The wren with little quill. [...]

And we see Bottom on the stage for the last time in the first scene of the fourth act, and at the end of this scene, Bottom betrays his wont clownery. Under the influence of the soporific juice of love-in-idleness, Bottom was asleep for some time, and in his sleep, he had had a dream. And, on waking, the lonely Bottom in the wood monologizes:

> *Bottom.* [Awaking] When my cue comes, call me, and I will answer. My next is 'Most fair Pyramus'. Heigh-ho! Peter Quince! Flute, the below-mender! Snout, the tinker! Starveling! God's my life, stol'n hence, and left me asleep!
>
> I have had a most rare vision. I have had a dream, past the wit of man to say what dream it was. Man is but an ass if he go about to expound this dream. Methought I was—there is no man can tell what. Methought I was, and methought I had, but man is but a patch'd fool, if he will offer to say what methought I had. The *eye of man hath not heard, the ear of man hath not seen, man's hand is not able to taste, his tongue to conceive, nor his heart to report*, what my dream was. I will get Peter Quince to write a ballad of this dream. It shall be call'd 'Bottom's Dream', because it hath no bottom; and I will sing it in the latter end of

the play, before the Duke. Peradventure, to make it the more gracious, I shall sing it at her death. [*Exit.*] (*italics mine*)

B. TRAGEDIES

Against Aristotle's dictum that in a dramatic presentation, the course of tragic emotion must not anywhere be baulked by any comic humour, Shakespeare has shown that the course of tragic emotion having judicious turns of comic humour is rather accentuated. This teaching of Shakespeare is really epochal, and the truth of it may be found in as many as seven plays of the bard: *Titus Andronicus, Hamlet, Macbeth, Antony and Cleopatra, Othello, King Lear* and *Julius Caesar*.

1. *Titus Andronicus*

The first ever tragedy of Shakespeare, *Titus Andronicus*, is a horrible tragedy and yet in it he has devised two scenes for clowning, to tone down the gruesomeness of blood-spilling that human mind cannot digest. The clown here, it is to be noted, is not named.

In IV, iii, we see Titus seemingly mad or on the verge of madness, due to his dire ire against the emperor and the heaven for the wrongs he is bowed to bear. He asks his allies to discharge rains of arrows in the courtyard of the emperor. At this moment the Clown arrives on the scene "*with a basket and two pigeons in it.*"

Titus. ....

Sirrah, what tidings? Have you any letters? Shall I have justice? What says Jupiter?

Clown. Ho, the gibbet-maker? He says that he hath taken them down again, for the man must be hang'd till the next week.

Titus. But what says Jupiter, I ask thee?

Clown. Alas, sir, I know not Jupiter; I never drank with him in all my life.

Titus. Why, villain, art not thou the carrier?

Clown. Ay, of my pigeons, sir; nothing else.

Titus. Why, didst thou not come from heaven?

Clown. From heaven! Alas, sir, I never came there. God forbid I should be so bold to press to heaven in my young days. Why I am going with my pigeons to the Tribunal Plebs, to take up a matter of brawl betwixt my uncle and one of the Emperal's men.

....

And, in the very next scene of the same act, the Clown appears for the second and last time. The scene is in front of the palace of the Emperor of Rome. The Emperor Saturninus, the Empress Tamora and her two sons—Demetrius and Chiron—and Lords and others are present. "*The Emperor brings the arrows in his hand that Titus shot at him.*" All those who assembled there are highly disturbed at Titus' effrontery. Presently the Clown arrives there. Tamora, the Empress, asks the Clown if he means to say something and the Clown replies:

Clown. Yes, forsooth, an your mistriship be Emperial.
Tamora. Empress I am, but yonder sits the Emperor.
Clown. 'Tis he.—God and Saint Stephen give you godden. I have brought you a letter and a couple of pigeons here. [*Saturninus reads the letter.*]
Saturninus. Go take him away, and hang him presently.
Clown. How much money must I have?
Tamora. Come, sirrah, you must be hang'd.
Clown. Hang'd! by'r lady, then I have brought up a neck to a fair end.
[*Exit guarded.*]

Against the gruesome course of the play uptill now, this raw buffoonery of the Clown well works as a short relief from the built-up tragic tension of the audience, and thus prepares them for the coming redoubled tragic catastrophe.

2. *Hamlet*

In *Hamlet*, there are two Clowns (shown as such and as grave-diggers in the *dramatis personae*) who appear only in the first scene of the fifth act. They are designated simply as "First Clown" and "Second Clown" in the body of the text. In the first scene of the fifth act, we see the two Clowns "*with spades and picks*" engaged in digging a grave for the internment of Ophelia's body. This scene, near a churchyard, begins with their conversation:

First Clown. Is she to buried in Christian burial when she wilfully seeks her own salvation?

Second Clown. I tell thee she is; therefore make her grave straight. The crowner hath sat on her, and finds it Christian burial.

First Clown. How can that be, unless she drown'd herself in her own defence?

Second Clown. Why, 'tis found so.

First Clown. It must be 'se offendendo'; it cannot be else. For here lies the point: if I drown myself wittingly, it argues an act; and an act hath three branches—it is to act, to do, to perform; argal, she drown'd herself wittingly.

Second Clown. Nay, but hear you, Goodman Delver.

First Clown. Give me leave. Here lies the water; good. Here stands the man; good. If the man go to the water and drown himself, it is, will he, nill he, he goes—mark you that; but if the water come to him and drown him, he drowns not himself. Argal, he that is not guilty of his own death shortens not his own life.

....

Hamlet and Horatio have presently arrived there. Hamlet asks First Clown: "How long hast thou been a grave-maker?"

First Clown. Of all the days i' th' year, I came to 't that day that our last King Hamlet overcame Fortinbras.

Hamlet. How long is that since?

First Clown. Cannot you tell that? Every fool can tell that: it was that very day that Young

	Hamlet was born—he that is mad, and sent to England.
Hamlet.	Ay, marry, why was he sent to England?
First Clown.	Why, because 'a was mad: 'a shall recover his wits there; or, if 'a do not, 'tis no great matter there.
Hamlet.	Why?
First Clown.	'Twill not be seen in him there: there the men are as mad as he.
Hamlet.	How came he mad?
First Clown.	Very strangely, they say.
Hamlet.	How strangely?
First Clown.	Faith, e'en with losing his wits.
Hamlet.	Upon what ground?
First Clown.	Why, here in Denmark. I have been sexton here, man and boy, thirty years.
	[...]

One special quality of First Clown in *Hamlet* is that, like Falstaff, for instance, he can sing. In V, i, he sings two snatches of a contemporary popular song:

(1) But age, with his stealing steps,
Hath clawed me in his clutch,
And hath shipped me intil the land,
As if I had never been such.

(2) A pickaxe and a spade, a spade,
For and a shrouding sheet:
O, a pit of clay for to be made
For such a guest is meet.

3. *Macbeth*

In *Macbeth*, Porter is a clownish character. It may be mentioned here that Shakespeare has four characters as porters in his four plays: *Macbeth; Henry VI, Part 1; Henry IV, Part 2* and *Henry VIII*. Excepting *Macbeth*, in all the other three plays, the Porters are either a servant (*Henry VI, Part 1*) or a doorkeeper, all of them are minor characters and none of them has any special significance in the plays. In *Macbeth*, on the other hand, the Porter alludes to the gatekeeper of the medieval morality plays. "Shakespeare's original audiences will have recognised immediately that the Porter [in *Macbeth*] was imitating a familiar figure of the medieval morality play: the gatekeeper of hell who admits Christ to Limbo in the ancient legend of the 'Harrowing of Hell'. This gatekeeper guarded the literal mouth of hell—a familiar image from the painted backdrops of gigantic, flaming lion's mouth (derived from Rev. xiii: 2) used in the morality plays. The Porter makes it clear that we are to see Macbeth's castle as hell, and leaves no doubt whatever that the enormity of Macbeth's evil is of the greatest importance in the play. When the Porter finally opens the door and admits Macduff, a subtle analogy between Macduff and Christ is suggested. This foreshadows Macduff's role as the final conqueror of the evil Macbeth" (Boyce, 511). Thus, the Porter in *Macbeth* performs a great dramatic role by alluding to the ambience of the medieval concept of Hell.

But, the Porter also performs two other things in *Macbeth*: one, he gives the audience a comic relief, and two, he serves as a chorus. Before we discuss these two functions of the Porter, let us see what he actually does on the stage. It should be noted here that the Porter appears only at the beginning of the third scene of the second act in the whole play, and that his comic part here is solo and very short. It is Macbeth's castle in Inverness and the Porter is within it. He hears a knocking. Knocking also was there before his coming in—knocking that Macbeth and then Lady Macbeth had earlier heard.

Porter. Here's a knocking indeed! If a man were porter of hell-gate, he should have [been] old turning key. [*Knock*] Knock, knock, knock! Who's there, i' th' name of Beelzebub? Here's a farmer that hang'd himself on th' expectation of plenty. Come in time; have napkins enow about you; here you'll sweat for't. [*Knock*] Knock, knock! Who's there, i' th' other devil's name? Faith, here's an equivocator, that could swear in both the scales against either scale; who committed treason enough for God's sake, yet could not equivocate to heaven. O, come in, Equivocator. [*Knock*] Knock, knock, knock! Who's there? Faith, here's an English tailor come hither for stealing out of a French hose. Come in, tailor, here you may roast your goose. [*Knock*] Knock, knock; never at quiet! What are you? But this place is too cold for hell. I'll devil-porter it no further. I had thought to have let in some of all professions that go the primrose way to th' everlasting bonfire. [*Knock*] Anon, anon! [*Opens the gate*] I pray you remember the porter.

Here, as we have said above, we may see how the Porter acts as a comic figure—"a typically humorous Shakespearean representation of unsophisticated humanity." (Boyce, 511)—and, in so far as he makes veiled comments on the evil doings of Macbeth and the ineluctable punishment thereof, he, like the Old Man of this play (II, iv), also serves as a chorus.

4. *Antony and Cleopatra*

In this play, as in *Macbeth*, the Clown appears but only in a single scene: in the second scene of the fifth act. Dolabella secretly informs Cleopatra that, after decisively defeating Antonio, Caesar has decided to ship her to Rome in three days. Cleopatra's love for Antonio is ocean-deep; she will not kotow before Caesar—she is "marble-constant". To escape the iron will of the Triumvir, she is bent upon killing herself (earlier she attempted to stab herself but Proculeius disarmed her), and she secretly arranged for that. On the appointed fatal day, the Clown appears before Cleopatra with a basket containing a poisonous snake ("worm"). She asks the Clown—

Cleopatra. [...] Hast thou the pretty worm of Nilus there
That kills and pains not?

Clown. Truly, I have him. But I would not be the party that should desire you to touch him, for his biting is immortal; those that do die of it do seldom or never recover.

Cleopatra. Remember'st thou any that have died on't?

Clown. Very many, men and women too. I heard of one of them no longer than yesterday: a very honest woman, but something given to lie, as a woman should not do but in the way of honesty; how she died of the biting of it, what she felt—truly she makes a very good report o' th' worm. But he that will believe all that they say shall never be saved by half that they do. But this is most fallible, the worm's an old worm.

Cleopatra. Get thee hence; farewell.

Clown. I wish you all joy of the worm. [*Sets down the basket.*]

Cleopatra. Farewell.

Clown. You must think this, look you, that the worm do his kind.

Cleopatra. Ay, ay; farewell.

Clown. Look you, the worm is not to be trusted but in the keeping of wise people; for indeed there is no goodness in the worm.

Cleopatra. Take thou no care; it shall be heeded.

Clown. Very good. Give it nothing, I pray you, for it is not worth the feeding.

Cleopatra. Will it eat me?

Clown. You must not think I am so simple but I know the evil himself will not eat a woman. I know that a woman is a dish for the gods, if the devil dress her not. But truly, these same whoreson devils do the gods great harm in their women, for in every ten that they make the devils mar five.

Cleopatra. Well, get thee gone; farewell.

Clown. Yes, forsooth. I wish you joy o' th' worm. [*Exit.*]

5. *Othello*

In *Othello*, the Clown is servant to Othello. He appears only in the third act, and there twice, for short whiles. In the first scene of the third act, the Clown does buffoonery with one of the musicians that Cassio has brought with him, and after that with Cassio himself.

Cassio. Masters, play here, I will content your pains. Something that's brief; and bid 'Good morrow, General'. [*Music.*]

Clown. Why masters, ha your instruments been in Naples, that they speak i' th' nose thus?

First Musician. How, sir, how?

Clown. Are these, I pray, call'd wind instruments?

First Musician. Ay, marry, are they, sir.

Clown. O, thereby hands a tail.

First Musician. Whereby hangs a tale, sir?

Clown. Marry, sir, by many a wind instrument that I know. But, masters, here's money for you; and the General so likes your music that he desires you, of all loves, to make no more noise with it.

First Musician. Well, sir, we will not.

Clown. If you have any music that may not be heard, to 't again; but, as they say, to hear music the General does not greatly care.

First Musician. We have none such.

Clown. Then put up your pipes in your bag, for I'll away. Go; vanish into air; away. [*Exeunt Musicians.*]

Cassio. Dost thou hear, my honest friend?

Clown. No, I hear not your honest friend; I hear you.

Cassio. Prithee keep up thy quillets. There's a poor piece of gold for thee. If the gentlewoman that attends the General's wife be stirring, tell her there's one Cassio entreats her a little favour of speech. Wilt thou do this?

Clown. She is stirring, sir; if she will stir hither, I shall seem to notify unto her.

Cassio. Do, good my friend. [*Exit Clown.*]

Next, the Clown appears in the fourth scene of the third act, and from here he retires forever. In the short beginning part of this scene, the Clown parleys exclusively with Desdemona, Emilia watching; not parleying, indeed, but jesting.

Desdemona. Do you know, sirrah, where the Lieutenant Cassio lies?

Clown. I dare not say he lies anywhere.

Desdemona. Why, man?

Clown. He's a soldier; and one to say a soldier lies, 'tis stabbing.

Desdemona. Go to. Where lodges he?

Clown. To tell you where he lodges is to tell you where I lie.

Desdemona. Can anything be made of this?

Clown. I know not where he lodges; and for me to devise a lodging, and say he lies there, were to lie in my own throat.

Desdemona. Can you inquire him out, and be edified by report?

Clown. I will catechize the world for him; that is, make questions, and by them answer.

Desdemona. Seek him; bid him come hither: tell him I have mov'd my lord on his behalf, and hope all will be well.

Clown. To do this is within the compass of man's wit; and therefore
I will attempt the doing it. [*Exit.*]

The verbal jestings of both the Clowns of *Antony and Cleopatra* and *Othello* rely principally on catachresis and malapropism.

6. *Julius Caesar*

Uniquely, *Julius Caesar*, a heart-harrowing tragedy against the backdrop of lofty ideals, begins with a comic parley between Flavius and Marullus, two tribunes, and a flock of Commoners or Citizens or Plebians (free Roman citizens, who were not patricians). We meet such people also in the second and third scenes of the second act but their humour exudes mostly in the beginning scene of the play. Flavius and Marullus meet certain commoners on a street of Rome.

Flavius.	Hence! Home, you idle creatures, get you home. Is this a holiday? What! Know you not, Being mechanical, you ought not walk Upon a laboring day without the sign Of your profession? Speak, what trade art thou?
First Citizen.	Why, sir, a carpenter.
Marullus.	Where is thy apron and thy rule? What dost thou with thy best apparel on? You, sir, what trade are you?
Second Citizen.	Truly, sir, in respect of a fine workman, I am but, as you would say, a cobbler.
Marullus.	But what trade art thou? Answer me directly.
Second Citizen.	A trade, sir, that I hope I may use with a safe conscience, which is indeed, sir, a mender of bad soles.
Marullus.	What trade, thou knave? Thou naughty knave, what trade?
Second Citizen.	Nay, I beseech you, sir, be not out with me; yet, If you be out, sir, I can mend you.
Marullus.	What mean'st thou by that? Mend me, thou saucy fellow!
Second Citizen.	Why, sir, cobble you.
Flavius.	Thou art a cobbler, art thou?
Second Citizen.	Truly, sir, all that I live by is with the awl. I meddle with no tradesman's matters nor women's matters, but with awl. I am indeed, sir, a surgeon to old shoes. When they are in great danger, I re-cover them. As proper men as ever trod upon neat's leather have gone upon my handiwork.

Flavius.	But wherefore art not in thy shop to-day? Why dost thou lead these men about the streets?
Second Citizen.	Truly, sir, to wear out their shoes, to get myself into more work. But indeed, sir, we make holiday to see Caesar, and to rejoice in his triumph.

7. *King Lear*

The Fool in *King Lear* is the court jester of Lear. Strictly speaking, this Fool should not be designated as a clown, for the two are not similar let alone same "The distinction between clown and fool is significant, although the Elizabethans tended to treat the terms as synonymous (Lavach and Feste—both professional jesters—are designated 'Clowns'). The clown tends to be outside the plot's main developments, while the fool is involved with the central characters. Whereas the clown's humour is unintentional, the fool's intellectual wit and trenchant observation are deliberate. With his blunt, earthly spontaneity, the clown lacks the fool's satirical edge" (Boyce, 199). That the fool on the stage is not a real-life fool is well expressed by Viola in *Twelfth Night* (III, i) when she comments about the witty Clown:

> This fellow is wise enough to play the fool;
> And to do that well craves a kind of wit.
> He must observe their mood on whom he jests,
> The quality of persons, and the time;
> And, like the haggard, check at every feather
> That comes before his eye. This is a practice
> As full of labour as a wise man's art;
> For folly that he wisely shows is fit;
> But wise men, folly-fall'n quite taint their wit.

The Fool in *King Lear* is, so to say, organically related to the play, in so far as he is a sort of jesting friend, philosopher and guide to the king who very rightly calls him "his yoke-fellow of equity" (III, vi, 37). The Fool's specio-temporal sphere in the play is noteworthy: he is present in as many as six scenes—I, iv;

I, v; II, iv; III, ii; III, iv; and III, vi. Another noteworthy thing about the Fool is that in no one of the above six scenes does he appear without Lear and Kent. And the third feature of the Fool is that he can sing.

In the fourth scene of the first act, for the first time we see the Fool on the stage. Lear, along with his royal train, earlier arrived in Albany's palace where Goneril received him and all his men very coldly. The banished Kent, being touched at heart by the beggarly condition of Lear, secretly accompanied Lear's train in disguise in order to serve him as a man Friday. Hurt at the core of his heart for the despicable plight of Lear, the Fool chastises the demented king with his mocking tongue for his lack of prudence in depriving Cordelia of her rightful share of parental love. Let us quote below a part of the parley between Lear and the Fool from the fourth scene of the first act to see the letter's foolery and wisdom.

Lear. How now, my pretty knave! How dost thou?

Fool. Sirrah, you were best take my coxcomb.

Kent. Why, fool?

Fool. Why? For taking one's part that's out of favour. Nay, an thou canst not smile as the wind sits, thoult catch cold shortly. There, take my coxcomb. Why this fellow has banish'd two on's daughters, and did the third a blessing against his will; if thou follow him, thou must needs wear my coxcomb.— How now, nuncle [my uncle]! Would I had two coxcombs and two daughters!

Lear. Why, my boy?

Fool. If I gave them all my living, I'd keep my coxcombs myself. There's mine; beg another of thy daughters.

Lear. Take heed, sirrah—the whip.

Fool. Truth's a dog must to kennel; he must be whipp'd out, when Lady the brach may stand by th' fire and stink.

Lear. A pestilent gall to me!

Fool. Sirrah, I'll teach thee a speech.

Lear. Do.

Fool. Mark it, nuncle:
Have more than thou showest,
Speak less than thou knowest,
Lend less than thou owest,
Ride more than thou goest,
Learn more than thou trowest,
Set less than thou throwest,
Leave thy drink and thy whore,
And keep in-a-door,
And thou shalt have more
Than two tens to a score.

Kent. This is nothing, fool.

Fool. Then 'tis like the breath of an unfee'd lawyer—you gave me nothing for't. Can you make no use of nothing, nuncle?

Lear. Why, no, boy; nothing can be made out of nothing.

Fool. *[To Kent]* Prithee tell him, so much the rent of his land comes to; he will not believe a fool.

Lear. A bitter fool!

Fool. Dost thou know the difference, my boy, between a bitter fool and a sweet one?

Lear. No, lad; teach me.

Fool. That lord that counsell'd thee
To give away thy land,
Come place him here by me—
Do thou for him stand.
The sweet and bitter fool
Will presently appear;
The one in motley here,
The other found out there.

Lear. Dost thou call me fool, boy?

Fool. All thy other titles thou hast given away; that thou wast born with.

....

Lear. When were you wont to be so full of songs, sirrah?

Fool. I have us'd it, nuncle, e'er since thou mad'st thy daughters thy mothers; for when thou gav'st them the rod, and put'st down thine breeches.

[*Sings*] Then they for sudden joy did weep,
And I for sorrow sung,
That such a king should play bo-peep
And go to the fools among. [....]

In the immediately following scene (I, v)—also in the palace of Albany—the three, i.e., Lear, Kent and the Fool converse.

Lear. Go you before to Gloucester with these letters. Acquaint my daughter no further with anything you know than comes from her demand out of the letter. If your diligence be not speedy, I shall be there afore you.

Kent. I will not sleep, my lord, till I have delivered your letter.

Fool. If a man's brains were in's heels, were't not in danger of kibes?

Lear. Ay, boy.

Fool. Then, I prithee, be merry; thy wit shall not go slipshod.

Lear. Ha, ha, ha!

Fool. Shalt see thy other daughter will use thee kindly; for though she's as like this as a crab's like an apple, yet I can tell what I can tell.

Lear. What canst tell, boy?

Fool. She will taste as like this as a crab does to a crab. Thou canst tell why one's nose stands i' th' middle one's face?

Lear. No.

Fool. Why to keep one's eyes of either side's nose, that what a man cannot smell out, he may spy into.

Lear. I did her wrong.

Fool. Canst tell how an oyster makes his shell?

Lear. No.

Fool. Nor I neither; but I can tell why a snail has a house.

Lear. Why?

Fool. Why, to put's head in; not to give it away to his daughters, and leave his horns without a case.

[....]

The above two snippets illustrate how the Fool, through jesting—that is his provided province—now cudgels, then teaches, and then sympathises with, his senile, demented, and innocent Sire.

In II, iv, the scene changes. Exasperated from the stunning ill-treatment received in Albany's palace, Lear has reached the castle of Gloucester, his second daughter Regan's husband, expecting a moity of the balm of sympathy for his lacerated soul. But his search for balm is in vain, his suffering relentlessly aggravating. Regan and Cornwall overtop Goneril and Albany in being atrocious to Lear. Kent, sent on an errand by Lear to Regan, is in the stocks. In sorrow and anger Lear braves out into storm, in his maddening fury and desperation, to meet Regan and Cornwall. But, before them, Lear becomes aghast to see Kent in the stocks. The king repines, his Fool, naturally, rejoices:

Kent. Hail to thee, noble master!

Lear. Ha!
Mak'st thou this shame thy pastime?

Kent. No, my lord.

Fool. Ha, Ha! He wears cruel garters. Horses are tied by the heads, dogs and bears by th' neck, monkeys by th' loins, and men by th' legs. When a man's over-lusty at legs, then he wears wooden nether-stocks.

When Kent narrates to Lear the sequence of events respecting his stocks, the Fool prognosticates Lear's further down-hill descent into desperation:

Fool. Winter's not gone yet, if the wild geese fly that way.
Fathers that wear rags
Do make their children blind;
But fathers that bear bags
Shall see their children kind.
Fortune that arrant whore,

Ne'er turns the key to th' poor.

But, for all this, thou shalt have as many dolours for thy daughters as thou canst tell in a year.

After this, when Lear left, Kent asks the Fool why the king has come with scant following. This question of Kent wrang stupid to the Fool and he retorted—

Fool. An thou hadst been set i' th' stocks for that question, thou'dst well deserv'd it.

Kent. Why, fool?

Fool. We'll set thee to school to an ant, to teach thee there's labouring i' th' winter. All that follow their noses are led by their eyes but blind men; and there's not a nose among twenty but can smell him that's stinking. Let go thy hold when a great wheel runs down a hill, lest it break thy neck with following; but the great one that goes upward, let him draw thee after. When a wise man gives thee better counsel, give me mine again. I would have none but knaves follow it, since a fool gives it.

That sir which serves and seeks for gain,
And follows but for form,
Will pack when it begins to rain,
And leave thee in the storm.
But I will tarry; the fool will stay
And let the wise man fly.
The knave turns fool that runs away;
The fool no knave, perdy.

Kent. Where learn'd you this, fool?

Fool. Not i' th' stocks, fool.

Thus, the Fool catechises the king and at the same time assures him that he serves him for no gain, and that he will not leave him in the lurch. Meantime, finding no receptive move from his daughter or son-in-law, Lear becomes uncontrollably exasperated but then controls himself; and the Fool then mocks at him to add salt to his wound:

Lear. O me, my heart, my rising heart!

But, down.

Fool. Cry to it, nuncle, as the cockney did to the eels when she put 'em i' th' paste alive; she knapp'd 'em o' th' coxcombs with a stick, and cried 'Down, wantons, down'. 'Twas her brother that, in pure kindness to his horse, butter'd his hay.

In III, ii of *King Lear*, we see Lear and the Fool (Kent appears a while later) in a heath where winds blow hard. Lear is undaunted of the storm; he rather wishes the winds blow harder and thunders shake everything, as though to punish nature and all that are ingrateful: "Blow, winds, and crack your cheeks; rage, blow. /..../ And though, all-shaking thunder,/ Strike flat the thick rotundity o' th' world;/ Crack nature's moulds, all garments spill at once,/ That makes ingrateful man." But the Fool's mockery does not abate:

Fool. O nuncle, court holy water in a dry house is better than this rain-water out o' door. Good nuncle, in; ask thy daughters' blessing. Here's a night pities neither wise men nor fools.

The maddened king, though utterly devastated by nature's fury, welcomes and encourages it submitting to it supinely, for it is gracious compared to his two daughters' satanic ingratitude: "Rumble thy bellyful. Spit, fire; spout rain./ Nor rain, wind, thunder, fir, are my daughters. /..../ O, ho! 'tis foul!" Here also the Fool mocks at Lear:

Fool. He that has a house to put's head in has a good head-piece.

The cod-piece that will house
Before the head has any.
The head and he shall louse;
So beggars marry many.
The man that makes his toe
What he his heart should make
Shall of a corn cry woe,
And turn his sleep to wake.

For there was never yet fair woman but she made mouths in a glass.

[*Enter* Kent.]

Lear. No, I will be the pattern of all patience; I will say nothing.

Kent. Who's there?

Fool. Marry, here's grace and a cod-piece; that's a wise man and a fool.

In III, iv, Lear, Kent and the Fool—the interlocked trio—are in front of a hovel in the same heath. The storm still is lashing out brutally. Kent tries to persuade him to enter the hovel but he will not. Edgar, in the guise of a madman, was inside the hovel and comes out. His eerie look frightens the Fool, who jitters and shouts at Lear:

Fool. Come not in here, nuncle, here's a spirit. Help me, help me!

Kent. Give me thy hand. Who's there?

Fool. A spirit, a spirit. He says his name's poor Tom. A spirit it is not but Edgar in a madman's guise and under the assumed name 'poor Tom' and giving out that he is being chased by a fiend (the reason of his being out of wits). Lear supposes Edgar's daughters have, like his ones, have driven him to a despondency like his own:

Lear. What, has his daughters brought him to this pass? Could'st thou save nothing? Would'st thou give 'em all?

Fool. Nay, he reserv'd a blanket, else we had been all sham'd.

Here, as in all the previous scenes, the Fool is showing Lear his lapses of judgments—his hamartia—and his pride or hubris with his mocking and jesting. But Lear is not to learn; he cannot make himself learn; he is hell-bound to self-destruction.

We see the Fool for the last time in the sixth scene of the third act—in the 'mock trial' scene, where the mad king imaginatively observes a trial of his two daughters, Edgar being the 'most learned justice', the Fool 'his yoke-fellow of equity' and Kent the 'commission'.

Enter Lear, Edgar, *and* Fool.

Edgar. Frateretto calls me, and tells me Nero is an angler in the lake of darkness.

Pray, innocent, and beware the foul fiend.

Fool. Prithee, nuncle, tell me whether a mad man be a gentleman, or a yeoman?

Lear. A king, a king!

Fool. No; he is a yeoman that has a gentleman to his son; for he's a mad yeoman that sees his a gentleman before him.

Lear. To have a thousand with red burning spits
Come hizzing in upon 'em—

Edgar. The foul fiend bites my back.

Fool. He's mad that trusts in the tameness of a wolf, a horse's health, a boy's love, or a whore's oath.

Lear. It shall be done; I will arraign them straight.

[*To Edgar*] Come, sit though here, most learned justicer. [*To the Fool*] Thou, sapient sir, sit here.—
Now, you she-foxes—

Edgar. Look where he stands and glare!
Want'st thou eyes at trial, madam?
Come o'er the bourn, Bessy, to me.

Fool. Her boat hath a leak, And she must not speak,
Why she dares not come over to thee. [....]

Lear. I'll will see their trial first. Bring in their evidence. [*To Edgar*] Thou robed men of justice, take thy place. [*To the Fool*] And thou, his yoke-fellow of equity,

Bench by his side. [*To Kent*] You are o' th' commission,

Sit you too. [....]

Lear. Arraign her first; 'tis Goneril. I here take oath before this honourable assembly she kick'd the poor King her father.

Fool. Come hither, mistress. Is your name Goneril?

Lear. She cannot deny it.

Fool. Cry you mercy, I took you for a joint-stool. [....]
Kent. Now, good my lord, lie here and rest awhile.
Lear. Make no noise, make no noise; draw the curtains.
So, so. We'll go to supper i' th' morning.
Fool. And I'll go to bed at noon.

C. HISTORY

Curious it is that while, following Aristotle, we generally do not expect comic humour in tragedies, Shakespeare has provided comic humour in as many as seven out of his ten tragedies. He is rather miserly in this regard in his histories—he has only three histories out of ten where there are occasions for us to laugh:

1. *Henry IV, Part One*: Five irregular (i.e. lawless) humourists:
   (i) Sir John Falstaff
   (ii) Poins (Edward)
   (iii) Bardolph
   (iv) Peto
   (v) Gadshill
2. *Henry IV, Part Two*: Five irregular humourists:
   (i) Sir John Falstaff
   (ii) Poins (Edward)
   (iii) Bardolph (not Lord Bardolph)
   (iv) Pistol
   (v) Peto
3. *Henry VI, Part Two*: Jack Cade (virtual clown or humourist)

We have said that Shakespeare is not generous in providing humour in his historical plays, compared to his comedies and tragedies. Yes, Shakespeare is so if we count the numbers of his comedies and tragedies in which he has drawn humourous characters. But in another sense, this can be controverted: the amount of risibility that he has generated in the rather narrow space of only two historical plays (for the nonce forget *Henry VI, Part 2*) is stupendous. Simply, consider the number of scenes where there are reviving humours:

1. *Henry IV, Part 1*:
   Act I—(I, ii)
   Act II—(II, i), (II, ii), (II, iv)
   Act III—(III, iii)
   Act IV—(IV, ii)
   Act V—(V, i), (V, iii), (V, iv)
2. *Henry IV, Part 2*
   Act I—(I, ii)
   Act II—(II, i), (II, ii), (II, iv)
   Act III—(III, ii)
   Act IV—(IV, iii), (IV, iii), (IV, iv)
   Act V—(V, i), (V, iii), (V, v)

In *Henry VI, Part 2,* there are no multiple clownish characters but only one—Jack Cade, who appears in only the fourth act. But, significantly, he is on the stage in as many as six of the ten scenes in that act to let us see his buffoonery. So, even in this play enough clowning or drollery is there. Ergo, the amount of the jesting in the historical plays is not noticeably less than that in the comedies or in the tragedies. However, let us look at the clownery in the historical plays in swift glances.

1. *Henry IV, Part 1*

The second scene of the first is dramatically important, because here we come to know of the present loose character of Hal, or the Prince of Wales, and his promise to rectify himself through 'reformation', from the conversation among Hal, Falstaff and Poins (Ned)—the three degenerates. Let us take an excerpt from the scene to see how the Prince degenerates and, especially, how the two irregular humourists, Falstaff and Poins, behave very lowly and clownishly. Falstaff enquires of the Prince about the time of the day now, and the Prince sees no reason why Falstaff requires to know the time.

Falstaff. Indeed, you come near me now, Hal; for we that take purses go by the moon and the seven stars, and not by Phoebus, he 'that wand'ring knight so fair'. And, I prithee, sweet wag, when thou art a king, as, God save thy Grace—Majesty, I should say; for grace thou wilt have none—

Prince. What, none?

Falstaff. No, by my troth; not so much as will serve to be prologue to an egg and butter.

Prince. Well, how then? Come roundly, roundly.

Falstaff. Marry, then, sweet wag, when thou art king, let not us that are squires of the night's body be called thieves of the day's beauty; let us be Diana's foresters, gentlemen of the shade, minions of the moon; and let men say we be men of good government, being governed, as the sea is, by our noble and chaste mistress the moon, under whose countenance we steal.

[....]

Prince. Good morrow, Ned.

Poins. Good morrow, sweet Hal. What says Monsieur Remorse? What says Sir John Sack and Sugar? Jack, how agrees the devil and thee about thy soul, that thou soldest him on Good Friday last for a cup of Madeira and a cold capon's leg?

Prince. Sir John stands to his word—the devil shall have his bargain; for he was never yet a breaker of proverbs; he will give the devil his due.

Poins. Then art thou damn'd for keeping thy word with the devil.

Prince. Else he had been damn'd for cozening the devil.

Poins. But, my lads my lads, to-morrow morning, by four o'clock early, at Gadshill! There are pilgrims going to Canterbury with rich offerings, and traders riding to London with fat purses. I have vizards for you all; you have horses for yourselves. Gadshill lies to-night in Rochester; I have bespoke supper to-morrow night in Eastcheap. We may do it as secure as sleep. If you will go, I will stuff your purses full of crowns; if you will not, tarry at home and be hang'd.

Falstaff. Hear ye, Yedward; if I tarry at home and go not, I'll hang you for going.

[....]

After both Falstaff and Poins leave the stage, the Prince (Hal) takes a u-turn and vow to eschew his present base life in the company of the lawless ("irregular") blackguardly persons, such as Falstaff, Poins, etc.:

> this loose behaviour I throw off
> ....
> And, like bright metal on a sullen ground,
> My reformation, glitt'ring o'er my fault,
> Shall show more goodly and attract more eyes
> Than that which hath no foil to set it off.

In II, i, we see only Gadshill clowning with two carriers, who are preparing to leave for London along with certain gentlemen who are carrying valuables. An excerpt from latter part of the scene, where Gadshill, a thief, boasts that he keeps company not with lowly ones but with great ones ("oneyers"):

Gadshill. [....] I am joined with no foot-land rakers, no long-staff six-penny strikers, none of these mad mustachio purple-hu'd malt-worms; but with nobility and tranquility, burgomasters and great oneyers, such as can hold in, such as will strike sooner than speak, and speak sooner than drink, and drink sooner than pray. And yet, zounds, I lie; for they pray continually to their saint, the commonwealth; or, rather, not pray to her, but pray on her; for they ride up and down on her, and make her their boots.

Chamberlain. What, the commonwealth their boots? Will she hold out water in foul way?

Gadshill. She will, she will; justice hath liquor'd her. We steal as in a castle, cocksure; we have the receipt of fern-seed, we walk invisible. ["Ferns were popularly supposed to produce an invisible seed which was capable of making the bearer invisible." (Cunliffe, 118)]

Gadshill. Give me thy hand: thou shalt have a share in our purchase, as I am a true man.

Chamberlain. Nay, rather let me have it, as you are a false thief.

Gadshill. Go to; 'homo' is a common name to all men. Bid the ostler bring my gelding out of the stable. Farewell, you muddy knave. [*Exeunt*]

The two following scenes—II, ii and II, iv—are exceptional, in that in each of the two all the five 'irregular humourists' are present: Falstaff, Poins, Bardolph, Peto, and Gadshill. In both these two scenes, Falstaff is the domineering humourist. In II, ii, all the five, except Falstaff, are heavily marginalized, and in II, iv, Bardolph and Peto somewhat surface. However, the following two snippets from the two scenes may illustrate the quality of the clowns, Falstaff's reaching down the lowest rung of vulgarity.

The second scene of the second act opens on the highway near Gadshill. Enter Prince Hall and Poins.

Poins. Come, shelter, shelter; I have remov'd Falstaff's horse, and he frets like a gumm'd velvet.

Prince. Stand close.

Enter Falstaff.

Falstaff. Poins! Poins! And be hang'd! Poins!

Prince. He is walk'd up to the top of the hill; I'll go seek him.

Falstaff. I am accurs'd to rob in that thief's company; the rascal hath removed my horse, and tied him I know not where. If I travel but four foot by the squier further afoot, I shall break my wind. Well, I doubt not but to die a fair death for all this, if I scape hanging for killing that rogue. I have forsworn his company hourly any time this two and twenty years, and yet I am bewitch'd with the rogue's company. If the rascal have not given me medicines to make me love him, I'll be hang'd. It could not be else: I have drunk medicines. Poins! Hal! A plague upon you both! Bardolph! Peto!

I'll starve ere I'll rob a foot further. An 'twere not as good a deed as drink to turn true man, and to leave these rogues, I am the veriest varlet that ever chewed with a tooth. Eight yards of uneven ground is three-score and ten miles afoot with me; and the stony-hearted villains know it well enough. A plague upon it, when thieves cannot be true one to another! [*they whistle*] Whew! A plague upon you all! Give me my horse, you rogues; give me my horse, and be hang'd.

Next, we see the five "irregular humourists" in the fourth scene of the same second act. Uniquely, this longish scene of some 531 lines is a free space for unbridled buffoonery of those humourists, Falstaff, though, enjoying the privileged share. For paucity of space, let us have just a short snippet of their dialogues:

Falstaff. Are not you a coward? Answer me to that—and Poins there?

Poins. Zounds, ye fat paunch, an ye call me coward, by the Lord, I'll stab thee.

Falstaff. I call thee coward! I'll see thee damn'd ere I call thee coward; but I would give a thousand pound I could run as fast as thou canst. You are straight enough in the shoulders—you care not who sees your back. Call you that backing of your friends? A plague upon such backing! Give me them that will face me. Give me a cup of sack; I am a rogue if I drunk to-day.

[....]

Falstaff. What's the matter! There be four of us here have ta'en a thousand pound this day morning.

Prince. Where is it, Jack? Where is it?

Falstaff. Where is it! taken from us it is: a hundred upon poor four of us.

Prince. What, a hundred, man?

Falstaff. I am a rogue if I were not at half-sword with a dozen of them two hours together. I have scap'd

> by miracle. I am eight times thrust through the doublet, four through the hose; my buckler cut through and through; my sword hack'd like a hand-saw—ecce signum! I never dealt better since I was a man—all would not do. A Plague of all cowards! Let them speak; if they speak more or less than truth, they are villains and the sons of darkness.

From the above about the five "irregular humourists" we may have gleaned some sense about their humour or clowning or buffoonery. The remaining scenes of *Henry IV, Part 2* where we meet them are: III, iii; IV, ii; V, i; V, iii and V, iv. These scenes only shed further light upon the quality—and not kind—of their buffoonery, but, as said earlier, due to paucity of space, let us remain this far.

2. *Henry IV, Part 2*

Like *Henry IV, Part 1*, this play is also flushed with the clowning of the same five "irregular humourists" ("irregular" meaning "lawless"): Sir John Falstaff, Edward Poins, Bardolph, Pistol and Peto. The reason is simple: *Henry IV, Part 2* is just a continuation of *Henry IV, Part 1*. And for the same reason any expatiation on the jestings or buffoonery of those five "irregular humourists" is here, perhaps, not called for. However, only this has to be mentioned that in *Henry IV, Part 2* they appear in the following scenes: I, ii (Falstaff); II, i (Falstaff); II, ii (Poins and Bardolph); II, iv (Falstaff, Pistol, Bardolph and Peto); III, ii (Falstaff and Bardolph); IV, iii (Falstaff); V, i (Falstaff and Bardolph); V, iii (Falstaff, Bardolph and Pistol); and V, v (Falstaff, Pistol and Bardolph).

3. *Henry VI, Part 2*

In the *dramatis personae* of this play, Jack Cade is designated simply as "*a rebel*", but he often behaves much like a clown or buffoon. *Henry VI, Part 2* is full of murders and conspiracies; so, probably, Shakespeare has introduced such a buffoonish character as Cade to tone down the horrors and suspenses encountered at times. Cade, though he is present only in the fourth act of the play, he appears in six of the ten scenes of it—in the second, third, sixth, seventh, eighth and tenth scenes. And near the beginning of the first scene of the fifth act, Alexander Iden, a gentleman from Kent, presents the head of Cade. Let us have a few queer, buffoonish ideas and behaviour of Cade, taking one or two instances of them from each one of the six scenes where he appears before us.

In IV, ii, Jack Cade discourses with George Bevis, John Holland, Dick, Smith and others, who have joined the rebellion against the king flaunting himself as the proper heir to the crown (falsely, he said earlier that his father was a Mortimer, mother a Plantagenet, and his wife "descended of the Lacies"), Cade assures them like a mountebank that when he ascends the throne he would institute a number of unheard of reformations.

Cade. Be brave then, for your captain is brave, and vows reformation. There shall be in England seven halfpenny loaves sold for a penny; the three-hoop'd pot shall have ten hoops; and I will make it felony to drink small beer. All the realm shall be in common, and in Cheapside shall my palfrey go to grass. And when I am king—as king I will be—

In the immediately next scene, Jack Cade takes stock of the skirmish between the royal and rebellious forces.

Cade. Where's Dick, the butcher of Ashford?

Dick. Here, sir.

Cade. They fell before thee like sheep and oxen, and thou behavedst thyself as if thou hadst been in thine own slaughter-house; therefore thus will I reward thee—the Lent shall be as long again as it is, and thou shall have a license to kill for a hundred lacking one.

In IV, vi of *Henry VI, Part 2*, we find Cade declares himself Lord of London. He now pronounces his intention of taking some highly fantastical and risible measures, such as making water fountains to flow wine and burning down the London Bridge and the London Tower.

Cade. Now is Mortimer [Cade himself] lord of this city. And here sitting upon London Stone, I charge and command that, of the city's cost, the pissing-conduit run nothing but claret wine this first year of our reign. And now henceforward it shall be treason for any that calls me other than Lord Mortimer.

[....]

Dick. My lord, there's an army gathered together in Smithfield.

Cade. Come then, let's go fight with them. But first go and set London Bridge on fire; and. If you can, burn down the Tower too. Come, let's away.

In the next scene, i.e., in the seventh scene of the fourth act, Cade's fantasticating becomes wilder and actions harsher and ragmatical.

Cade. So, sirs. Now go some and pull down the Savoy; others to the Inns of Court; down with them all.

Dick. I have a suit unto your lordship.

Cade. Be it a lordship, thou shalt have it for that word.

Dick. Only that the laws of England may come out of your mouth. [....]

Cade. I have thought upon it; it shall be so. Away, burn all the records of the realm. My mouth shall be the Parliament of England. [....]

[Enter George Bevis, along with Lord Say whom Cade pulls up for some of his progressive works]

Cade. Well, he shall be beheaded for it ten times. Ah, thou say, thou serge, nay, thou buckram lord! Now art thou within point blank of our jurisdiction regal. What canst thou answer to my Majesty for giving up Normandy unto Mounsieur Basimecu the Dauphin of France? Be it known unto thee by these presence, even the presence of Lord Mortimer, that I am the besom that must sweep the court clean of such filth as thou art. Thou hast most traitorously corrupted the youth of the realm in erecting a grammar school; and whereas, before, our forefathers had no other books but the score and the tally, thou hast caused printing to be us'd, and, contrary to the King, his crown, and dignity, thou hast built a paper-mill. It will be proved to thy face that thou hast men about thee that usually talk of a noun and a verb, and such abominable words as no Christian ear can endure to hear. Thou hast appointed justices of peace, to call poor men before them about matters they were not able to answer. Moreover, thou hast put them in prison, and because they could not read, thou hast hand'd them, when, indeed, only for that cause they have been most worthy to live. Thou dost ride in a foot-cloth, dost thou not? ["foot-cloth" means an "ornamented saddle-cloth hanging to the ground" (Cunliffe, 124)]

In IV, viii, we see Cade's rebellion almost completely crushed and his followers—the "rabblement" or the "multitude"—switching over to the side of King Henry VI. Cade, therefore, curses them and takes to his heels, his ludicrous boasting still remaining with him.

Cade. Was ever feather so lightly blown to and fro as this multitude? The name of Henry the Fifth hales them to an hundred mischiefs and makes them leave me desolate. I see them lay their heads together to surprise me. My sword make way for me for here is no staying. In despite of the devils and hell, have through the very midst of you! And heavens and honour be witness that no want of resolution in me, but only my followers' base and ignominious treasons, make me betake me to my heels.

And, lastly, in the tenth scene of the fourth act, Cade resorts to reflexive sarcasm when he sees his end quite clear. In the garden of Alexander Iden, a gentleman of Kent, he has ensconced himself to evade being caught by the forces of King Henry VI, and is staying there for five days, famishing. Now Iden has come to catch him for dispatching. Suddering, Cade blabs, and then more does he blab when slain by Iden in a duel.

Cade. By my valour, the most complete champion [Iden] that ever I heard! Steel, if thou turn thy edge, or cut not out the burly-bon'd clown [it is here that Cade identifies himself as clown] in chines of beef ere thou sleep in thy sheath. I beseech God on my knees thou mayst be turn'd to hobnails. [*Here they fight; Cade falls.*] O, I am slain! famine and no other hath slain me. Let ten thousand devils come against me, and give me but the ten meals I have lost, and I'd defy them all. Wither, garden, and be henceforth a burying place to all that do dwell in this house, because the unconquered soul of Cade is fled. [....]

Cade. Iden, farewell; and be proud of thy victory. Tell Kent from me she hath lost her best man, and exhort all the world to be cowards; for I, that never feared any, am vanquished by famine, not by valour.

[*Dies.*]

5
Dance

I

In the Preface to the first edition of his *The Tao of Physics*, Fritjof Capra wrote: "Five years ago, I had a beautiful experience which set me on a road that has led to the writing of this book. I was sitting by the ocean one late summer afternoon, watching the waves rolling in and feeling the rhythm of my breathing, when I suddenly became aware of my whole environment as being engaged in the gigantic cosmic dance. Being a physicist, I knew that the sand, rocks, water, and air around me were made of vibrating molecules and atoms, and that these consisted of particles which interacted with one another by creating and destroying other particles.... All this was familiar to me from my research in high-energy physics, but until that moment I had only experienced it through graphs, diagrams, and mathematical theories. As I sat on that beach my former experiences came to life; I 'saw' cascades of energy coming down from outer space, in which particles were created and destroyed in rhythmic pulses; I 'saw' the atoms of the elements and those of my body participating in this cosmic dance of energy; I felt its rhythm and I 'heard' its sound, and at that moment I *knew* that this was the Dance of Shiva, the Lord of Dancers worshiped [*sic*] by the Hindus" (Capra, xix). Something like this we hear in *The Merchant of Venice* (V, i, 58-61) where Lorenzo asks Jessica to sit and enjoy the dancing ("motion") and singing of the heavenly bodies:

> Sit, Jessica. Look how the floor of heaven
> Is thick inlaid with patines of bright gold:

There's not the smallest orb which thou behold'st
But in his *motion* like an angel sings,
(*emphasis added*)

Shakespeare had at least some knowledge of the medieval cosmogony, according to which all the heavenly bodies—even the tiniest ones—are never in *stasis* but move all the while ever and ever. Our scientists also tell us that even the tiniest subatomic particles are not fixed but are in motion. This *motion* Shakespeare called not movement but dance.

Shakespeare knew the great part that music and dance might play in dramatic performances. He wrote for the stage, and he knew that however much potency there might lie in words, words alone could not bestow the desired level of intensity to the emotion or passion unless it is backed by embellishments, such as music, song or dance. When, in *Hamlet* (II, ii, 190-91), Polonius asks Hamlet: "What do you read, my lord?", Hamlet retorts: "Words, words, words." What meaning do these three heavy words bear in this cryptic rebuttal is not clear, but it is true that words that lie dead on the pages of a play are not the play on the stage. And so Hamlet, in his soliloquy (*Hamlet*, II, ii, 600) very wisely says: "The play's the thing", the actual play.

Unfortunately, till to-day very few scholars have earnestly taken up the task of assessing the functions of dance, and, for that matter, of song and music, in the sphere of dramaturgy. So long dance has been understood as unintellectual, unacademic, naïve, and lowly, as one may gather, for instance, from the book *Bodies of the Text: Dance as Theory, Literature as Dance*, edited by Ellen W. Goellner and Jacqueline Shea Murphy (Rutgers University Press, 1995, New Brunswick, NJ). Hopefully, in 1982, the UNESCO declared 29th April as the International Dance Day, as it also declared in the same year 21st June as the International Music Day. Further, dance, by now, has been able to carve out at least a minor place in the academia, and now researches are being undertaken about the topicality and problematics of dance in drama as well as about how the meaning of the play may be illustrated by dance. Academics are now progressively engaging themselves in such other central issues around dance as: flux and fluidity of meaning and identity and dance; rhythm of language and dance; meaning and the dancing body, etc.

However, in our limited task here we would try to see how Shakespeare has employed dances in his plays and to what end. To start with, in nineteen out of his thirty-seven plays, he presents us with dances.

1. *A Midsummer Night's Dream*
2. *The Winter's Tale*
3. *Much Ado About Nothing*
4. *The Merry Wives of Windsor*
5. *Pericles*
6. *Romeo and Juliet*
7. *Henry VIII*
8. *The Tempest*
9. *Macbeth*
10. *Love's Labour's Lost*
11. *All's Well that Ends Well*
12. *Twelfth Night*
13. *Henry V*
14. *Troilus and Cressida*
15. *The Two Noble. Kinsmen*
16. *The Two Gentlemen of Verona*
17. *Antony and Cleopatra*
18. *Titus Andronicus*
19. *Hamlet*

And the following five plays either close with a dance, or there is a dance just before the epilogue, or the epilogue is spoken by a dancer, or by a chorus who is supposedly a dancer, or with a song that naturally suggests the rhythms of dance:

1. *As You Like It* (a dance immediately before the Epilogue)
2. *Much Ado About Nothing* (Benedick dances to close the play)

3. *Henry IV, Part Two* (the Epilogue is spoken by a Dancer)
4. *Henry V* (the Epilogue is spoken by the Chorus who is supposedly a dancer)
5. *Twelfth Night* (the Clown sings, supposedly with the accompaniment of a dance).

II

However, let us now get some idea about the major kinds of dances that were popular during the Elizabethan era, and which Shakespeare might have had in his mind while he wrote simply "dance" in the stage direction and did not always explicitly name it.

1. *Antic Dance.* This is a capering and grotesque dance, which originated in Italy (Latin *antiques* means fantastic decorations). In *Macbeth* (IV, i, 127-30) the witches dance an "antic round" which is this antic dance. The First Witch calls out to the other two witches:

> Come, sisters, cheer we up his sprites,
> And show the best of our delights;
> I'll charm the air to give a sound,
> While you perform your *antic round;*
>
> (*italics mine*)

In *Love's Labour's Lost* (V, i, 9-98 and V, i, 127), the "fantastical Spaniard" Adriano de Armado boasts to the wiseacre schoolmaster Holofernes that the King has asked him to arrange an entertainment for the Princess. Armado tells Holofernes: ".... The very all of all is—but, sweet heart, I do implore secrecy—that the King would have me present the Princess, sweet chuck, with some delightful ostentation, or show, or pageant, or *antic*, or firework..." (*italics mine*). Armado thinks of presenting a pageant of the nine Worthies, but if that do not succeed, he will present an antic: "We will have, if this fadge not, an *antic*" (*italics mine*).

2. *Bergomask.* Like the antic, this dance also was imported from Italy. It is a peasant dance, a country dance. In *A Midsummer Night's Dream* (V, i, 343 and V, i, 350-51), Bottom and Theseus, Duke of Athens, speak of Bergomasks. In the ultimate scene of the play, when the four pairs of lovers—Helena and Demetrius, Hermia and Lysander, Titania and Oberon, and Theseus and Hippolyta—are happily reunited, and the play-within-play of Pyramus and Thisby is about to be over, Bottom asks Theseus whether the play-within-play will be followed by an epilogue or a Bergomask dance—

Bottom. Will it please you to see the Epilogue, or to hear a *Bergomask* dance between two of our company?

Theseus. No Epilogue, I pray you; for your play needs no excuse.... But come, your *Bergomask;* let your epilogue alone. *A dance.*

(*italics mine*)

3. ***Brawl.*** In the 12th-century France, there was a type of dance whose chief characteristic was side-to-side movement of a chain of dancers. In the course of time, this type of popular dance which was known as *branle*—a French term, meaning 'to sway'—travelled to England around 1450, getting its name anglicised to brawl. Brawl was a dance not for the upper class but for the lower class of people of England, along with jig and morris dance. In brawl, dancers unite in a circle and with one another and do continual shakes and perform occasional kisses, and change steps to changes of the tune. In *Love's Labour's Lost* (III, i, 7-8), we hear of brawl in the conversation between Moth and Armado:

Moth. Master, will you win your love with a French *brawl*?

Armado. How meanest thou? Brawling in French? (*italics mine*)

4. ***Canary.*** This dance perhaps originated in the Canary Islands. It is a Spanish dance that in its remote past had a tinge of barbarism. To the civilised audience the canary seems a fantastic dance. From the canary islands the canary was imported to France and then from France to England. In *Love's Labour's Lost* (III, i, 11), Moth refers Armado to canary. And in *All's Well That Ends Well* (II, i, 71-74), Lafeu tells the King:

I have seen a medicine
That's able to breathe life into a stone,
Quicken a rock, and make you dance *canary*
With spritely fire and motion; whose simple touch
Is powerful to araise King Pepin, nay,
To give great Charlemain a pen in's hand
And write to her a love-line.

5. ***Cinque-Pace.*** It is a dance of five steps (*cinque* = five; and *pace* = step). Cinque-pace or Cinquepace was the name of the original galliard, because galliard is also a dance of five steps. It is also called Cinque pas. In *Much Ado About Nothing* (II, i, 60-67), Beatrice quibbles to Hero: "For, hear me Hero: wooing, wedding, and repenting, is a Scotch jig, a measure, and a *cinquepace*: the first suit is hot and hasty, like a Scotch jig, and full as fantastical; the wedding, mannerly modest, as a measure, full of state and ancientry; and then comes repentance, and, with his bad legs, falls into the cinquepace faster and faster, till he sink into his grave." Again, in *Twelfth Night* (I, iii, 122), Sir Toby Belch, while in conversation with Sir Andrew Aguecheek, mentions sink-a-pace (cinquepace) (*italics mine*).

6. ***Coranto.*** Coranto is the Italian form of English country dance. Coranto simply means 'country' dance or 'rustic' dance (Naylor, 122). Coranto is a very rapid and lively dance immensely appreciated by the public in the Elizabethan age. In *Henry V* (III, v, 33), the Duke of Britain mentions coranto while conversing with the Dauphin about how 'madams' in France urges French youths to go to Britain and teach in "English dancing schools" "lavoltas high and swift corantos". In *All's Well That Ends Well* (II, iii, 38-41), there is a reference to coranto in the conversation between Parolles and Lafeu:

Parolles. Here comes the King.
Lafeu. Lusting [funny], as the Duchman says: I'll like a maid the better, whilst I have a tooth in my head. Why, he's able to lead her a *coranto*.

And, in *Twelfth Night* (I, iii, 116-25), Sir Toby Belch refers to coranto when he talks to Sir Andrew Aguecheek.

7. ***Fading.*** Fading is a pretty Irish dance that is done in cheerful occasions. For this dance, a king and a queen are chosen

from among the assembled dancers—the best ones, of course. The dance then begins, and then another pair of king and queen is chosen, and the dance goes on. In this way, the fading goes on in undulating, serpentine movements. In *The Winter's Tale* (IV, iv, 190-94), the servant tells the Crown about the pedlar: "He hath songs for man or woman of all sizes; no milliner can so fit his customers with gloves. He has the prettiest love-songs for maids; so without bawdry, which is strange; with such delicate burdens of dildos and *fadings*, 'jump her and thump her';....." (*italics mine*)

8. ***Hay.*** This country dance was brought to England from France, and it is classed among the brawls. In this country dance, the performers stand in a circle and then "'wind round *handing* in passing until you come to your places'" (Naylor, 131). In *Love's Labour's Lost* (V, i, 133-34), Dull, the constable, tells Holofernes, the schoolmaster:

> I'll make one in a dance, or so; or I will play
> On the tabor to the Worthies, and let them dance the *hay. (italics mine)*

9.***Jig***. Jig was a lively dance, a "farcical afterpiece or interlude sung and danced to popular tunes" (*Chambers Twentieth Century Dictionary*). John H. Long, in his *Shakespeare's Use of Music*, writes that "Jigs were usually song-dances involving much pantomimic satire" (Long, 96). Jig is a sprightly but coarse sort of dance, as may be gathered from what Hamlet (*Hamlet*, II, ii, 493) satirically says about Polonius: "He's for a *jig*, or a tale of bawdry, or he sleeps." Here Hamlet is castigating Polonius' indifference to the play-within-play (the mouse-trap). However, in *Twelfth Night* (I, iii, 121), Sir Toby Belch refers to jig when he tells Sir Andrew: "...my very walk should be a *jig*;...". Such a reference to jig is also made by Beatrice when she tells about wooing, wedding and repenting in *Much Ado About Nothing* (II, i, 60): ".... For, hear me Hero: wooing, wedding, and repenting, is as a Scotch *jig*, a measure, and a cinquepace;..." And in *Love's Labour's Lost* (III, i, 10-11), Moth refers to jig when he tells Armado: "No, my complete master; but to *jig* off a tune at the tongue's end,..." (*italics mine*).

10. ***Lavolta.*** This dance is also called lavolta. Lavolta is an ancient dance which involves much turning and high jumping. Lavolta came to England from Italy via France. This dance is performed by couples, and in it the man turns his woman several times and then helps the woman jump high up. In *King Henry V* (III, v, 32-35), the Duke of Britain refers to lavolta when he tells the Dauphin about the French women who mock their husbands:

> They bid us to the English dancing schools.
> And teach *lavoltas* high, and swift *corantos*,
> Saying our grace is only in our heels
> And that we are most lofty runaways.

In *Troilus and Cressida* (IV, iv, 84-85), Troilus tells Cressida: "I cannot sing,/ Nor heel the high *lavolt* [lavolta],..." In *The Two Gentlemen of Verona* (I, ii, 82), Julia tells Lucetta: "Best sing it to the tune of '*Light o' Love*'." The song 'Light o' Love' best concords with lavolta. In *Much Ado About Nothing* (III, iv, 38-40), Margaret also refers to the song '*Light o' Love*', which concords with lavolta, in her conversation with Beatrice: "Clap into '*Light o' Loves*'; that goes without a burden. Do you sing it, and I'll dance it" (*italics mine*).

11. ***Pavan.*** This a slow dance, much enjoyed by the Spaniards. The term 'pavan' originated in the Spanish *pavo* which means peacock. It came to England from Spain, as it may be easily guessed from the name of the dance. Pavan is not only slow but also grave and majestic. Edward W. Naylor writes about pavan: "It was a stately dance, with a stately name, for the derivation is most probably from *Pavo*, a peacock, with a reference, no doubt, to the majestic strut and gay feathers of that bird. It was *de rigueur* for gentlemen to dance the Pavan in cap and sword; for lawyers to wear their gowns, princes their mantles; and ladies to take part in the fullest of full dress, the long trains of their gowns being supposed to correspond in appearance and movement to the peacock's tail" (Naylor, 134). In *Twelfth Night* (V, i, 192), Sir Toby Belch tells the Clown about Dick Surgeon who is drunk and is sleeping at eight in the morning: "Then he's a rogue and a passy measures *pavin* [pavan]" (*italics mine*).

12. ***Roundel.*** In this dance, the performers move in a circle, as the name of the dance suggests. In *A Midsummer Night's Dream* (II, ii, 1), Titania tells her train: "Come now, a *roundel* and a fairy song;..." (*italics mine*).

13. ***'Saltiers' dance.*** In *The Winter's Tale* (IV, iv, 318-22), Shakespeare presents us with another kind of dance—the dance of 'Saltiers'. At the particular place of *The Winter's Tale*, mentioned above, the Servant announces: "Master, there is [sic] three carters, three shepherds, three neat-herds, three swine-herds, that have made themselves all men of hair; they call themselves Saltiers, and they have a dance which the wenches say is a gallimaufry of gambols,..." "Shakespeare's saltiers (*The Winter's Tale* IV, iv, 353) is perh. meant to mark a rustic confusion of satyr and saultier (jumper)". (*Chambers Twentieth Century Dictionary*, entry: satyr, pp. 1200-01) [gallimaufry means a medley of persons or things; and "themselves all men of hair" alludes to the satyr].

14. ***Sword-Dance.*** A kind of dance performed with sword in hand. In *Antony and Cleopatra* (III, xi, 35-36), Antony refers to the sword-dance when he tells about Cassius:

> Yes, my lord, yes. He at Philippi kept
> His *sword e'en like a dancer*, while I struck
> The lean and wrinkled Cassius;

In *All's Well That Ends Well* (II, i, 30-33), Bertram, who has been kept away from the frontline of the war, is lamenting:

> I shall stay here the forehorse to a smock,
> Creaking my shoes on the plain masonry,
> Till honour be brought up, and no sword worn
> But one to dance with.

And in *Titus Andronicus* (II, i, 38-40), Demetrius tells his brother Chiron:

> Why, boy, although our mother, unadvis'd,
> Gave you a *dancing-rapier* by your side,
> Are you so desperate grown to threat your friends?

15. ***Measure.*** Measure is a slow and stately dance. Edward W. Naylor writes about the nomenclature of this dance: "The term Measure certainly seems to have been used to signify a particularly staid and formal dance" (Naylor, 126). This dance used to be performed mostly at public entertainments in the Inns of Court and at such other places and occasions. In *Love's Labour's Lost* (V, ii, 184-87), this dance is mentioned twice in the talk between the King of Navarre (Ferdinand) and Boyet, a lord attending on the Princess of France, with whom the King has fallen in love:

King. Say to her we have measur'd many miles
To trade a *measure* with her on this grass.
Boyet. They say that they have measur'd many a mile
To trade a *measure* with you on this grass.

Besides all these dances, there are some other dances mentioned by Shakespeare in his plays. For instance, in *Love's Labour's Lost* (IV, ii, 132), the schoolmaster Holofernes refers to the dance, known by the name '*trip and go*', when he asks Jaquenetta to swiftly go and deliver to the King a paper: "... *Trip and go*, my sweet; deliver this paper into the royal hand of the King;...." Again, in *Hamlet* (I, iv, 8-9), Hamlet tells Horatio about King Claudius:

The King doth wake to-night and takes his rouse,
Keeps wassail, and the swagg'ring *up-spring reels*,
Up-spring reels is also the name of a particular style of dance. (*italics mine*)

III

The great value of dance in human life, in many of its manifestations, as we have said, was internationally and formally recognized only in 1982 when the UNESCO declared the 29th of April as the International Dance Day. But love of dance was not only a fact of the twentieth century, but it was also a fact in the pre-historic times as well. The Hindu God Shiva, the third of the Trinity of Brahma, Vishnu and Shiva, has been being recognized as the cosmic dancer since time immemorial. He is also called *Nataraj* (*nata*, meaning dancer or actor, and *raj*, meaning king), meaning the King of dancers or actors. In this sense, in the Hindus dramaturgy, dance has had a legitimate place since pre-historic times. Four hundred years before Christ, Plato, in his *Laws* (*BK II*), claimed that the knowledge of dance should be a part of an educated man's connotation. In *Laws* (*BK II*), Clinius and an Athenian are engaged in a conversation on (good) education:

Athenian: So by an uneducated man we shall mean one who has no choric training, and by an educated man one whose choric training has been through?

Clinius: Exactly.

Athenian: And, mark you, the choric art as a whole embraces both dance and song.

Clinius: No doubt.

Athenian: Thus it follows that a well-educated man can both sing well and dance well.

Their conversation again turns to dance (and song and music) in *Laws* (*BK VII* where, keeping in view their aim of founding the utopian state—Magnesia—the Athenian delivers on the need to instruct boys and girls in *physical culture* which includes *dancing and wrestling*.

Perhaps mostly due to Plato's influence, in the Elizabethan educational and cultural system dance could have carved out a comfortable niche. The theatre-goers were very interested in all sorts of dances, especially in the jig. During Shakespeare's time, William Kempe and Richard Tarlton were almost legendary performers of the jig, generally to the tune of the simple pipe and the tabor. It was the common fashion to conclude the performance of a play with a dance, though not recommended in the text. In some cases of plays, there are definite directions in the texts to conclude the performances with dances. In *Much Ado About Nothing*, Benedick ignores the prioritised tidings of the Messenger and orders instead a dance to the music, with which the play concludes:

Messenger. My lord, your brother John is ta'en in flight,
And brought with armed men back to Messina.

Benedick. Think not on him till to-morrow.
I'll devise thee brave punishments for him.
Strike up, pipers. (*italics mine*)

In *A Midsummer Night's Dream*, the dance and singing do not, in fact, conclude the performance of the play, in one sense, but in another sense, the dance and singing close the play, because after the dance and singing every character leaves the stage but not Puck, who delivers the Epilogue. The dance and singing is there in the stage-direction itself: "*Oberon leading, the Fairies sing and dance.*"

It may be said here that in the 17th century the demand for more dances compelled introduction of various dances in performances of the plays. F.E. Halliday writes: "It may be that in the 17th century the adult companies followed the Children of Paul's and the Chapel in giving musical interludes, and sometimes dances between the acts. Certainly, dances were frequently introduced into the plays themselves, as in *The Winter's Tale* and *The Tempest*" (Halliday, 126). In the later centuries, the importance of dance was gradually minimized in the theatres, yet dance continued to attract the attention of a good number of dramatists, poets and novelists and even philosophers well beyond the 17th century. For example, T.S. Eliot was showing his keen interest in the rhythm of dance in his *Waste Land,* and Thomas Hardy employed dancing scenes in a few of his novels, such as *Far From the Madding Crowd.* And, curiously, the philosopher Friedrich Wilhelm Nietzsche (1844-1900) was much influenced by dance via the music of Richard Wagner, so much so that his celebrated theory of the birth of tragedy, as enunciated in his *The Birth of Tragedy*, heavily leans on his conception of the wild Dionysian dance tamed by the Apollonian order.

Since Rene Descartes' dichotomy between the mind and the body, we had been used to thinking that the mind and the body are two absolutely separate entities, and that the two works separately and independently, such that when we do physical works only the body is doing the works and not our mind, and likewise when we are thinking only the mind is working and not the body. But now we know that we are psychophysical phenomena, such that the body cannot do anything without the connivance of the mind, and the other way round. Now, therefore, we can say that while we are dancing (a physical activity) we are also thinking (a mental activity), or that dancing is a sort of physical expression of certain thought. And so as we can express our thinking through language so also can we express our thoughts through dance. And, further, as we can express ourselves through writing, so we can express ourselves through dancing. *Ergo*, dancing is a kind of writing.

However, presently hundreds of researches are being done on the problematics of the relation between drama and dance, or, on the contribution of dance in the domain of drama. Researchers are now trying to answer such questions as: Can dance present what a play wants to present through language (or verbal media)? or can dance express what a play fails to present through language? or can dance co-operate with the language of drama in the matter of enhancing the dramatic effect? Such researches will certainly enrich our knowledge of the place of dance in the field of drama, but even by now we know much more than earlier about the importance of dance in drama from our experiences of pantomime; dance drama; No (or Noh) play, and such others in which dance is an essential component. Our knowledge of the Japanese No or Noh play has initially come from W.B. Yeats' *Four Plays Chiefly for Dancers* which comprises *At the Hawk's Well* (1917), *The Only Jealousy of Emer* (1919), *The Dreaming of the Bones* (1919), and *Calvary* (1920). Yeats understood the value of dance, as did Antonin Artaud who recognised the essence of drama in the Balinese dance of the island of Bali in the south east Asia. Language is the universal medium of drama, but language has wide limitations as a tool of expression. Friedrich Nietzsche even denied language as the appropriate medium of dramatic expression. J.P. Stern writes that Nietzsche had a "contempt for language as an inferior medium, inadequate to the task of conveying the deepest mystery of life" (Stern, 47). Should anybody doubt the limitations of language as a medium of expression, let him observe how people move their hands and eyes and makes facial expressions while using language to express some idea or emotion, and let him see how their body parts aid their language. Antonin Artaud went even further.

He said that the body first form the words before they are released as language. The use of dances in plays has not been phenomenally diminished, let alone obliterated in our days; rather, astonishingly, we find that even in absurd plays dances are not absolutely absent. Samuel Beckett, for instance, has dances in some of his plays.

Dance is a phenomenon where we see how mind and body meld into one another. Nietzsche's Zarathustra considered dance as a metaphor. He compared dance to a bird that escapes the gravity of the earth and becomes free. Like the bird, the dancer disentangles himself/herself from social restrictions and becomes free. This idea we may find in the conversation between Florizel and Perdita in *The Winter's Tale* (IV, iv, 140-46). Florizel tells her:

Florizel. When you do dance, I wish you
A wave o' th' sea, that you might ever do
Nothing but that; move still, still so,
And no other function. Each your doing,
So singular in each particular,
Crowns what you are doing in the present deeds,
That all your acts are queens.

Dance is perhaps the oldest form of human expression. When men used to hunt for consuming raw meat, even then they danced. E.B. Tylor, in his *Dictionary of Anthropology*, writes: "It has been generally accepted that dance is an almost universal expression of man in all ages and nations. The dance is probably the most ancient art expression and has sometimes been called the major recreation of early man. Since birds and animals have been observed dancing and since the rhythm can be provided by clapping, etc., dance must have been an almost universal form of pre-cultural play" (Tylor, 154). Next, in the biblical period we see dance for religious and private purposes. Sir William Smith, in his *A Smaller Dictionary of the Bible*, writes: "The dance is spoken of in Holy Scripture universally as symbolical of some rejoicing, and is often coupled for the sake of contrast with mourning, as in Eccl. iii.4 (...).... The 'feast unto the Lord,' which Moses proposed to Pharaoh to hold, was really a dance.

Women, however, among the Hebrews made the dance their especial means of expressing their feelings; and so welcomed their husbands or friends on their return from battle" (Smith, 116).

IV

Shakespeare's love of dance is obvious. His use of the words 'dance', 'dancer', etc. and dance-related words in his plays may evince his love of dance. In *Shakespeare Concordance*, the word 'dance' occurs 77 times, 'danced' six times, 'dancer' two times, 'dances' ten times, 'danceth' once, 'dancing' 19 times, 'dancing rapier' once and 'dancing schools' once. However, how in his own days did Shakespeare thought to profitably utilize dance in his drama, keeping in mind the uncivil major section of his audience? Dance in his plays contributes in three important ways. Firstly, dance provides entertainment with its intrinsic quality of pleasing people. Sometimes a dance is provided for the merriment of some characters of the play and thus, indirectly, for the amusement of the audience. For instance, in *The Tempest* (IV, i, 134-38), to celebrate the engagement of Miranda and Ferdinand, Prospero arranges for a dance, and for a group of spectators orders Ariel: "Go bring the rabble". Then he asks every one present to keep silence, and the spirit Iris orders the nymphs or Naiads, in habits of reapers, to present a dance:

> You sun-burnt sicklemen, of August weary,
> Come hither from the furrow, and be merry.
> Make holiday. Your rye-straw hats put on,
> And these fresh nymphs encounter every one
> In *country footing*. (*Italics Mine*)

Secondly, in five of his plays, Shakespeare draws the curtain either expressly with a dance at the very ending or with a dance very near to the end. *The Much Ado About Nothing* closes explicitly with a dance, as we have already seen. But *As You Like It* ends with Rosalind's Prologue, but just before the Prologue there is a dance ordered by the Senior Duke (in exile):

> Proceed, proceed. We will begin these rites,
> As we do trust they'll end, in true delight.
> [*A Dance. Exeunt.*]

2 Henry IV closes with an Epilogue, but in the Epilogue there are allusions to dance, twice: "Will you command me to use *my legs*?" and "My tongue is weary; when *my legs* are too, I would bid you good night" (*italics mine*). The Chorus performs very important parts in *King Henry V*. He appears before each act, as well as closes the play with a (untitled) prologue. Now, the word 'chorus' was derived from the Greek *chorus*, meaning 'dance'. So, the Chorus, or the single-person chorus character, in *King Henry V* slantingly alludes to so much of dancing. *Twelfth Night* is closed neither with an epilogue nor with a dance; it ends with a song sung by Feste, the clown. And considering the heavy rhythmic stresses of the song who would say it is not accompanied by a dance? Mark the song—

> When that I was and a little tiny boy,
> With hey, ho, the wind and the rain,
> A foolish thing was but a toy,
> For the rain it raineth every day....

Why so, why some of the plays end with a dance? For one thing, and the most important at that, in Shakespeare's time it was the general vogue to conclude a dramatic performance with a dance, no matter whether the dance had any relevance to the play or no. And this was so because the Elizabethans were much fond of dance as they were of music and song. Shakespeare sometimes followed the vogue or pleased the people with songs for profit, ignoring the question of relevance. For instance, the dance at the close of *As You Like It* (but immediately before the Prologue) has no noticeable relevance to the play itself. The dance is commanded by Duke Senior as a 'rite', but, in fact, the dance is just for "true delights" of the audience:

> Proceed, proceed. We will begin these rites,
> As we do trust they'll end, in true delights.

The dance in *The Tempest* (IV, i) and the dance in *As You Like It* (V, iv) do not serve the same purpose. In the former case, the dance is for the celebration of the betrothal between Miranda and Ferdinand, which is dramatically relevant; but in the latter case, the dance does not serve any dramatic necessity: it is merely a "rite" and for "delight". We should notice here that in most of these five plays discussed so far, the dances are dramatically required within the plays, i.e. the dances are organically integrated within them.

Thirdly, dance is a powerful medium of expression or a language of thought, as we have earlier said. The Cartesian dichotomy is not applicable in the case of dance, for in it mind and body work in unison. Dance is a sort of language that goes beyond language, and expresses what language is incapable to do. Look—and we are repeating here—how a man speaks to you, trying to express some of his complex thoughts, feelings or emotions. He talks, of course, but he also takes the aid of the motions of his hands, head, eyes and mouth. Why? Because his language (and the language of all of us as well) has its limitation and so he fails to express what wants to express with the help of only his language, and so he takes the aid of his body-parts in motion. Frederick Nietzsche went further than this. According to him, dance is a metaphor for thought. We express a thought through language; likewise we may express a thought through dance. Not only this, he called dance 'anti-gravity', or freedom from the pull of the earth or from the iron laws of life. The gravity of life cannot rein in the dancer, because he is like the wheel that revolves on itself, free. Dance is *unconscious* free-flowing movements of the body, not *Delsartisme* in which thought, feeling or emotion is *consciously* converted into bodily postures. Dance is not inspired by the outside world but from within. The language of dance is not conditioned by the world and so is not limited by it. The language of dance can express the inexpressible: for instance, the dance of Vaslav Nijinsky or of Rudolf Nureyv, or the Andalusian flamenco (fury) dance, or the dance of the whirling fakir. In *The Winter's Tale* (IV, iv, 140-46), Florizel (a.k.a. Doricles) wishes Perdita's dance to be such (we repeat here, for illustration):

> when you do dance, I wish you
> A wave of the sea, that you might ever do
> Nothing but that; more still, still so,
> And own no other function. Each your doing,
> So singular in each particular,
> Crowns what you are doing in the present deeds,
> That all your acts are queens.

Fourthly, Shakespeare sometimes very ingeniously employs in his plays speeches in prose, or in stichomythic dialogues, crafted in the very rhythm of dance. One example of this is to be found in the conversation among Phebe, Silvius, Orlando and Rosalind in the second scene of the final act of *As You Like It* (ll. 76-101):

Phebe. Good shepherd tell this youth what 'tis to love.
Silvius. It is to be all made of sighs and tears;
And so am I for Phebe.
Phebe. And I for Ganymede.
Orlando. And I for Rosalind.
Rosalind. And I for no woman.
Silvius. It is to be all made of faith and service;
And so am I for Phebe.
Phebe. And I for Ganymede.
Orlando. And I for Rosalind.
Rosalind. And I for no woman.
Silvius. It is to be all made of fantasy,
All made of passion, and all made of wishes;
All adoration, duty, and observance,
All humbleness, all patience, and impatience,
All purity, all trial, all obedience;
And so am I for Phebe.
Phebe. And so am I for Ganymede.
Orlando. And so am I for Rosalind.
Rosalind. And so am I for no woman.
Phebe. If this be so, why blame you me to love you?
Silvius. If this be so, why blame you me to love you?
Orlando. If this be so, why blame you me to love you?
Rosalind. Why do you speak too 'Why blame you me to love you?
Orlando. To her that is not here, nor doth not hear.

J.L. Styan very truly writes about the above speeches: "The patterned speech marks the beat appropriate to the dance, and the dance marks the beat appropriate to the speech" (Styan, 153-54). The "blind repetition of phrase" by the different speakers adds to the covert choreography of the dialogue. Shakespeare must have a sound knowledge of choreography, indeed.

And now, before we move on to the next chapter, one last thing about dance: music and song may be both for joy and sorrow, both for light and shadow, but dance is only for joy, never for sorrow—it is the brightest thing of life.

6
Music

I
(MUSIC IN THE PLAYS)

The quantum of music Shakespeare has invested in his works one can guess from the simple fact that among his 37 plays there is only one, *The Comedy of Errors*, where there is no music. The *Shakespeare Concordance* tells us that the term 'music' has been used 221 times in the whole canon of Shakespeare. Shakespeare has employed music in all the genres of his plays: comedy, romance, tragedy and history, of course mostly in the comedies. In a few plays of his, the presence of music is almost imperceptible, as in *Timon of Athens*, but a few others are redolent of it, such as *Romeo and Juliet*. Edward W. Naylor, an authority on music, in his book *Shakespeare and Music*, writes: "Out of thirty-seven plays of Shakespeare, there are no less than thirty-two which contain interesting references to music and musical matters *in the text itself*. There are also over three hundred stage directions which are musical in their nature, and these occur in thirty-six out of thirty-seven plays" (Naylor, 3-4).

There are at least three reasons of Shakespeare being lavish of music in his plays. For one thing, the Elizabethan people were very fond of music, vocal and instrumental, such that it was "the habit of playing on an instrument in a barber's shop while waiting one's turn to be shaved" (Naylor, 18). Secondly, music was highly favoured in the purple sphere, before as well as after Elizabeth I. Henry VIII himself composed church music and enjoyed singing. Anne Boleyn was an 'enthusiastic musician', and so was Queen Catherine and Edward VI. Edward W. Naylor writes that "if ever a country deserved to be called 'musical,' that country was England, in the 16th and 17th centuries. King and courtier, peasant and ploughman, each could 'take his part,' with each music was a part of his daily life; while so far from being above knowing the difference between a minim and a crotchet, a gentleman would have been ashamed not to know it" (Naylor, 20). Musicians were in high demand in the court of kings and queens and nobles: "Bands of musicians, consorts as they were usually called, were a regular part of the household of the Queen [Elizabeth I], and of all the great nobles, and even of lesser private gentlemen. In 1571 the Queen's musicians consisted of eighteen trumpeters, seven violins, six flutes, six sackbuts, and singers. King James's musicians numbered twenty-six in 1606, and twenty-two in 1617" (Stephenson, 221).

Thirdly, we may believe that very probably in his school days, Shakespeare was trained in music and singing, if we believe that being influenced by Latinism his school course included music as per the quadrivium, i.e. arithmetic, geometry, astronomy and music. We are also told that in his boyhood Shakespeare used to participate in the choir of the parish church as well.

However, Aristotle, the first commentator on the drama, spoke of six elements of it: plot, character, thought, diction, music, and spectacle. Joseph Addison (1672-1719), the author of the blank-verse tragedy *Cato*, gave full marks to music in his poem "A Song for St Cecilia's Day, At Oxford":

> Music, the greatest good that mortals know
> And all of heaven we have below.

But then why did Aristotle give music the fifth place in drama, a place even below thought and diction? Because, according to him, the 'burden' of drama rests principally on its plot and the function of music in drama is only to sharpen or intensify the generated emotion. However, it should not be overlooked that Aristotle has kept music above the 'spectacle' of the drama, nonetheless. Yet, to be fair, Aristotle perhaps could not properly weigh the value of music, an intellectualist as he was. To Aristotle, music in drama was an embellishment, an adornment. More than a century before Aristotle, the Chinese philosopher Confucius (551-479 B.C.) could justly appreciate the worth of music. He said: "Music produces a kind of pleasure which human nature cannot do without."

In any case, like Confucius, though Shakespeare could realize the power of music, as after him John Dryden could. In his poem "A Song for St Cecilia's Day" in which he extolled St Cecilia, the patron of musicians and music, John Dryden writes: "What passion cannot Music raise and quell?" Here is the point of music in drama. Drama's business is to generate and then quench passion and emotion. And this Shakespeare, like Dryden after him, well understood, and well kept in mind while writing his plays. This is why Shakespeare has not employed music either merely as an entertainment or as a device to delay action or to find time for players to get ready for the next scene. His music is integral to the plays, such that one cannot pluck it off without a harm to the play. Shakespeare was also well aware of the fact that the Elizabethan audience had a taste for music; nay, he knew that any normal human being was pleased to hear music, and, withal, he fancied that even sub-human species were positively affected by a dulcet tune. In *The Merchant of Venice* (5.1), when Jessica complains that she does not enjoy music, Lorenzo explains to her the power of music:

> The reason is your spirits are attentive;
> For do but note a wild and wanton herd,
> Or a race of youthful and unhandled colts,
> Fetching mad bounds, bellowing and neighing loud,
> Which is the hot condition of their blood—
> If they but hear perchance a trumpet sound,
> Or any air of music touch their ears,
> You shall perceive them make a mutual stand,
> Their savage eyes turn'd to a modest gaze
> By the sweet power of music. Therefore the poet
> Did feign that Orpheus drew trees, stones, and floods;
> Since naught so stockish, hard, and full of rage
> But music for the time doth change his nature.
> The man that hath no music in himself,
> Nor is not mov'd with concord of sweet sounds,
> Is fit for treasons, stratagems, and spoils;
> The motions of his spirits are dull as night,

And his affections dark as Erebus.
Let no such man be trusted.

The supernatural power of Orpheus's music we also find in the song of the women attending on the Queen in *Henry VIII* (3.1):

Orpheus with his lute made trees,
And the mountain tops that freeze,
Bow themselves when he did sing;
To his music plants and flowers
Ever sprung, as sun and showers
There had made a lasting spring.
Every thing that heard him play,
Even the billows of the sea,
Hung their heads and then lay by.
In sweet music is such art,
Killing care and grief of heart
Fall asleep or hearing die.

Mythology apart, Shakespeare perhaps believed that music had curative effect on madness or insanity, and modern psychiatry seems to support this. In *Pericles* (V.i), Pericles is in a "melancholy state" for his daughter Marina is reportedly dead in shipwreck. But when he finds her alive, he becomes maddened with overmuch of joy: "I am wild in my beholding./ O heavens bless my girl!" At this moment, Pericles hears the "heavenly music" or the "the music of the spheres" and falls to sleep, and becomes cured of his hyper-excitement or sort of insanity. Pericles, in his utter wonderment ejaculates:

Most heavenly music!
It nips me unto list'ning, and thick slumber
Hangs upon my eyes: let me rest.

The curative effect of music on insanity or madness was not an invention of Shakespeare, it was woven into the belief system of the Elizabethan people. And, to go further back in history, it was present even in the philosophy of Pythagoras, Plato and Aristotle, whence perhaps it was brought to England in the wake of Julius Caesar's *vini vidi vici* in England. Pythagoras is credited for being the first philosopher to speak of *musica universalis*—that is, music in the universe, due to the motions of the planets,—which he called the music of the spheres. After him, Boethius thought of three kinds of music: *musica mundana, musica humana*, and *musica instrumentalis*. The first is the music of the spheres; the second the 'reflection of the indivisible human essence' or, simply, the harmony of the soul; and the third is the concord of tune and rhythm produced on musical instruments. Plato and Aristotle generally agreed with this philosophy of music, and Shakespeare illustrated these three kinds of music in his plays.

Now let us see the occurrences of music in Shakespeare's plays. But before that we must be clear about what we mean by the term 'music'. *Chambers Twentieth Century Dictionary* (1981) defines music as "the art of expression in sound, in melody, and harmony, including both composition and execution: sometimes specially instrumental performance to the exclusion of singing". The same dictionary speaks of two kinds of music (see there entry "vocable"): *vocal music,* music produced by the human voice alone, as opposed to *instrumental music*. However, in this chapter we will deal with the instrumental music, that goes along with, or without, singing, and try to evaluate their dramatic impact. The songs in the plays will be considered in a separate chapter.

In Shakespeare, instrumental music has conspicuous and influential presences in nine comedies (out of 15), two tragedies (out of 10), two histories (out of 10) and in two romances—*Pericles* and *The Tempest*. The nine comedies are: *As You Like It, Twelfth Night, Measure for Measure, The Merchant of Venice, A Midsummer Night's Dream, Much Ado About Nothing, The Taming the Shrew, The Two Gentlemen of Verona, Love's Labour's Lost* and *Comedy of Errors*. The two tragedies are: *Antony and Cleopatra* and *Timon of Athens*. And the two histories are: *Richard II* and *Henry VIII*. Let us discuss (randomly, without regard to their groupings) below the impact of music in these 15 plays.

1. ***As You Like It*** **(Comedy).** The most part of this play happens in the idyllic Forest of Arden with love-making, songs, dances, clownery, and music. As is appropriate for a high jinks comedy, *As You Like It* is vibrant with songs and vocal music that accompany the songs. It is very appropriate that the setting of the play being a forest we should not expect any instrumental music there but only vocal music. In the stage direction also, there is no instrumental music. In the stage performance, of course, of necessity, instrumental music may be added to the songs sung. Besides the songs and vocal music, there are many references to music in the play; for instance, the term 'broken music' is repeated therein more than once. We come across this term for the first time in the second scene of the first act, where Rosalind says: "But is there any else longs to see this broken music in his sides?" The eldest son of an old man, reports Le Beau, wrestled with Charles, the wrestler of Frederick, the usurper brother of the Duke, and got three of his ribs broken. Rosalind is jocularly analogizing between broken ribs and broken music. A.H. Moncur-Sime illustrates the term 'broken music' thus: "The best explanation of the term seems to be that given by Elson: 'The employment of the instruments, either in accompanying vocal music, or in purely instrumental forms, had one peculiar restriction in the sixteenth and seventeenth centuries. It was the habit of keeping each family of instruments by itself in a 'consort'. Thus, there could be a 'consort' of viols 'consort of hautboys', but if one kind of instrument entered into a 'consort' of other instruments than those of its own family, the result was called 'broken music'" (Moncur-Sime, 37).

In the fifth act of *As You Like It*, there are explicit mentions of music twice. In the fourth scene of the fifth act, when Hymen (the handsome youthful god of marriage) sings on the occasion of the marriage of Rosalind to Orlando, the stage direction is "Still Music" (soft music). And after the singing of Hymen, to celebrate the marriage, Duke Senior asks Jaques de Boys, brother of Orlando (de Boys) and all others musicians to play:

> Welcome, young man.
> ....
> And fall into our rustic revelry.
> Play, music; and you brides and bridegrooms all,
> With measure heap'd in joy, to the measures fall.

This is not all about music in *As You Like It*. There are in this play six songs which, we may suppose, must be accompanied by instrumental music. And in the end but before the Epilogue, the Senior Duke orders a dance in which all, except only the melancholic Jaques, participate, and dance without music is inconceivable.

2. *Twelfth Night* (Comedy). In the "*dramatis Personae*" of *As You Like It*, there is no mention of "Musicians", but in that of *Twelfth Night* "Musicians" are explicitly stated. Not only this, but the play also even begins with a music ordered by the love-torn Orsino, the Duke of Illyria:

> If music be the food of love, play on,
> Give me excess of it, that surfeiting,
> The appetite may sicken and so die.

A.C. Bradley once rightly observed about *Twelfth Night* that "To think of *Twelfth Night* is to think of music." We may also say that the play is full of songs (all sung by the Clown) and clownery. However, in the very first act (scenes ii and iii) we come across references—straight or oblique—to music dance and songs, in such terms and words as "sing", "music", "viol-de-gamboys", "dancing", galliard and coranto.

Next, in the fourth scene of the second act of the play, we see the Duke yearning for music, in the company of Viola-Cesario, Curio and others: "Give me some music." The Duke orders Curio to seek out Feste, the jester or fool, for singing, and music to be struck. And after Feste is found and brought in, he sings, with the accompaniment of music: "Come away, come away, death,..." Act III begins with a reference to music. Viola [in man's attire] asks Feste, the Clown, with his tabor: "Save thee friend, and thy music! Dost thou live by thy tabor?" Feste wittily cuts a joke: "No, sir, I live by the church." Next we hear in the first scene of the third act not of mundane music, but of heavenly. Viola, as Cesario, pleads love to Olivia on behalf of Orsino, the Duke, but Olivia confesses her love, very slyly, to Viola-Cesario, saying that her (Viola-Cesario's) requited love she (Olivia) would prefer to the celestial music:

> O, by your leave, I pray you:
> I bade you never speak again of him;

But would you undertake another suit,
I had rather hear you to solicit that
Than music from the spheres.

After this we do not hear of music till the end of the second scene of the fourth act where Feste first sings catches of the old song "Hey, Robin, jolly Robin", perhaps with the accompaniment of instrumental music, and then a full song "I am gone, sir,/ And anon, sir.", again perhaps with instrumental music. Lastly, the Clown, Feste, concludes the play with a 20-linesong, understandably with instrumentally emphatic rhythmic music:

When that I was and a little tiny boy,
With hey, ho, the wind and the rain, [....]

3. ***The Merchant of Venice* (Comedy).** This play begins with extreme discord (about blood or a pound of flesh from Antonio's front) but ends with a concord nonpareil (three couples united in wed-locks plus a cascade of conversations around music, and music played). Nowhere in Shakespeare's plays do we find so much of praise of music in so short a space as the beginning half of the fifth act of *The Merchant of Venice*. Within the space of 58 lines, the word 'music' is pronounced 10 times by Lorenzo, Jessica, Portia and Nerissa, and in the second scene of the third act (casket scene), four times in sixth lines.

We first come across music in the second scene of the third act where Bassanio is to choose the right casket from the three cascades in order to win Portia. Bassanio confesses his love for her. Then Portia—

Away, then! I am lock'd in one of them.
If you do love me, you will find me out.
Nerissa and the rest, stand all aloof;
Let *music* sound while he doth make his choice;
Then if he loose, he makes a swan-like end,
Fading in *music*. That the comparison
May stand more proper, my eye shall be the stream
And wat'ry death-bed for him. He may win;
And what is *music* then? Then *music* is
Even as the flourish when true subjects bow
To a new-crowned monarch; such it is

As are those dulcet sounds in break of day
That creep into the dreaming bridegroom's ear
And summon him to marriage. (*italics mine*)

After this, when Bassanio meditates on which casket to choose and, withal, sings, music is struck to accompany his song:

Tell me where is fancy bred,
Or in the heart or in the head?
How begot, how nourished?
Reply, reply.
It is engend'red in the eyes,
With gazing fed; and fancy dies
In the cradle where it lies.
Let us all ring fancy's knell:
I'll begin it—Ding, dong, bell.

After a long gap in the play, we again hear music itself, or about it, in the lone scene of the fifth Act. Lorenzo and Jessica are alone in the moonlit night in the romantic Belmont, remembering ancient love tales in such a lovely night. After a while Stephano and Launcelot approach them. Lorenzo asks Stephano to bring in musicians. Stephano gone, Lorenzo ruminates on the music in the universe as well as in human souls, which music (or harmony) we do not perceive so long as we are swaddled in flesh. Lorenzo tells Jessica:

How sweet the moonlight sleeps upon this bank!
Here will we sit and let the sounds of *music*
Creep in our ears; soft stillness and the night
Become the touches of sweet harmony.
Sit, Jessica. Look how the floor of heaven
Is thick inlaid with patines of bright gold;
There's not the smallest orb which thou behold'st
But in his motion like an angel sings,
Still quiring to the young-ey'd cherubins;
Such *harmony* is in immortal souls,
But whilst this muddy vesture of decay
Doth grossly close it in, we cannot hear it. (*italics mine*)

What Lorenzo is describing is nothing else than the mystic "music of the spheres".

Meantime, musicians of mundane music have arrived and are ready to play. Lorenzo welcomes them:

Come, ho, and wake Diana with a hymn;
With sweetest touches pierce your mistress' ear,
And draw her home with *music*, (*italics mine*)

And the musicians are striking up music but Jessica complains that she cannot enjoy it:

Jessica. I am never merry when I hear sweet *music*.
Lorenzo. The reason is your spirits are attentive;
For do but note a wild and wanton herd,
Or race of youthful and unhandled colts
Fetching mad bounds, bellowing and neighing loud,
Which is the hot condition of their blood—
If they but hear perchance a trumpet sound,
Or any air of *music* touch their ears,
You shall perceive them make a mutual stand,
Their savage eyes turn'd to a modest gaze
By the sweet power of *music*. Therefore the poet
Did feign that Orpheus drew trees, stones and floods;
Since nought so stockish, hard, and full of rage,
But *music* for the time doth change his nature.
The man that hath no *music* in himself,
Nor is not mov'd with concord of sweet sounds,
Is fit for treasons, stratagems, and spoils;
The motions of his spirit are dull as night,
And his affections dark as Erebus.
Let no such man be trusted. Mark the *music*.

At this point of time Portia and Nerissa enter, and Portia, in her wonderment at the same as mellifluous music interjects: "*Music*! Hark!" Nerissa returns: "It is your *music*, madam, of the house" (*italics mine*). A.C. Bradley, we repeat, said that "To think of *Twelfth Night* is to think of music." He was absolutely right.

4. *A Midsummer Night's Dream* (Comedy). Music is rather sparse in this play (though it is a fantasy, it has love as a theme, and the highest number of female characters are in it—three things that may make one expect more music). However, we hear of music for the first time in the first scene of the fourth act where Titania, under the spell of the magic juice, asks Bottom, who has been metamorphosed into an ass, if he would like to hear some music, and he consents:

Titania. What, wilt thou hear some *music*, my sweet love?
Bottom. I have a reasonable good ear in *music*. Let's have the tongs and the bones. (*italics mine*)

According to Richard John Cunliffe's *A New Shakespearean Dictionary*, "tongs" probably refers to "an instrument like a triangle, played with a key" and "bones" perhaps refers to "Bobbins made of bone for weaving bonelace" (Cunliffe, pages 39 and 32).

Be it as it may, after a while, but in the same scene, Titania comes out of the magic spell, and Oberon asks Robin to take the ass's head (mask) off his head and desires music.

Titania. My Oberon! What visions have I seen!
Methought I was enamour'd of an ass.
Oberon. There lies your love.
Titania. How came these things to pass?
O, how mine eyes do loathe his visage now!
Oberon. Silence awhile, Robin, take off this head.
Titania, *music* call; and strike more dead
Than common sleep of all these five the sense.
Titania. *Music*, ho, *music*, such as charmeth sleep.
Puck. Now when thou wak'st with thine own fool's eyes peep.
Oberon. Sound, *music*. Come, my Queen, take hands with me, [*Music*.]
And rock the ground whereon these sleepers be. (*italics mine*)

Next, in the lone scene of the fifth act, there are one song and two dances which, we may presume, are accompanied by appropriate music. After the play-within-play is done, Bottom asks Theseus if there will be an epilogue or a dance. Theseus tells him that as all the characters of the play-within-play are dead, no epilogue is necessary: "No epilogue, I pray you; for your play needs no excuse. Never excuse; for when the players are all dead there need none to be blamed.... But come, your Bergomask; let your epilogue alone." Richard John Cunliffe writes about Bergomask: "*Bergomask dance*, a rustic dance in imitation of the clownish people of Bergamo in Italy" (Cunliffe, 27). The bergomask, we may understand, is accompanied by music.

5. *Much Ado About Nothing* (Comedy). In this play, we first come across music in the first scene of the second act where, first, we hear terms about music and dance and then hear music and see dance. Beatrice would not marry but her uncle Leonato persuades her to get wedded.

> *Leonato.* Daughter, remember what I told you: if the prince do solicit you in that kind, you know your answer.
>
> *Beatrice.* [to Hero]. The fault will be in the *music*, cousin, if you be not wood in good time. If the Prince be too important, tell him there is measure in everything, and so dance out the answer. For, hear me, Hero: wooing, wedding, and repenting, is as a Scotch jig, a measure, and a cinquepace; the first suit is hot and hasty, like a Scotch jig, and full as fantastical; the wedding, mannerly modest, as a measure, full of state and ancientry; and then comes repentance, and, with his bad legs, falls into the cinquepace faster and faster, till he sink into his grave. (*italics mine*).

Now, the previously arranged masque is about to begin and all—Don Pedro, Claudio, Benedick, Balthasar, Don John, Borachio and Antonio—wear masks. The *drum* is struck. The dance begins with [*Music*].

The next stoppage for music is the third scene of the second act. Here we find Benedick in Leonato's orchard. Benedick, who is avers to marriage, is musing: ".... I do much wonder that one man, seeing how much another man is a fool when he dedicates his behaviours to love, will, after he hath laughed at such shallow follies in others, become the argument of his own scorn by falling in love; and such a man is Claudio. I have known when there was no *music* with him but the *drum* and the *fife*, and now had he rather hear the *tabor* and the *pipe*,..." (*italics mine*). His musing over, Benedick hides himself in a corner of the arbour.

Now, Don Pedro, Claudio and Leonato arrive in the orchard of Leonato to hear music.

Don Pedro. Come, shall we hear this *music*?
Claudio. Yea, my good lord. How still the evening is,
As hush'd on purpose to grace *harmony!*
Don Pedro. See you where Benedick hath hid himself?
Claudio. O, very well, my lord: the *music* ended,
We'll fit the kid-fox with a pennyworth.
Enter Balthasar, *with music.*
Don Pedro. Come, Bathasar, we'll hear that song again.
Balthasar. O, good my lord, tax not so bad a voice,
To slander *music* any more than once.
Don Pedro. It is the witness still of excellency
To put a strange face on his own perfection.
I pray thee, sing, and let me woo no more.
....
Balthasar. Note this before my *notes*:
There's not a *note* of mine that's worth the noting.
[Balthasar begins playing the "air" on the instrument.]
Don Pedro. Why, these are very *crotchets* that he speaks;
Note *notes,* forsooth, and nothing! [*Music*]
Benedick. Now, divine air! now is his soul ravished! Is it not strange that sheeps' guts should hale souls out of men's bodies?
Well, a horn [a drinking vessel] for my money, when all's done. (*italics mine*)

We again hear of music in the third scene of the fifth Act, where we see Don Pedro and Claudio and other three or four persons with tapers near a church, by which, it is believed, is the tomb of Hero. Claudio reads an epitaph for Hero, believing she lies in that tomb. That done, Claudio urges all aloud: "Now, *music*, sound, and sing your solemn hymn." And, lastly, the play ends with music and dance.

Benedick. Come, come, we are friends, let's have a dance ere we are married;
Therefore play, *music*....
Enter a Messenger.
Messenger [to Don Pedro]. My Lord, your brother John is ta'en in flight
And brought with armed men back to Messina.
Benedick. Think not on him till to-morrow.
I'll devise thee brave punishment for him.
Strike up, pipers. [*Dance. Exeunt.*] (*italics mine*)

6. *Pericles, Prince of Tyre* (Comedy). *Pericles* is a play where more than once miracles happen. And so, appropriately, the music that we hear here is not mundane but divine or heavenly—the "*music* of the spheres". And this happy music Pericles hears in the first scene of the fifth act. Buffeted by fortune several times, the "heavy Pericles" has arrived at Mytilene in search of Marina. He is so depressed that he has become aphasiac—speechless. Lysimachus, Governor of Mytilene, asks Marina to sing in order to bring Pericles out of his grave depression. She sings but to no avail (V, i).

Lysimachus. Mark'd he your *music*?
Marina. No, nor looked on us.

This was in the earlier part of the first scene of the fifth act. But after that event, in the same scene, when Pericles has had recognition of Marina and has come out of his "melancholy state", he hears music celestial. Helicanus has brought in Lysimachus, Governor of Mytilene, who is desirous of seeing the present condition of Pericles.

Helicanus. Sir, 'tis the Governor of Mytilene,
Who, hearing of your melancholy state,
Did come to see you.
Pericles. I embrace you.
Give me my robes. I am wild in my beholding.

O heavens bless my girl! But hark, what *music*?
Tell Helicanus, my Marina, tell him
O'er, point by point, for yet he seems to doubt,
How sure you are my daughter. But what *music*?

Helicanus. My lord, I hear none.

Pericles. None? The *music of the spheres*! List, my Marina.

Lysimachus. It is not good to cross him; give him way.

Pericles. Rarest *sounds*! Do ye not hear?

Lysimachus. My lord, I hear. [*Music.*]

Pericles. Most heavenly *music*!
It nips me into list'ning, and thick slumber
Hangs upon mine eyes: let me rest. [*Sleeps.*]
(*italics mine*)

7. ***The Taming of the Shrew* (Comedy).** This play has only one scene where we come across several references to music, and that is the first scene of the third act. Hortensio and Lucentio are in love with Bianca. Lucentio disguises as her schoolmaster, and Hortensio gives her lessens in music. The two suitors are mutual rivals.

Lucentio. *Fiddler*, forbear; you grow too forward, sir:
Have you so soon forgot the entertainment
Her sister Katherine welcomed you withal?

Hortensio. But, wrangling pedant, this is
The patroness of heavenly *harmony*;
Then gave me leave to have prerogative;
And when in *music* we have spent an hour,
Your lecture shall have leisure for as much.

Lucentio. Preposterous ass, that never read so far
To know the cause why *music* was ordain'd!
Was it not to refresh the mind of man
After his studies or his usual pain?
Then give me leave to read philosophy.

Hortensio. Sirrah, I will not bear these braves of thine.

Bianca.	Why, gentlemen, you do me double wrong, To strive for that which resteth in my choice: I am no breeching scholar in the schools; I'll not be tied to hours nor 'pointed times, But learn my lessons as I please myself. And to cut off all strife: here sit we down; Take you your *instrument*, *play* you the whiles; His lecture will be done ere you have *tun'd.*
Hortensio.	You'll leave his lecture when I am in *tune*?
Lucentio.	That will be never—*Tune* your *instrument*.
Bianca.	Where left we last?
Lucentio.	Here, madam: 'Hic ibat Simois, hic est Sigeia tellus, Hic steterat Priami regia celsa senis'.
Bianca.	Construe them.
Lucentio.	'Hic ibat' as I told you before—'Simois' I am Lucentio—'hic est' son unto Vincentio of Pisa—'Sigeia tellus' disguised thus to get your love—'Hic steterat' and that Lucentio that comes a-wooing—'Priami' is my man Tranio—'regia' bearing my port—'celsa senis' that we might beguile the old pantaloon.
Hortensio.	Madam, my instrument's in *tune*.
Bianca.	Let's hear. O fie! the *treble jars*.
Lucentio.	*Spit* in the hole, man, and *tune* again.
	....
Hortensio.	Madam, 'tis now in *tune*.
Lucentio.	All but the *bass*.
	....
Hortensio.	[*To Lucentio*]. You may go walk and give me leave awhile; My lessons make no *music in three parts*.
Lucentio.	Are you so formal, sir? Well, I must wait. [*Aside*] And watch withal; for, but I be deceiv'd, Our fine *musician* groweth amorous.

Hortensio. Madam, before you touch the *instrument*
To learn the order of *fingering*,
I must begin with rudiments of art,
To teach you *gamut* in a briefer sort,
More pleasant, pithy, and effectual,
Then hath been taught by any of my trade;
And there it is *in writing fairly drawn*

Bianca. Why, I am past my *gamut* long ago. (*italics mine*)

The last music we hear is in the very next scene where the banquet is prepared to celebrate the marriage of Petruchio and Katherina. The music is played by minstrels, and Gremio is drawing the attention of all to that music: "Hark, hark! I hear the minstrels *play*" (*italics mine*).

8. ***The Two Gentlemen of Verona* (Comedy).** In this play, only in the second scene of the fourth act do we hear music, but there are references to music in the second scene of the first act and the second scene of the third act. In I, i, Julia and her waiting-woman Lucetta converse about poetry, singing and music:

Julia. Some love of yours hath writ to you in rhyme.
Lucetta. That I might sing it, madam, to a *tune*.
Give me a *note*; your ladyship can set.
Julia. As little by such *toys* as may be possible.
Best sing it to the tune of 'Light o' Love'. (*italics mine*)

In III, ii, Proteus explains to the Duke the potential power of music (compare with what Lorenzo tells Jessica in *The Merchant of Venice*, V, i):

....
For Orpheus' *lute* was strung with poets' sinews,
Whose golden touch could soften steel and stones,
Make tigers tame, and huge leviathans
Forsake unsounded deeps to dance on sands.
After your dire-lamenting elegies,
Visit some sweet *consort*; to their *instruments*

Tune a deploring dump—the night's dead silence
Will well become such sweet-complaining grievance. (*italics mine*)

We actually hear music in the second scene of the fourth act. Proteus raves that Silvia spurns all his love-gifts. At this time Thurio enters with the musicians, as was pre-arranged, supposedly by Proteus, in order to draw Silvia's musically-mollifed love to himself. Proteus announces: "Now must we to her window,/ And give some evening *music* to her ear." Julia, in boy's dress, and her Host, that is, in whose house Julia takes temporary residence, arrive there.

Host. Come, we'll have you merry; I'll bring you where you shall hear *music*, and see the gentleman that you ask'd for.
Julia. But shall I hear him speak?
Host. Ay, that you shall. [*Music plays.*]
Julia. That will be *music.* (*italics mine*)

Along with the music the song is sung: "Who is Silvia? What is she,...".

Host. How now, you are sadder than you were before? How do you, man?
The *music* likes you not.
Julia. You mistake; the musician likes me not.
Host. Why, my pretty youth?
Julia. He plays false, father.

....

Host. I perceive you delight not in *music.*
Julia. Not a whit, when it *jars* so. (*italics mine*)

9. *The Tempest* (Romance). *The Tempest* is one of a few Shakespearean plays that is replete with songs, music and dance. But it has one things more—sleep and drinking. However, *The Tempest* has some eight or nine songs (*As You Like It* and *Twelfth Night* each has seven). *The Tempest* is the most musically vibrant of Shakespearean plays. And, to some critics this is befittingly so, because it is in the form of a masque. We should not forget the phrase "our revels now are over" of this play, and revels are not revels without music. So, the last revel of Shakespeare's life is befittingly musical. Further, in writing three of his plays Shakespeare, perhaps, kept his motive concentrated on the vegetative enjoyment of his play-goers: *As You Like It* (c. 1600), *Twelfth Night* or *What You Will* (c. 1601) and this one *The Tempest* (1611/12). (The expressions "as you like it" and "what you will" plead for the first two plays as two jolly pieces of the jovial dramatist Shakespeare, who, perhaps, wanted to say goodbye to his audience in the year 1610 or 1611 drowning them in the tempest of jolly revelry.)

Howbeit, in *The Tempest* we first hear the song and music of Ariel in the second scene of the first act. Here the stage direction is: "Ariel, *invisible, playing and singing*; Ferdinand *following*."

Ariel's Song.
Come unto these yellow sands,
And then take hands;....

Ferdinand. Where should this *music* be? I' th' air or th' earth?
It sounds no more; and sure it waits upon
Some god o' th' island. Sitting on a bank,
Weeping again the King my father's wreck,
This *music* crept by me upon the waters,
Allaying both their fury and my passion
With its sweet *air*; thence I have follow'd it.
Or it hath drawn me rather. But 'tis gone.
No, it begins again.
Ariel's Song.
Full fathom five thy father lies;....

Next, we hear music in the second scene of the third act, where Stephano sings and Ariel plays on a tabor and pipe.

Stephano. Come on, Trinculo, let us sing.
Flout 'em and scout 'em,
And scout 'em and flout 'em;
Thought is free.
Caliban. That's not the *tune.*

[*Ariel plays the tune on a tabor and pipe.*] (*italics mine*)

The next music in *The Tempest* is in the third scene of the third act. The stage direction runs thus: "*Solemn and strange music; and* Prospero *on the top, invisible. Enter several strange Shapes, bringing in a banquet; and dance about it with gentle actions of salutations*; etc."

Alonso. What *harmony* is this? My good friends, hark!
Gonzalo. Marvellous sweet *music*! (*italics mine*)

But soon Ariel enters in thunder and lightning and the banquet vanishes, and then Ariel too vanishes. Even after that we hear music and see dancing of strange shapes. Note the stage direction: "*He* [Ariel] *vanishes in thunder; then to soft music, enter the Shapes again, and dance, with mocks and mows, and carrying out the* [banquet] *table.*"

In the first scene of the fourth act, we hear music for the penultimate time in the play. On the happy occasion of the betrothal of Miranda to Ferdinand, Prospero has arranged a masque, for which he orders Ariel to gather an audience—"Go bring the rabble". And, then, when a supernumerary audience ("corollary") has arrived, Prospero asks everyone around to keep silent and witness the production of the masque that now begins along with gentle music.

Prospero...
No tongue! All eyes! Be silent. [*Soft music.*]

And the ultimate music of *The Tempest* is to be heard in the last scene of the play. Prospero is happy: Miranda will unite with Ferdinand in wedlock and Prospero's wrong-doers are repentant. He forgives them all, and henceforth his "Every third thought shall be my grave." And now he is desirous of only one thing—"some heavenly *music*" and so "*Solemn music*" is played: a "solemn air", "the best comforter/ To an unsettled fancy, cure thy brains".

10. *Antony and Cleopatra* (Tragedy). The Duke's beginning line of *Twelfth Night* (I, i) is repeated by Cleopatra in *Antony and Cleopatra* (II, v) almost verbatim. Both are burning in the fire of love and both are hungry for music. The Duke said:

If *music* be food of love, play on:
Give me excess of it, that, surfeiting,
The appetite may sicken, and so die.

And Cleopatra begins the scene thus:

Give me some *music—music*, moody food
Of us that trade in love.

And Charmian, Iras and Alexas shout out:

The *music*, ho!

Soon Cleopatra becomes impatient with the music and seeks another sort of music:

Give me mine angle—we'll to th' river. There,
My *music* playing far off, I will betray
Twany-finn'd fishes; my bended hook shall pierce
Their slimy jaws; and as I draw them up
I'll think them every one an Antony,
And say 'Ah ha! Y're caught'.

Next, we hear music twice in the seventh scene of the second act; once, during the banquet on board Pompey's galley, off Misenum, and, next, after the banquet and during the drinking bout. On the earlier occasion, the stage direction is "*Music plays*" and, understandably, the banquet went on along with music. In the latter occasion, Enobarbus proposes to Antony "the Egyptian Bacchanals" and the same is held.

Enobarbus. [To Antony] Ha, my brave emperor!
Shall we dance now the Egyptian Bacchanals
And celebrate our drink?

Pompey. Let's ha't, good soldier.

Antony. Come, let's all take hands,
Till that the conquering wine hath steep'd our sense
In soft and delicate Lethe.

Enobarbus. All take hands.
Make battery to our ears with the loud *music*,
The while I'll place you; then the boy shall sing;

The holding every man shall bear as loud
As his strong sides can volley.
[*Music plays.*] *Enobarbus places them hand in hand.* (*italics mine*)

Two further references to music are there in the third scene of the fourth act and in the second scene of the fifth act of *Antony and Cleopatra.* In the earlier scene, a few soldiers converse when music is heard. The stage direction tells us: "*Music of the hautboys is under the stage.*"

Second Soldier. Peace, what *noise*?
Third Soldier. List, list!
Second Soldier. Hark!
Third Soldier. *Music* i' th' air. (*italics mine*)

And, lastly, Cleopatra, in the second scene of the fifth act, compares Antony's voice with the 'music of the spheres': "His legs bestrid the ocean; his rear'd arm/ Crested the world. His voice was propertied/ As all the *tuned spheres*, and that to friends;..." (*italics mine*).

11. ***King Henry VIII*** **(History).** In six scenes of four acts of this play we hear music, and in this sense, we can call *Henry VIII* a musical play. We first hear of music in the third scene of the first act where there is a reference to music by Sandys, a lord. Next, in the banquet thrown by Cardinal Wolsey, there is a masque in which there are dance and *music* galore. This happens in the fourth scene of the first act. The guests choose ladies for the masque and the King, Henry VIII, chooses Ann Bullen. All wear masks and music plays. But, before the masque, when the guests are treated with drink, we hear *drum* and *trumpet.* The fourth scene of the second act is the divorce scene where the King, Henry VIII, divorces his earlier queen Katherine in a hall in Black Friars. Before the beginning of the divorce proceedings, *trumpets*, *sennets* and *cornets* are sounded.

In the first scene of the third act, the divorced and broken down Katherine, surrounded by her women, asks one of them—

Queen Katherine. Take thy *lute*, wench. My soul grows sad with troubles;

Sing and disperse 'em, if thou canst. Leave working.

And then a song is sung:

Orpheus with his *lute* made trees,
And the mountain tops that freeze,
....
In sweet *music* is such art,
Killing care and grief of heart
Fall asleep or hearing die. (*italics mine*)

In the immediately following scene, we again see Katherine, when she is utterly depressed, now being a dowager. She is morbidly hungry for sad music and asks her gentleman-usher, Griffith, to arrange for music:

Good Griffith,
Cause the *musicians* play me that sad *note*
I nam'd my knell, whilst I sit meditating
On that *celestial harmony* I go to.
[*Sad and solemn music.*]

Music is playing. She falls into sleep and sees in s vision "*six* Personages *clad in white robes.*" They congee to Katherine, garland her, and then "*dancing* vanish". The music does not stop but continues. Katherine narrates to Griffith what she has seen in the vision and asks to stop the music: "Bid the *music* leave,/ They are harsh and heavy to me." The music ceases. (*italics mine*)

12. *Timon of Athens* (Tragedy). In the second scene of the first act of this play, Timon has arranged a banquet in which *hautboys* are playing loud *music*. During the banquet, a masque is played, in which Cupid and a band of ladies participate. It is a "Masque of Ladies as Amazons". The ladies, with masks, play on their *lutes* and dance. The masque over, each one of the guests of the banquet single out an Amazon, and all dance to "*a lofty strain or two to the hautboys, and cease.*"

13. *Love's Labour's Lost* (Comedy). Ferdinand, the king of Navarre, and his lords, who have put out their oath not to see women for three years in order to study, have, however, arranged a pageant in which they plan to meet the French princess and her ladies, who have come to Navarre, wearing masks. The French princes and her ladies, too, wear masks with a view to confuse the gentlemen as to who will woo whom. In the early part of the long second scene of the fifth act, the event happens in the park, in a romantic environment. Both the parties meet. The masque begins. Stage direction: "*Trumpet sounds within*".

Boyet. The *trumpet sounds*; be masked; the maskers come. [*The ladies mask.*]

Enter Blackamoors *with music*, Moth *as Prologue, the* King *and his* Lords *as Maskers, in the guise of Russians.*

Moth. All hail, the richest beauties on the earth!...

14. ***King Richard the Second*** **(History).** Like in *Love's Labours Lost*, in this play also we hear music in only a single scene—in the fifth scene of the fifth Act. The king is thrown into prison by Bolingbroke (the future King Henry IV), and he is fuming at the hellish prison:

I have been studying how I may compare
This prison where I live unto the world;
....
[*The music plays.*]
Music do I hear?
Ha, ha! *Keep time*. How sour sweet music is
When time is broke and no proportion kept!
So is it in the *music* of men's lives. (*italics mine*)

15. ***The Comedy of Errors*** **(Comedy).** In this play, we do not hear any music; we only hear a reference to a musical instrument. In the third scene of the fourth Act of this play, Dromio of Syracuse tells his master Antipholus of Syracuse about an unidentified man he calls "old Adam":

Antipholus of Syracuse. What Adam dost thou mean?

Dromio of Syracuse. Not that Adam that kept the Paradise, but that Adam that
Keeps the prison; he that goes in the calf's skin that was kill'd for the Prodigal;....

Ant. S. I understand thee not.

Dro. S. No? Why, 'tis a plain case: he that went, like a *bass-viol*, in a case of leather;.... (*italics mine*)

The man ("Adam") Dromio of Syracuse is referring to is wearing a loose leather shirt or such apparel, and so he is looking like a bass-viol (that appears like the digit 8) in a bag of leather. The thing that is to be noted here is that Shakespeare was so very familiar with the bass-viol (and other musical instrument) that the analogy between the man and a bass-viol in a leather bag swiftly came to his imagination.

II
(MUSICIANS)

So far we have heard music, or at least heard references to music, in 15 plays of Shakespeare, but in only five plays out of these 15, musicians are mentioned in the *dramatis persone*, which musicians we see on stage and playing. That is, these musicians visibly participate in the performance on stage, and the other musicians participate *incognito*. Those musicians who play on stage are to be found in *The Two Gentlemen of Verona*, *The Merchant of Venice*, *Romeo and Juliet*, *Othello* and *Cymbeline*. They are mentioned in the stage-directions in the particular places of the plays as follows:

1. *The Two Gentlemen of Verona* (IV, ii):
   Stage direction: "*Enter* Thurio *and* Musicians."
2. *The Merchant of Venice* (V, i):
   Stage direction: "*Enter* Musicians."
3. *Romeo and Juliet* (IV, v):
   Stage direction: "*Enter* Friar Lawrence *and* County Paris *with* Musicians."
4. *Othello* (III, i):
   Stage direction: "*Enter* Cassio, *with* Musicians."
5. *Cymbeline* (II, iii):
   Stage direction: "*Enter* Musicians."

III
(MUSICAL INSTRUMENTS)

The Elizabethan people, as told earlier, were very musical—were lovers of music—so much so that some critics and scholars even say that they were more music-lovers than any people of the Western world, though the Elizabethan musical instruments were not that much developed. Elizabethan music culture received the patronage of Queen Elizabeth. She employed 70 musicians and she herself could play on at least two musical instruments, one of them being verginal and the other lute. Her interest in vocal and instrumental music was not amateurish, for she could sing and dance and could even compose dance music. Her love of music naturally made her courtiers drawn to the art of music, so much so that most, if not all, of them knew the preliminaries of one or two musical instruments and a smack of singing.

However, in the Elizabethan era, a good number of musical instruments prevailed, some of them are the following (I am quoting from John H. Long, *Shakespeare's Use of Music: A Study of the Music and Its Performance in the Production of Seven Comedies*, 1955, University of Florida Press, pp. 17-26):

1. *The Lute.* "The lute was a stringed instrument which was plucked like a guitar or a mandolin. In shape it resembled one half of a pear, cut lengthwise, having fretted finger-board which extended from the smaller end and over which the strings were placed along the flat side. There were several types of lutes, which differed in size, number of strings, and method of tuning. During the reign of Elizabeth the most common type was the treble lute with eleven gut strings" (p. 17).

2. *The Cittern.* "The cittern, or cithern, resembled the lute, in frontal outline, but, unlike the lute, had a flat back. It was strung with four single wire strings, or four pairs, which were often played with a plectrum or with the fingernails.... The cittern was played mostly among the lower-class Elizabethans because it was easy to master and...because its simpler construction made it much less expensive" (p. 18).

3. *The Viol.* "The viols were bowed string instruments. Two types were in use during the late English Renaissance, the *viol da gamba* and the *viol da braccio*. The dominant type in sixteenth and seventeenth century England was the gamba, or 'leg' viol.... The tonal volume of this instrument was not so great as that of the modern violin, nor did it have the brilliance of the violin family. Its tone was distinguished, however, by a mellowness and a clear, singing quality" (p. 18).

4. ***The Rebec.*** "The rebec was a country cousin of the viols. In shape it resembled an oblong lute, though generally the rebec was smaller. By the middle of the sixteenth century, it was considered by many to be a rustic instrument. It generally had three strings, was played with a short, arched bow, and was held against the shoulder of the player" (p. 19).

5. ***The Violin.*** "The violins and the other members of the family—the viola and the bass violin (an instrument which we now call violoncello)—belong to the *viola da braccio*, or 'arm viol' side of the viol instruments. In contrast to the gamba viols, the tone of the violins was brilliant, loud and harsh. The members of the violin family were late in being accepted in England; not until the Restoration did they come into general use" (pp. 19-20).

6. ***The Shawm.*** "The name 'shawms' here includes the hautboys, waits, curtails, and bombards. These instruments were all of the wood-wind-with-double-reed variety similar to the modern oboe, English horn, and bassoon.... "The volume of sound produced by a shawm was almost as great as that of a trumpet. Its tone quality was harsher than the tones produced by modern double-reed instruments; when several shawms were played together, the result was a skirling sound similar to that produced by a band of bagpipes" (p. 20).

7. ***The Recorder.*** "The recorders were vertical flutes, having a mouthpiece in the end rather than on the side as is the case with the modern cross flute. The recorder mouthpiece also contained a fipple [see *infra*], the device found in many penny whistles and organ pipes which produces the musical tone.... The recorders were often referred to as pipes or flutes" (p. 21).

8. ***The Flute.*** "The flute (cross flute, or German flute), used in England during the sixteenth and seventeenth centuries, was an early version of the present flute. It was found in several forms, although the variations were slight. Its cousin, the fife, was pitched an octave higher than the flute. The fife was generally used, with a drum, in military formations" (p. 22).

9. ***The Pipe.*** "The pipe, or three-hole recorder, was played with one hand. It was actually a member of the recorder family in that it was a vertical flute with fipple [an arrangement of a block], and a sharp edge against which it directs the wind, in the recorder, etc.: *Chambers Twentieth Century Dictionary*, 1981, p. 490.... Although it was considered a vulgar instrument by the upper-class Elizabethans, it was, at the same time, quite versatile. Along with the labour it accompanied songs, dances, and jigs, and it was in fact the poor man's orchestra" (p. 22).

10. ***The Cornet.*** "Early cornets, unlike the modern brass instruments, were tapered tubes made of horn, ivory, or wood covered with leather. They had simple cup mouthpieces, very much like those of trumpets, and the tube was pierced with seven finger-holes—six in front and one behind, as was the case with the recorders and shawms" (p. 23).

11. ***The Racket.*** "The racket was a peculiar, shawm-like instrument of bass pitch. It consisted of a tube bent back and forth eight times, pushed together, and then enclosed by a cylinder. Both the mouthpiece, with its double reed, and the terminal end of the tube projected from the top of the cylinder. The cylinder itself was short and was pierced by a complicated system of finger holes. The tonal quality of this musical platypus [footlike thing] was muffled and reedy; it was sometimes used in place of the curtal [a musical instrument]" (p. 24).

12. ***The Sackbut.*** "Sackbuts are now called trombones, and despite the passage of time there is very little difference between the old and the new. The Elizabethan sackbuts were made in the usual three pitches—treble, tenor, and bass; but since the treble sackbut actually produced notes in normal alto range, the treble cornet was often added to the consort of sackbuts in order to attain a complete tonal range within the group. "Like the cornets, sackbuts were usually employed with choral groups, although they were also popular with the waits, or watchmen...." In comparison with the modern trombone the sackbut had a softer tone, which made it suitable for smaller ensembles" (p. 25).

13. ***The Trumpet.*** "The trumpet was the nobleman of sixteenth and seventeenth century instruments. Trumpeters belonged to a special group guild and did not play in combination with other instruments.... In shape the Elizabethan trumpet resembled the modern trumpet and was about four feet long. The tone produced from it was softer than that of the modern trumpet because of its thicker metal and narrower bell. There was no family or set of trumpets. "The functions of the trumpet were, in England, apparently limited to the presentation of flourishes, fanfares, and military signals. By reason of its use in royal households, it was commonly associated with scenes of stately pomp and ceremony" (p. 25).

14. ***The Horn.*** "Like the trumpet, the horn was not made in sets, although it varied slightly in shape and size. In its larger form the horn had the appearance of a French horn without valves. Also, like the trumpet, the horn was reserved for signals and flourishes, usually in connection with hunting. Its tone was probably strident, as the practice of rounding the tone did not prevail until about the beginning of the eighteenth century" (p. 25).

15. ***The Drum.*** "Of the several varieties of drums used in Elizabethan England, three kinds were common. The kettledrums, shaped and constructed almost like their modern counterparts, were used in military formations and in processions.... "A smaller and more common drum, made of wood, was the tabor. The tabor was a barrel-shaped instrument of various depths, having a skin cover at each end. In its larger forms the tabor was used by foot soldiers; in its smaller forms it was the almost inseparable companion of the three-hole.... "A third type of drum was the timbrel, or tambourine—a small hoop of wood covered with skin on one side only—whose principal purpose was to accentuate the rhythm of dance music" (pp. 25-26).

16. ***The Regal.*** "The regal was a small portable organ. The keyboard, pipes, and two bellows were sometimes so disposed on a hinged frame that the instrument could be split in half and folded together. When thus closed, it resembled a large book; the source of a common name applied to it, the 'Bible regal', is thus explained.... The regals were generally used with vocal choirs. Their tone was similar to that of our clarinet, though harsher" (p. 26).

Besides, there were some other minor musical instruments, such as, crumhorn, lizard, mandora, pandora, theorbo, etc. However, which ones of all these instruments were mostly used in the dramatic performances during the Elizabethan and Jacobean era we cannot categorically say, except that the musical instruments that we have described above were popular in the theatres.

IV
(POWERS AND FUNCTIONS OF MUSIC)

Shakespeare has, in his plays, demonstrated different powers and functions of music—powers over the nature and human and non-human beings, and functions in different human needs.

1. *Power of Music over the Nature and Human and non-Human Beings.*

In *The Merchant of Venice* (V, i, 69-82), Lorenzo is ebullient while praising the of power of music to Jessica:

Jessica. I am never merry when I hear sweet music.
Lorenzo. The reason is your spirits are attentive;
For do but note a wild and wanton herd,
Or race of youthful and unhandled colts,
Fetching mad bounds, bellowing and neighing loud,
Which is the hot condition of their blood—
If they but hear perchance a trumpet sound,
Or any air of music touch their ears,
You shall perceive them make a mutual stand,
Their savage eyes turn'd to a modest gaze
By the sweet power of music. Therefore the poet
Did feign that Orpheus drew trees, stones, and floods;
Since naught so stockfish, hard, and full of rage,
But music for the time doth change his nature.

This story of the power of Orpheus' music we again find in the song of the women attending on the Queen in *Henry VIII* (III, i, 3-14):

Orpheus with his lute made trees,
And the mountain tops that freeze,
        Bow themselves when he did sing;
To his music plants and flowers
Ever sprung, as sun and showers
        There had made a lasting spring.

Everything that heard him play,
Even the bellows of the sea,
        Hung their heads and then lay by.
In sweet music is such art,
Killing care and grief of heart
        Fall asleep or hearing die.

Orpheus' music we hear for the third time in *The Two Gentlemen of Verona* (III, ii, 78-81) where Proteus tells the Duke about the power of music:

> For Orpheus' *lute* was strung with poets' sinews,
> Whose golden touch could soften steel and stones,
> Make tigers lame, and huge leviathans
> Forsake unsounded deeps to dance on sands. (*italics mine*)

Music has also the power to change the character or mood or motivation of human beings. In *Measure for Measure* (IV, i, 11-15), the unhappy Mariana was hearing a song of the Boy: "Take, O, take those lips away". Suddenly, the Duke (Vincentio) disguised as a friar, enters there. Mariana excuses herself saying she was enjoying the song—vocal music, that is—only to get rid of her woe. The Duke understood:

Mariana. ....
I cry you mercy, sir, and well could wish
You had not found me here so *musical.*
Let me excuse me, and believe me so,
My mirth it much displeas'd, but pleas'd my woe.

Duke. 'Tis good; though *music* oft hath such a charm
To make bad good and good prove to harm. (*italics mine*)

Shakespeare's last play is the most musical: *The Tempest* (perhaps, he wanted his ultimate exit from the stage to be the most musical, a most music-lover as he was). Music has a magnetic power not only on human beings but also over sub-human beings, like Caliban, the "Abhorred slave" (Miranda) "not honour'd with a human shape"—a savage litter of the witch Sycorax (and, perhaps, Prospero). This most uncivilized creature also enjoys music, slips into sleep under the embalming influence of the sweet harmony of music. Caliban reports this to Stephano in *The Tempest* (III, ii, 130-38):

> Be not afeard. This isle is full of *noises*,
> Sounds, and sweet airs, that give delight and hurt not.
> Sometimes a thousand *twanging instruments*
> Will hum about mine ears; and sometimes *voices*,
> That, if I then had wak'd after long sleep,
> Will make me sleep again; and then, in dreaming,
> The clouds methought would open and show riches
> Ready to drop upon me, that when I wak'ed,
> I cried to dream again.

This soporific property of music is to be found in two other places of the Shakespearean canon: in *A Midsummer Night's Dream* (IV, i, 80) and in *Pericles* (V, i, 231-33). In the earlier place, Titania, the Queen of the fairies cries out to the musicians: "*Music*, ho, *music*, such as charmeth sleep!" In the latter place, Pericles hears the "*music* of the spheres" and interjects at it and is overcome by its soporific influence:

> Most heavenly music!
> It nips me unto list'ening, and thick slumber
> Hangs upon my eyes: let me rest.

Love and music are mutually consonant as we see in *Twelfth Night* (I, i, 1-3) and *Antony and Cleopatra* (II, v, 1-2). Interestingly, *Twelfth Night*, that spins around the theme of love, even begins with the consonance between love and music. Orsino, the Duke of Illyria, is sick for love of the young widow Olivia, and orders music:

If *music* be the food of love, play on,
Give me excess of it, that, surfeiting,
The appetite may sicken and so die.

Like Orsino, Cleopatra in *Antony and Cleopatra* is also seething in the heat of love and is asking her attendants:

Give me some *music—music*, moody food
Of us that trade in love.

Music is an intrinsic property of human kind, and so if one wants the love of music he should be treated as a suspect of belonging to the inhuman kind. This Lorenzo teaches Jessica in *The Merchant of Venice* (V, i, 83-88):

The man that hath no *music* in himself,
Nor is not mov'd with concord of sweet sounds,
Is fit for treasons, stratagems, and spoils;
The motions of his spirit are dull as night,
And his affections dark as Erebus.
Let no such man be trusted. (*italics mine*)

Music is not only a component of the human being, but also a co-ordinate of man's life. Music and life are such that a turn in the one turns the course of the other. So co-related the two are that the beauty of each is based on the harmony between the two. In *King Richard the Second* V (V, v, 41-48), the incarcerated Richard muses on this philosophy of life:

Music do I hear?
Ha, ha! Keep time. How sour sweet *music* is
When time is broke and no proportion kept!
So is it in the *music* of men's lives. (*italics mine*)

Musi is delectable to even to sub-human species, as we have seen above in *The Tempest* (III, ii, 130-38) where Caliban falls asleep with "*sweet airs*" and dreams, and to dream again desires to fall to sleep with "*sweet airs*".

The curative value of music is an ancient wisdom as it is a modern. In *King Richard the Second* (V, v, 62), Richard speaks like an alienist (psychoanalyst) about music: "it have help madmen to their wits". Music is a quick medicine for heart's malady—for grief-stricken heart-ache. In *Romeo and Juliet*

(IV, v, 123-29), Juliet abhors her proposed marriage to Paris, because she is in deep love with Romeo. To find no alternative way to escape the wedding, she takes a soporific potion on an advice of the friar and falls into deepest sleep and looks as if dead. Alarmed, her nurse asks the assembled musicians to depart, when one of them tells her that this "pitiful case" of Juliet might be "amended", meaning Juliet might be restored to life and joy with music. Just at that moment, Peter a servant to Juliet's nurse, enters and asks the musicians to play out the popular song 'Heart's ease', and they comply:

"When griping grief the heart doth wound
And doleful dumps the mind oppress,
Then *music* with her silver sound"—
....
"Then *music* with her silver sound
With speedy help doth lend redress." (*italics mine*)

Music is vegetative, not rational; and so when the brain or mind is oppressed by too much of ratiocination for too long, music refreshes it and restores it to its former state. In *The Taming of the Shrew* (III, i, 9-13), Lucentio, the pedant, and Hortensio, the fiddler, wrangle over why there should be music beside philosophy or intellection. Lucentio superciliously explains to Hortensio:

Preposterous ass, that never read as far
To know the cause why *music* was ordain'd!
Was it not to refresh the mind of man
After his studies or his usual pain?
Then give me leave to read philosophy. (*italics mine*)

In *The Tempest* (I, ii, 386-95), Ferdinand experiences how music has swept away his sorrow for the loss of his father in the shipwreck. Sitting on the bank, he was sorrowing, when a music, from where he could not identify, came to him, and momentarily he forgot his sorrow.

Sitting on a bank,
Weeping again the King my father's wreck,
The *music* crept by me upon the waters,

Allaying both their fury and my passion (*italics mine*)
With its sweet air; thence I have follow'd it
Or it hath drawn me rather.

The curative power of music is also spoken of by Prospero in *The Tempest* (V, i, 58-59). Prospero abjures his "rough magic" and hungers for "some heavenly *music*" and then hears a "*Solemn music*". At this moment, Ariel and others gather there in a circle, as directed by Prospero who edifies them on the benefits of music:

A solemn *air*, and the best comforter
To an unsettled fancy, cure thy brains,
Now unless, boil'd within thy skull! (*italics mine*)

Shakespeare believed in the Elizabethan myth that the whole universe is musical, that everything contained in it is also musical, and that all of the universe are in concordance. But when this concordance or harmony breaks down, destruction, discord and evil break out. This philosophy we hear from Lorenzo in *The Merchant of Venice* (V, i, 60-65), where Lorenzo says that the universal music is present even in the souls of human beings. Lorenzo educates Jessica about this metaphysics of music:

There's not the smallest orb which thou behold'st
But in his motion like an angel sings,
Still quiring to the young-ey'd cherubins;
Such *harmony* is in immortal souls,
But whilst this muddy vesture of decay
Doth grossly close it in, we cannot hear it. (*italics mine*)

Such is the "music of the spheres" which Pericles, even his "muddy vesture", perceives (*Pericles*, V, i, 227). Music is a frequent and recurrent idea of Shakespeare, and he has littered his plays with it. Interestingly, he concludes many of his plays with music and, also of interest is the fact that music occurs more frequently in the last acts of his plays, and that his last play, *The Tempest*, is marvelously musical throughout. Besides employing music in his plays for dramatic purposes, Shakespeare has made innumerable references to music and musical instruments in his plays. Just one instance may illustrate the point. In *Hamlet* (III, ii, 354), Hamlet is protesting that Guildenstern is treating him as a 'thing', having no sense or sagacity. While thus protesting, he is fancying himself to be a musical instrument. He tells Guildenstern:

> Why, look you now, how unworthy a thing you make of me! You would play upon me; you would seem to know my *stops*; you would *pluck out* the heart of my mystery; you would *sound* me from my lowest *note* to the top of my *compass*; and there is much *music*, excellent *voice*, in this little *organ*, yet cannot you make it speak. 'Sblood, do you think I am easier to be *play'd* on than a *pipe*? Call me what *instrument* you will, though you can *fret* me, yet you cannot *play* upon me. (*italics mine*)

V

So far we have succinctly dealt only with the major functions of music in Shakespeare's plays and not touched upon the minor ones. Music is played each time a king enters the stage (but not always when he leaves it), and generally a sennet is sounded or a flourish (a highly ornamental passage of music) is done. 'Alarum', i.e. a call to arms for war, is sounded with a mélange of musical instruments, including, especially, drums and clarinets (clarionets). And dances, always, and songs, almost always, are accompanied by music. Music is also sounded during 'dead march', i.e. marching off from the stage with a dead body; for instance, the 'dead march' when Lear's dead body is being taken away from the stage at the very last moment of *King Lear* (V, iii, 326). And, lastly, in some playhouses of the Elizabethan era, a musical 'consort' (concert) separated two successive acts of the plays. And, further, outside the performance of the play, a music or musical concert announced to the public the beginning of a performance. Lastly, in certain playhouses in the Elizabethan age, even if in the text there was no direction to the effect that the play would be ended with a musical *ouvre*, directors used to close the play with a musical flare.

We have yet two vital functions of music to discuss. Firstly, in most cases, vocal music or singing, is accompanied by instrumental music, in order to intensify the mood generated by the singing of a song. Music is also related to dance, for it does not only accompany dance but also modulates it. Secondly, music makes the appropriate atmosphere for an event or a scene. In the casket scene of *The Merchant of Venice*, for instance, why is there music though there is neither singing nor dancing? The answer perhaps is that here music creates the appropriate atmosphere of utmost solemnity and seriousness, driving away all extraneous interfering stimuli from Bassanio who is going to choose the right casket. Bassanio is situated between life (with Portia) and death (without her). The concern of Bassanio requires extremely deep meditation on his part, to which music is an aid.

VI

Shakespeare had a peculiar taste for weird music—music whose source is invisible and whose source changes direction: it now comes from above, now from below, now from this direction, now from that. In *The Tempest* (I, ii and II, i), Ariel's music is such. In *The Tempest* (II, ii), Caliban tells Stephano that the island of Prospero is "full of *noises*":

> Be not afeared. This isle is full of *noises*,
> Sound, and *sweet airs*, that give delight, and hurt not.
> (*italics mine*)

Why does Caliban ask Stephano not to be "afeared"? Because those "noises" or "airs" mostly are weird, i.e. are invisible and are emanating from ever-changing directions. In *The Tempest* (III, iii), again, we hear weird or "strange" music. Prospero has thrown a magical banquet, where there is, as the stage direction tells us, "*Solemn and strange music.*" In the *scena solus* of the fifth act of *The Tempest*, Prospero hungers for another sort of weird music—the "heavenly *music*"—that is extra-terrestrial music that comes down from above. Another kind of weird music can be heard in *Antonio and Cleopatra* (IV, iii, 12-14) where a company of soldiers shows up before Cleopatra's palace. The stage direction says: "*Music of hautboys is under the stage*".

2nd *Soldier.* Peace, what noise?
3rd *Soldier. List, list!*
2nd *Soldier.* Hark!
3rd *Soldier.* Music in th' air.
4th *Soldier.* Under the earth.

The soldiers cannot figure out where from the music comes. The 3rd Soldier understands that it comes down from above, but the 4th Soldier says it comes up from below the earth.

As told before, Shakespeare had belief in the prevailing myth about music. In the Elizabethan age, people at large believed in the Pythagorean philosophy of music. Shakespeare's concept of 'music of the spheres' perhaps came from Pythagoras' (570-495 B.C.) philosophy of music which taught that music is of spiritual nature and that the whole of the creation is pervaded with spiritual music. When the harmony or concordance of this music is disrupted, disorder in the universe ensues. Pythagoras taught that music is the window to the spirituality of the upper regions of the whole creation—of the heavens. That Shakespeare was acquainted with the Pythagorean philosophy of music is understandable from *Twelfth Night* (IV, ii, 49) where to judge the sanity of Malvolio, the Clown asks him: "What is the opinion of Pythagoras concerning wild foul?" Pythagoras believed in transmigration of soul; believed that when, for instance, a man dies, his disembodied soul may enter into the body of a fowl at its birth. From the Clown's question to Malvolio we may presume that Shakespeare had at least a passing knowledge of Pythagoras. "This [music of the sphere], Pythagoras, first of all the Greeks conceived in his mind; and understood that the spheres sounded something concordant, because of the necessity of proportion, which never forsakes celestial beings" (Naylor, 152-53). However, Shakespeare has employed the concept of 'the music of the spheres' in three of his plays:

(i) ***Twelfth Night*** (III, i, 103-07). Olivia has fallen in love of Viola-Cesario, and when the latter tries to persuade Olivia to "whet" her past love of Orsino,

Olivia tells Viola-Cesario:

O, by your leave, I pray you:

I bade you never speak again of him;
But, would you undertake another suit,
I had rather hear you to solicit that
Than *music from the spheres.*

(ii) ***Antony and Cleopatra*** (V, ii, 82-84). Cleopatra describes to Dolabella the features of Antony thus:

His legs bestrid the ocean; his rear'd arm
Crested the world. His voice was propertied
As all the *tuned spheres,*

(iii) ***Pericles*** (V, i, 226-27). Pericles has found out Marina after long search and much worry. He is now over-joyed and prays to the heavens to bless her. At this moment, Pericles hears extra-terrestrial or heavenly music, and asks Helicanus if he too hears that music. Helicanus says he does not. Pericles wonders why Helicanus does not hear it, and then asks Marina to listen to that heavenly music. Afterwards, though, Helicanus listens to that music:

Helicanus. My lord, I hear none.
Pericles. None? The *music of the spheres*! List my Marina. [*Music.*]
Pericles. *Most heavenly music*! (*italics mine*)

After Pythagoras (c. 570-495 B.C.), Anicius Manlius Severius Boethius (c. 477-524 A.D.) wrote two important books, one of them on music: *De Consolatione Philosophiae* and *De Institutione Musica.* In the earlier book, which he wrote while in prison and before his execution, Boethius held philosophy as the loadstar of man's life. In the second book, he, as we have earlier stated, talks of three kinds of music: *musica mundana*, *musica humana*, and *musica instrumentalis*. *Musica mundana* is what Shakespeare calls the music of the spheres; *musica humana* is the harmony between man's corporal body and his non-corporeal reason or spirit; and *musica instrumentalis* is the concordance that we create with musical instruments—it is, simply, what today we call instrumental music. However, Shakespeare, probably, got the concept of the music of the spheres from the works both of Pythagoras and of Boethius.

VII

Music is famously a very powerful modulator of human moods and emotions, and so it can be employed as a powerful dramatic device or dramatic embellishment, because drama primarily deals in human moods and emotions. Shakespeare knew this full well and devised his dramas accordingly. No dramatist has yet employed music in his plays so much and so profitably as Shakespeare has done. A few of his plays—such as *Twelfth Night* and *The Tempest*—are so stuffed with music that they may be called operettas. Not only his instrumental music mightily contributes to the beauty of his plays but also his musical words, which even his most caustic critic G.B. Shaw famously praised. Yes, words may be musical, and dialogues too, as Granville-Barker tells us of "the harmony and clash of the music of the dialogue" (Styan, 4). It is this musicality of Shakespeare's plays that went a good long way to make them most popular in his days, and in ours too, and, too, will go a long way in the long future to come. One pleasing thing to conclude this chapter with: Shakespeare well knew the value of, and had the fervour for, music about 400 years ago, and only after about 400 years since Shakespeare we have begun to recognize the value of, and to develop the zeal for, music, as is apparent from the UNESCO declaring 21 June as the International Music Day—the day that is celebrated in more than 120 countries across the wide world.

7
Songs

Shakespeare has a plenty of songs in his plays, unlike any other of his contemporary dramatists. This may point to his own love of songs and his possible training in vocal music in young age. His songs, arguably, have contributed much to the excellence of his plays. Edgar Fripp, in his *Shakespeare: Man and Artist,* writes: "Shakespeare, we may be sure, was both a vocalist and an instrumentalist. His lovely songs prove it; nor otherwise could he have attained his eminence as an actor and pre-eminence as a playwright" (Fripp, 126-27). This is a very emphatic statement, indeed. However, in his love of music, Shakespeare was understandably influenced by the music-loving Elizabethan society. John H. Long in his *Shakespeare's Use of Music*, writes: "The Elizabethan age is often referred as the golden age of English song. Vocal music pervaded the life of the time to an extent which we hardly realize" (Long, 1). The vogue of vocal music—of singing, that is—came to England from France in the 14th century, as Edward W. Naylor tells us in his *Shakespeare and Music*: "It is impossible to give even an outline of the history of Songs and Singing in England. The general statement must suffice that vocal music, accompanied by viols and harps, with songs and catches, were common in the year 1230 in France; and any reader of Chaucer and Gower may see for himself that vocal music was flourishing in the 14th century in England" (Naylor, 65). This great growth of song continued to sustain through the 15th and 16th centuries and then, as the fickle public taste changed, the song faded out, but, of course, not before Shakespeare retired from the stage.

In Section VI of his *Poetics*, Aristotle counted six elements in a tragedy (in a play, that is): plot, characters, thought, diction, song, and spectacle—in that order. And in Section VII, he writes that of the six elements, the first four are of superior importance and of the remaining two elements—song and spectacle—song holds the chief place, among dramatic embellishments. The truth of this Shakespeare well knew and so he stuffed his plays, so to say, with songs. He has employed a total of 92 songs in his plays as per the "items listed in the Oxford Shakespeare's *Index of First Lines of Songs,* etc." (Fox, 222). But certainly all the 92 songs were not composed by Shakespeare himself; many of them he borrowed from the extant popular ballads. But which ones of the 92 are composed by himself we do not perhaps know for certain. However, F.E. Halliday is certain of 23 songs among the 92 to have been composed by the bard himself. Halliday's inventory (Halliday, 460-61) of the 23 songs and the specific plays in which they occur is given bellow:

1. 1594: *The Two Gentlemen of Verona*
   Who is Silvia? (IV, ii)
2. 1594: *Love's Labour's Lost*
   When daisies pied (V, ii)
3. 1595: *A Midsummer Night's Dream*
   You spotted snakes (II, ii)
4. 1596: *The Merchant of Venice*
   Tell me, where is fancy bred? (III, ii)
5. 1598: *Much Ado About Nothing*
   Sigh no more, ladies (II, iii)
   Pardon, goddess of the night (V, ii)
6. 1599: *As You Like It*
   Under the Greenwood Tree (II, v)
   Blow, blow, thou winter wind (II, vii)
   What shall he have that killed the deer? (IV, ii)
   It was a lover and his lass (V, iii)
7. 1600: *Twelfth Night*
   O mistress mine (II, iii)
   Come away, come away, death (II, iv)
   When that I was and a little tiny boy (V, i)
8. 1603: *Measure for Measure*
   Take, O take those lips away (IV, i)

9. 1609: *Cymbeline*
   Hark, hark, the lark (II, iii)
   Fear no more the heat o' the sun (IV, ii)
10. 1610: *The Winter's Tale*
    When daffodils begin to peer (IV, iii)
    Get you hence, for I must go (IV, iv)
    Lawn as white as driven snow (IV, iv)
11. 1611: *The Tempest*
    Come unto these yellow sands (I, ii)
    Full fathom five thy father lies (I, ii)
    Where the bee sucks (V, i)
12. 1612: *King Henry VIII*
    Orpheus with his lute (III, i)

Now, let us see the above songs themselves—the full songs only and not the catches of contemporary ballads or songs—and then consider the aesthetic and dramatic values of these songs in the plays.

1. *The Two Gentlemen of Verona* (IV, ii)

Proteus loved Julia in Verona, but after coming to Milan he falls headlong in love of Silvia, the daughter of the Duke of Milan. Under Silvia's window, Proteus sings in serenade the following song, Julia (in boy's clothes and now come from Verona to Milan to retrieve Proteus) and her Host in Milan hearing the music-accompanied song of Proteus from a distance.

Who is Silvia? What is she,
    That all our swains commends her?
Holy, fair, and wise is she;
    The heaven such grace did lend her,
That she might admired be.

Is she kind as she is fair?
    For beauty lives with kindness.
Love doth to her eyes repair,
    To help him of his blindness;
And, being help'd inhabits there.

Then to Silvia let us sing
    That Silvia is excelling;

She excels each mortal thing
Upon the dull earth dwelling.
To her let us garlands bring.

As a submissive appeal of an eager and desperate lover to his beloved, the song is dramatically lovely and the atmosphere appropriate.

2. *Love's Labour's Lost* (V, ii)

At the end of this play, an Interlude of the Nine Worthies is presented for the entertainment of the travelling French Princes. But the news of the death of her father arrives and she orders arrangements to be made for her immediate return to France. The Interlude is abandoned instantaneously. Armado, the fantastical Spaniard, persuades the sad Princess to hear the 'dialogue' of the Cuckoo and the Owl. The 'dialogue' is in the form of two parts of a song. The part of the Cuckoo is Ver or Spring, and the part of the Owl is Heim, or Winter.

Spring

When daisies pied and violets blue
And lady-smocks all silver white
And cuckoo-buds of yellow hue
Do paint the meadows with delight,
The cuckoo then on every tree
Mocks married men, for thus sings he:
'Cuckoo;
Cuckoo, cuckoo' O word of fear,
Unpleasing to a married ear!

When shepherds pipe on oaten straws,
And merry larks are ploughmen's clocks;
When turtle tread, and rooks and daws,
And maidens bleach their summer smocks;
The cuckoo then on every tree
Mocks married men, for thus sings he:
'Cuckoo;
Cuckoo, cuckoo'-----O word of fear,
Unpleasing to a married ear!

Winter

When icicles hang by the wall,
And Dick the shepherd blows his nail,
And Tom bears logs into the hall,
And milk comes frozen home in pail,
Then nightly sings the staring owl:
'To-who;
To-whit, To-who'—A merry note,
While greasy Joan doth keel the pot.

When all aloud the wind doth blow,
And coughing drowns the parson's saw,
And birds sit brooding in the snow,
And Marian's nose looks red and raw,
When roasted crabs hiss in the bowl,
Then nightly sings the staring owl:
'To-who;
To-whit, To-who'----A merry note,
While greasy Joan doth keel the pot.

The two parts of the song—the song of the Cuckoo and the song of the owl—suggest two seasons: spring and winter. And the two seasons symbolically refer to the two parts of the plot of the play: the romantic first part—which occupies the whole of the first four acts and also the major portion of the fifth act—where the three avowed celibates fall in love of three spinsters including the Princess of France; and the other brief saddening part where on the sudden demise of the King of France, the French Princess returns home. The first part is like spring (Cuckoo) and the second part is like winter (Owl). The song, as a whole, beautifully illustrates the play, the play of life's changing seasons.

3. *A Midsummer Night's Dream* (II, ii)

To celebrate the wedding of Theseus and Hipolyta, a performance of the old play of Pyramus and Thisbe is planned in the wood near Athens, and to that end rehearsal is going on in the same place. Two other cross pairs have also repaired to the same wood: Demetrius (who loves Hermia), Helena (who loves Demetrius) and Lysander (who loves Hermia). In the same wood, again, Oberon, the King of the fairies, and Titania, the Queen of the fairies, quarreled a lot, and now Titania asks the fairies to dance and sing to make her fall into sleep: "Sing me now asleep;/ Then to your offices, and let me rest."

The fairies sing.

First Fairy. You spotted snakes with double tongue,
Thorny hedgehogs, be not seen;
Newts and blind-worms, do no wrong,
Come not near our fairy Queen.

Chorus. Philomel with melody
Sing in our sweet lullaby.
Lulla, lulla, lullaby; lulla, lulla, lullaby.
Never harm
Nor spell nor charm
Come not our lovely lady nigh.
So good night, with lullaby.

Second Fairy. Weaving spiders, come not here;
Hence, you long-legg'd spinners, hence.
Beetle black, approach not near;
Worm nor snail do no offence.

Chorus. Philomel with melody,...

The whole of the second, third and fourth acts of *Midsummer Night's Dream* are set in the wood near Athens. It is in this lovely bucolic scenario that Titania asks the fairies to sing her to sleep. The wood, understandably, is infested with spotted snakes having bifurcated tongues, hedgehogs, newts, spiders and beetles—all that may harm Titania, and so the fairies are beseeching them not come near her. The song expresses the love of the fairies for their queen Titania, and so is very appropriate for the occasion, and is so very realistic.

4. *The Merchant of Venice* (III, ii)

Portia secretly loves Bassanio but Bassanio loves her openly. The pairing will fructify only if he chooses the right casket from amongst three. While he is mulling on which is the right casket, Portia orders music to play, and Bassanio muses on the birth and growth of love in a song:

Tell me where is fancy bred,
Or in the heart or in the head,
How begot, how nourished?
        Reply, reply.
It is engend'red in the eyes,
With gazing fed; and fancy dies
In the cradle where it lies.
        Let us all ring fancy's knell;
        I'll begin it—Ding, dong, bell.

Bassanio knows that love is but fancy (he is here light-hearted, indeed, and not as serious as Portia), and so he asks himself whether fancy is born in the head or in the heart. He answers his own question thus: fancy is bred in the eyes of the beholder (or lover) and it grows with the beholder's (or lover's) gazing on the object beheld. Bassanio tells himself that fancy is ephemeral. (he thinks that in case he fails in his choosing the right casket, his fancy for Portia will swiftly fly away). At the last moment, bracing himself, Bassanio proceeds to choose the casket that he thinks to be the right one, all through thinking that his love of Portia is but a fancy.

The song well describes the anxious indecision of Bassanio, which he tries to palliate with his trifling light song. As a dramatic device, the song must be appreciated, for the choosing must take some time for the anxiously mulling Bassanio. The time elapsed is wisely filled up with the song. Had there been no song for the actionless passage of time, the elapsed time would seem vacant and feel tedious. The stage management with the song is a witty ploy.

5. *Much Ado About Nothing* (II, iii and V, iii)

The marriage of Claudio and Hero has already been settled. Now Don Pedro strives, with the help of Leonato and Claudio, to reconcile the warring Benedick and Beatrice and make them fall in love with one another. The team of Don Pedro arrives in Leonato's orchard, along with Don Pedro. Earlier, Benedick went into the orchard and, on the appearance of Don Pedro and his team, hides himself in the bush. As plotted beforehand, Don Pedro and his companions begin talking loudly and colourfully about Beatrice's love of Benedick, so that Benedick will hear their conversation and will fall in love with her. Their conversation is going to prove the inconstancy of Benedick and the deep love Beatrice for him. Balthazar, an attendant on Don Pedro, sings the following song that slyly points to men's (particularly to Benedick's) inconstancy (and, by implication, Beatrice's constancy in her love of Benedick). Thus the following song of Balthazar, in the third scene of the second act of *Much Ado About Nothing* is dramatically very effectual.

Sigh no more, ladies, sigh no more,
Men were deceivers ever,
One foot in sea and one foot on shore,
To one thing constant never.
Then sigh not so, but let them go,
And be you blithe and bonny;
Converting all your sounds of woe
Into Hey nonny nonny.

Sing no more ditties, sing no more
Of dumps so dull and heavy;
The feud of men was never so,
Since summer first was leavy.
Then sigh not so,...

In the third scene of the fifth act of *Much Ado About Nothing,* there is another song (the stage direction does not name the singer) sung by the same Balthazar. John Pedro, the bastard brother of Don Pedro, has a design to mar the settled marriage of Claudio and Hero. He enlists the aid of his follower Borachio who goads one of Hero's gentlewomen to disguise herself as Hero and meet Claudio. This fake Hero lures Claudio to be offended by her. As a result, Claudio changes his opinion about Hero, and consequently Hero breaks down in grief. Friar Francis promptly takes her away and hides her. Leonato, hero's father and governor of Messina announces that Hero died of grief. Afterwards, Don Pedro, Claudio, and other three or four persons "with tapers" visit Hero's fake statue in the churchyard. Claudio reads out the scroll that says that Hero died of "slanderous tongues". This done, Claudio asks all to "sing your solemn hymn [song]":

Pardon, goddess of night,
Those that slew thy virgin knight;
For the which, with songs of woe,
Round about her they go.
Midnight, assist our moan;
Help us to sigh and groan,
Heavily, heavily.
Graves, yawn, and yield your dead,
Till death be uttered,
Heavily, heavily.

The dramatic function of this song is to enhance Claudio's grief and repentance, and thus, in effect, help bring Hero and Claudio far closer for their wedlock.

6. *As You Like It* (II, v; II, vii; IV, ii; V, iii)

This play has the greatest number of songs composed by Shakespeare himself (Halliday, 460-61)—four in all. The first song is in the fifth scene of the second act. Duke Senior (the exiled Duke), Touchstone, La Beau, Rosalind (disguised as Ganymede), Celia (now known as Aliena), Jaques, Amiens—all are now away from the civilized courtly ambience and are in the pastoral or bucolic environ of the forest of Arden, all happy and full of jollity. Amiens notices, as, understandably, all the others also do, the difference between the past courtly life, infested with oppression, jealousy, usurpation and enmity on the one hand, and, on the other, the present peaceful, pastoral, lovely life about which Amiens and others sing. First, the song of Amiens (II, v) portrays the stark contrast between the two lives of the two places and loudly praises the pastoral one.

Under the greenwood tree
Who loves to lie with me,
And turn his merry note
Unto the sweet bird's throat.
Come hither, come hither, come hither.
Here shall we see
No enemy
But winter and rough weather.

Amiens' song seems to invite every man to leave behind the life of the "painted civilization" and lie on the lap of the utopian green pasture. His song may remind one of the beautiful pastoral poem of W.B. Yeats: "Come away O human child,/ To the waters and the wild,/ With a fairy hand in hand,/ For the world is more full of weeping/ Than you can understand."

The second song of *As You Like It*, composed by Shakespeare himself, occurs in the seventh scene of the second act. In the previous song, the burden was pointed to the wide difference between the purple but uneasy life of the court and the simple but delightful life of the green pasture. In this present song sung this time as well by Amiens, we are told that the inhumane human beings are more evil than occasional calamities of nature.

Blow, blow, thou winter wind,
Thou art not so unkind
As man's ingratitude;
Thy tooth is not so keen,
Because thou art not seen,
Although thy breath be rude.
Heigh-ho! Sing heigh-ho! unto the green holly.
Most friendship is feigning, most loving mere folly.
Then, heigh-ho, the holly!
This life is most jolly.
Freeze, freeze, thou bitter sky,
That dost not bite so nigh
As benefits forgot:
Though thou the waters warp,
Thy sting is not so sharp
As friend rememb'red not.
Heigh-ho! sing, &c.

The next song of *As You Like It* is in the second scene of the fourth act, and is sung by one of the lords attending on the banished Duke, all of them in the habits of foresters. Perhaps it is Amiens, one of the lords, who sings the song and the others sing only the refrain or burden—"Then sing him home."

What shall he have that kill'd the deer?
His leather skin and horns to wear.
Then sing him home.

[*The rest shall bear this burden*]

Take thou no scorn to wear the horn;
It was a crest ere thou wast born.
Thy father's father wore it;
And thy father bore it.
The horn, the horn, the lusty horn,
Is not a thing to laugh to scorn.

As You Like It is a unique play, in the sense that out of its total 22 scenes, 16 are set in the Forest of Arden. Only the first act of the play is outside the Forest and the last two acts are all in the Forest. The above song is a hunting ditty, and very appropriate it is, for in the forest it is only natural to hunt. At the very beginning of the second scene of the fourth act, we learn that someone has hunted down a deer. Jaques asks: "Which is he that killed the deer?" And one of his accompanying lords answers: "Sir, it was I." The hunting of the deer and the song have added realism to the scene. But, more than that, the song, or rather the whole scene (IV, ii) provides Celia time to sleep, at the end of the previous scene (IV, i: where she says: "And I'll sleep.") and appear in the third scene of the fourth act, along with Rosalind. If the present song, or the whole of the second scene, had not been there as a wedge between the first and the third scenes, there would have been a great flaw. So this song is a necessary dramatic manoeuvre.

The last song of *As You Like It* is a beautiful romantic song that is "almost certainly composed by Shakespeare himself" (Halliday, 1969, 460). This song occurs in the third scene of the fifth act. A romantic song in a pastoral setting with a delightful rhythmic dance—what a beautiful combination!

It was a lover and his lass,
With a hey, and a ho, and a hey nonino,
That o'er the green corn-field did pass
In the spring time, the only pretty ring time,
When birds do sing, hey ding a ding, ding.
Sweet lovers love the spring.

Between the acres of the rye,
With a hey, and a ho, and a hey nonino,
These pretty country folks would lie,

In the spring time, & c.

This carol they began that hour,
With a hey, and a ho, and a hey nonino,
How that a life was but a flower,
In the spring time, & c.

And therefore take the present time,
With a hey, and a ho, and a hey nonino,
For love is crowned with the prime,
In the spring time, & c.

The last two scenes of *As You Like It* are appropriately—because it is romantic play—full of songs, dance and merriment, for there are four couples whose marriages are to be solemnized next day: Orlando and Rosalind, Oliver and Celia, Silvius and Phebe and Touchstone and Audrey. In the short third scene of the fifth act, though, only the banns of the jester Touchstone with the simple country girl Audrey is being celebrated with the beautiful song, "It was a lover and his lass". The song, therefore, is dramatically very appropriate for the occasion. Its rhythm is enchanting and, expectedly, it is to be accompanied by a dance.

7. *Twelfth Night; or, What You Will* (II, iii; II, iv; and V, i)

In the third scene of the second act of *Twelfth Night*, Sir Toby, Sir Andrew and Feste (the Clown) are doing a carousal, where Feste is singing the following song:

O mistress mine, where are you roaming?
O stay and hear; your true love's coming,
That can sing both high and low.
Trip no further, pretty sweeting;
Journeys end in lovers meeting,
Every wise man's son doth know.

....

What is love? 'Tis not hereafter;
Present mirth is present laughter;
What's to come is still unsure.
In delay there lies no plenty,
Then come kiss me, sweet and twenty;
Youth's a stuff will not endure.

The carousal is going on in Olivia's house. When all are heavily drunk, Maria arrives there and warns them of tough measures by her lady Olivia for their uncivil tumult, but to no avail. Next, there comes the hard-core Puritan Malvolio and cautions them likewise, but in vain. Meantime, Malvolio has attracted the ire of all of carousal party for his Puritanical fastidiousness, and so Maria plans to beguile Malvolio as an imaginary lover of Olivia. Maria will send "epistles of love" from Olivia to Malvolio—the "epistles" written by herself, imitating Olivia's handwriting. Malvolio will fall madly in the love of Olivia, but his love will not be requited.

The above song has two dramatic relevances. First, it is appropriate for the occasion of the carousal. Second, it builds a situation for the eruption of Malvolio's Puritanical *temper tantrum,* to mollify which Olivia entraps him with fake letters to fall in love with Maria. This dramatic manoeuvre gives a Philip to the tenor of the play.

The immediately next song is simply a balm for the love-lorn lascerated soul of Orsino, the Duke of Illyria. Love, when it grabs the hold of one, is smashing. So, to soothe himself, Orsino asks Feste to sing once more "the song we had last night." Orsino himself describes last night's song (II, iv) to Cesario:

> Mark it Cesario; it is old and plain;
> The spinsters and the knitters in the sun,
> And the free maids that weave their thread with bones,
> Do use to chant it; it is silly sooth,
> And dallies with the innocence of love,
> Like the old age.

And then Feste, the Clown, sings. The love-lorn and dejected Duke Orsino naturally invites death, which is the theme of our present song.

> Come away, come away, death;
> And in sad cypress let me be laid;
> Fly away, fly away, breath,
> I am slain by a fair cruel maid.
> My shroud of white, stuck all with yew,
> O, prepare it!

My part of death no one so true
Did share it.

Not a flower, not a flower sweet,
On my black coffin let there be strown;
Not a friend, not a friend greet
My poor corpse where my bones shall be thrown;
A thousand thousand sighs to save,
Lay me, O, where
Sad true lover never find my grave,
To weep there.

The last song of *Twelfth Night* is virtually the epilogue of the play. The song, supposedly, should be sung with music and dance jovially though its burden bears a streak of some sadness: "For the rain it raineth every day."

When that I was and a little tiny boy,
With hey, ho, the wind and the rain,
A foolish thing was but a toy,
For the rain it raineth every day.

But when I come to man's estate,
With hey, ho, the wind and the rain,
'Gainst knaves and thieves men shut their gate,
For the rain it raineth every day.

But when I came, alas! to wive,
With hey, ho, the wind and the rain,
By swaggering could I never thrive,
For the rain it raineth every day.

But when I came unto my beds,
With hey, ho, the wind and the rain,
With toss-pots still had drunken heads,
For the rain it raineth every day.

A great while ago the world began,
With hey, ho, the wind and the rain,
But that's all one, our play is done,
And we will strive to please you every day.

This song may be deemed to have two parts: the last four lines of it may be taken to be the epilogue of the play, but the rest of the song is a sort of a parody of the romance that the play is. Charles Boyce writes about this song of Feste: "Feste provides a final statement of the play's anti-romantic undertone in his bitter song (V, i, 388-407), which outlines the sorry life of a drunkard. For him, the loving of the main plot seems to count for nothing: 'the rain it raineth every day'. Feste's song expresses the jester's loneliness, for he remains outside the lovers' world, but it also reminds us of the limitations of comedy,... Tellingly, another stanza of the same song is sung by the tragic Fool of *King Lear* (III, ii, 74-77)" (Boyce, 669).

8. *Measure for Measure* (IV, i)

Mariana is still in deep love of Angelo who promised to marry her and gave her a ring to that effect, but Angelo now disowns his promise for her dowry being lost in her brother's shipwreck. Duke Vincentio tells Isabella about Mariana: "She should this Angelo have married; was affianced to her by oath, and the nuptial appointed; between which time of the contract and limit of the solemnity her brother Frederick was wreck'd at sea, having in that perished vessel the dowry of his sister" (III, i). The Duke further tells her: "This forenamed maid hath yet in her the continuance of her first affection; his unjust unkindness, that in all reason should have quenched her love, hath, like an impediment in the current, made it more violent and unruly." So to tame herself, while in the "*mooted grange at Saint Luke's*", she asks Boy to sing and Boy sings.

Take, O, take those lips away,
That so sweetly were forsworn;
And those eyes, the break of day,
Lights that do mislead the morn;
But my kisses bring again, bring again;
Seals of love, but seal'd in vain, seal'd in vain.

The song is dramatically very appropriate because it sharply illustrates the love-lorn Mariana's utterly deplorable state and sharpens the audience's empathy for her.

9. *Cymbeline* (II, iii and IV, ii)

Posthumus Leonatus, affianced to Imogen, is driven by King Cymbeline out of Britain and so Cloten, the villain, who was many times abjectly rejected by her, now finds an opportunity to mollify her and offer her proposal of marriage once more. With this end in view, Cloten has hired musicians whom he now orders to play near the ante-chamber adjoining Imogen's apartment: "Come on; tune: if you can penetrate her with your fingering, so; we'll try with tongue too: if none will do, let her remain; but I'll never give o'er. First, a very excellent good-conceited thing; after, a wonderful sweet air, with admirable rich words to it: and then let her consider." The song (II, iii) that is then sung (understandably along with the tune of musical instruments) verily obeys Cloten's instruction.

Hark, hark! The lark at heaven's gate sings,
And Phoebus 'gins arise,
His steeds to water at those springs
On chalic'd flow'rs that lies;
And winking Mary-buds begin
To open their golden eyes;
With every thing that pretty bin,
My lady sweet, arise:
Arise, arise.

The next song of *Cymbeline* is in the second scene of the fourth Act. Imogen disguises herself in man's attire, assumes the name of Fidele, and goes to Milford Haven (in order to meet Posthumus, as he falsely asked her to find him there). Feeling ill, she takes the potion that the Queen got prepared as a poison (to kill Pisanio) which in fact was a soporific agent, and is deeply asleep. Meanwhile, Cloten, in a habit like Posthumus', is killed by Guiderius (Polydore) and his body lies near Imogen. When Imogen wakes, she supposes that the dead body is of Posthumus and swoons. She seems dead, and Guiderius and Arviragus (Cadwal) prepare to bury her, singing the following song:

Guiderius. Fear no more the heat o' the sun,
Nor the furious water's rages;
Thou thy worldly task hast done,
Home art gone, and ta'en thy wages:
Golden lads and girls all must,
As chimney-sweepers, come to dust.

Arviragus. Fear no more the frown o' the great;
Thou art past the tyrant's stroke;

Care no more to clothe and eat
To thee the reed is as the oak:
The scepter, learning, physic must
All follow this, and come to dust.

Guiderius. Fear no more the lightning-flash,
Arviragus. Nor the all-dreaded thunder-stone;
Guiderius. Fear not slander, censure rash;
Arviragus. Thou hast finish'd joy and moan.
Both. All lovers young, all lovers must
Consign to thee, and come to dust.
Guiderius. No exorciser harm thee!
Arviragus. Nor no witchcraft harm thee!
Guiderius. Ghost unlaid forbear thee!
Arviragus. Nothing ill come near thee!
Both. Quiet consummation have,
And renowned be thy grave!

Guiderius and Arviragus take Imogen to be really dead. Hamlet may be afraid of death ("But the dread of something after death,/ The undiscover'd country from whose bourn/ No traveler returns, puzzles the will [to die]"), but he also knows that death ends (for ever) the summation of all the pains of life ("To die; to sleep/ No more; and by sleep to say we end/ The heart-ache and the thousand natural shocks/ That flesh is air to"). Guiderius and Arviragus' song is echoic of Hamlet's meditation on death. The two brothers, Guiderius and Arviragus, sing this song very appropriately because they are going to bury their mother.

10. *The Winter's Tale* (IV, iii; IV, iv; and IV, iv)

In *The Winter's Tale*, there are four songs, all sung by the vagabond rogue Autolycus, the first two (IV, iii and IV, iv) singly and the last one (IV, iv) with the young shepherdess Mopsa. The first and second songs happen to be in the third scene of the fourth act. This third scene of the fourth act even begins with Autolycus' song.

When daffodils begin to peer,
With heigh! the doxy over the dale,
Why, then comes in the sweet o' the year,
For the red blood reigns in the winter's pale.

The white sheet bleaching on the hedge,
With heigh! the sweet birds, O, how they sing!
Doth set my pugging tooth on edge,
For a quart of ale is a dish for a king.

The lark, that tirra-lirra chants,
With heigh! with heigh! the thrush and the jay,
Are summer songs for me and my aunts,
While we lie tumbling in the hey.

....

But shall I go mourn for that, my dear?
The pale moon shines by night;
And when I wander here and there,
I then do most go right.

If tinkers may have leave to live,
And bear the sow-skin budget,
Then my account I well may give
And in the stocks avouch it.

The song is a daguerreotype of Autolycus' character: he is care-free and happy-go-lucky, and a rogue insouciant about moral injunctions. His roguery is instantiated in his next four-line song. The Clown is going to the market to buy things for the upcoming shepherds' feast. Autolycus notices him and is bent to 'hent' his purse. With a trick, Autolycus snatches away the Clown's purse. Delighted, he sings:

Jog on, jog on, the foot-path way,
And merrily hent the stile-a;
A merry heart goes all the day,
Your sad tires in a mile-a.

This song further portrays Autolycus's character: he is a carefree rogue and a happy-go-lucky popinjay.

Next, there are two (or three) more songs in the fourth scene of the fourth Act. It may be noted here that there are very few scenes in Shakespeare's plays which are so vibrant with music and dance and song as this single scene. The setting of this scene is in the care-free bucolic Bohemia and in the cottage of a shepherd. It is not only a pastoral scene, it is a scene so full of (winter) flowers that it is absolutely unique even in the Shakespearean canon. However, here in this romantic scene, Florizel and Perdita are celebrating their nuptial avowal. Shepherds and shepherdresses, including Mopsa and Dorcas, clown, and Camilo and Polixenes (in disguise) have assembled here. After some dancing by Perdita, with the shepherds and shepherdresses, a servant tells the Clown that a pedlar (Autolycus) of ribbons, etc. is come nearby—a pedlar that can sing excellently. The Clown asks the servant to "let him approach singing." Accordingly, Autolycus enters singing—

Lawn as white as driven snow;
Cypress black as e'er was crow;
Gloves as sweet as damask roses
Masks for faces and for noses;
Bugle bracelet, necklace amber,
Perfume for a lady's chamber;
Golden quoifs and stomachers,
For my lads to give their dears;
Pins and pocking-sticks of steel—
What maids lack from head to heel.
Come, buy of me, come; come buy, come buy;
Buy, lads, or else your lasses cry.
Come, buy.

Autolycus is pedlar of varieties of things for ladies' decorations. This song details all that, and by so doing truly portrays his profession.

The fourth song, written, we are told by F.E. Halliday, "almost certainly" by Shakespeare (Halliday, 460), is a fragmentary three-part ballad sung by Autolycus, Mopsa and Dorcas in the same scene (IV, iv). Autolycus sells not only ladies' things of beautification but ballads as well, and he briefs the Clown, Mopsa and Dorcas about a few popular ballads, including the one about "Two maids wooing a man". Mopsa says that she and Dorcas can sing this three-part ballad if Autolycus joins them. Autolycus consents, saying "'tis my occupation". And they sing:

Autolycus. Get you hence, for I must go
Where it fits not you to know.

Dorcas. Whither?
Mopsa. O, whither?
Dorcas. Whither?
Mopsa. It becomes thy oath full well
Thou to me thy secrets tell.
Dorcas. Me too! Let me thither.
Mopsa. Or thou goest to th' grange or mill.
Dorcas. If to either, thou dost ill.
Autolycus. Neither.
Dorcas. What, neither?
Autolycus. Neither.
Dorcas. Thou hast sworn my love to be.
Mopsa. Thou hast sworn it more to me.
Then whither goest? Say, whither?

This ballad beautifully suggests the love between the two wenches, Mopsa and Dorcas. Autolycus here is playing the part of a clown. However, after the above song is over, Autolycus, as he came in singing, singing out he goes—

Will you buy any tape,
Or lace for your cape,
My dainty duck, my dear-a?
Any silk, any thread,
Any toy for your head,
Of the new'st and fin'st wear-a?
Come to the pedlar
That doth utter all men's ware-a.

This song gives the finishing touch to the unforgettable character of the ever buoyant and jolly Autolycus who, as if, swims on the surfs of life.

11. *The Tempest* (I, ii; I, ii and V, i)

In the second scene of the first Act of the play, we see that sea-storm, magically raised by Prospero, has subsided and all aboard the ship—Alonso, Sebastian, Ferdinand and others have made it to the shore of Prospero's island in scattered groups. Ariel, invisible but playing on a musical instrument and singing, is guiding Ferdinand who has strayed away from other groups, towards Prospero's cell. Ferdinand can hear Ariel's music and song but cannot see him. Ariel sings the lovely song (I, ii):

Come unto these yellow sands,
And then take hands;
Curtsied when you have and kissed,
The wild waves whist,
Foot it featly here and there,
And, sweet sprites, the burden bear.
Hark, hark!
Burden dispersedly. Bow-wow.
The watch dogs bark.
Burden dispersedly. Bow-wow.
Hark, hark! I hear
The strain of strutting chanticleer
Cry, Cock-a-diddle-dow.

As told before, Ferdinand cannot see Ariel, nor can he figure out from where the music (vocal music or song, perhaps accompanied by instrumental music) is coming. He muses: "Where should this music be? I' th' air or th' earth?" Ferdinand cannot make out anything of the invisible Ariel's song (vocal music), and, consequently, he is all the more flummoxed. May be, he thinks, the music is mourning his "father's wreck." However, the above song of Ariel makes us visualize the colour and psychological eeriness of Prospero's strange island—"yellow sand", "The wild waves whist", "The watch-dogs bark", "The strain of strutting chanticleer" and the "sweet sprites". At a certain point of time, Ariel's song stops, and Ferdinand ejaculates: "But 'tis gone."

No sooner does Ferdinand say that Ariel's music is no more ("'tis gone"), Ariel once more sings another song in the same second scene of the first Act. This time the theme of his song is the metamorphosis of Ferdinand's father under the saline sea. But this is quite untrue, for his father is now roaming in another part of the strange island of Prospero. Ariel sings:

Full fathom five thy father lies;
Of his bones are coral made;
Those are pearls that were his eyes;
Nothing of him that doth fade

But doth suffer a sea-change.
Into something, rich and strange.
Sea-nymphs hourly ring his knell:
Burden. Ding-dong
Hark! Now I hear them—Ding-dong bell.

Ferdinand's grief from losing his father in the ship-wreck, as he supposes, is already heavy on him. And this song aggravates the grief and casts a shadow on his bright beauty, such that Prospero calls his grief "beauty's canker".

The last song of *The Tempest* happens in the lone scene of the fifth act, and is sung also by Ariel. Every event of the play is now pushing towards a happy ending. All are happy now, reconciled and harmonized: Ferdinand and Miranda are mutually affianced; Alonso, Sebastian and Antonio have been exculpated; and Caliban and Trinculo have been manumitted. Prospero now will break his magical staff, 'discase' himself, and become his former self as the Duke of Milan. He orders Ariel:

Fetch me the hat and rapier in my cell;
I will discase me, and myself present
As I was sometime Milan. Quickly, spirit;
Thou shalt ere long be free.

Ariel brings the hat and the rapier, and while helping Prospero in attiring himself sings:

Where the bee sucks, there suck I;
In a cowslip's bell I lie;
There I couch when owls do cry.
On the bat's back I do fly
After summer merrily.
Merrily, merrily shall I live now
Under the blossom that hangs on the bough.

This song is an almost full-scale self-description of Ariel, who is a unique creation of Shakespeare—an invisible being that talks and works like human beings—a creation germane to which another is very rare in the history of world literature to find. However, before this song, we have only seen what he does but did not know what he is himself—what he feeds on, where he sleeps and when, etc. Only after we have heard this song, has Ariel a "local habitation" in addition to his name.

12. *King Henry VIII* (III, i)

This play has just one song in it. King Henry VIII is determined to divorce Queen Katherine because earlier she married her brother once removed and because Henry is in love with Anne Bullen. In her apartments, the morose Katherine asks one of her attending women who are at work: "Take thy lute, wench. My soul grows sad with troubles;/ Sing and disperse 'em, if thou canst./ Leaving working." The particular woman complies, leaves her work and sings:

> Orpheus with his lute made trees,
> And the mountain tops that freeze,
> Bow themselves when he did sing;
> To his music plants and flowers
> Ever sprung, as sun and showers
> There had made a lasting spring.
>
> Everything that heard him play,
> Even the billows of the sea,
> Hung their heads and then lay by.
> In sweet music is such art,
> Killing care and grief of heart
> Fall asleep or hearing die.

The song is simply intended to bring solace to the lacerated soul of Katherine, and this the song does and that commendably, for immediately after the song Queen Katherine talks placidly or nonchalantly with the two Cardinals—Wolsey and Campeius.

These are the 23 songs that, as told before, are, according to F.E. Halliday, "almost certainly" composed by Shakespeare himself. The total number of songs in the 37 plays of Shakespeare, as said previously, is 92. So, we may presume that either all of the rest 69 songs he borrowed from popular songs and ballads or some of them were interpolated by other hands while the plays were staged or were published. And, we shall remain here only repeating that Shakespeare—if, again, we may depend on Halliday—himself composed most songs for his four plays: *As You Like It* (4), *The Twelfth Night* (3), *The Winter's Tale* (3) and *The Tempest* (3). And these 23 most delectable ditties certainly betray Shakespeare as a superb song-writer as well.

8
Dumb Show and Play-Within-Play

Shakespeare has employed the device of the dumb show in two of his plays: *Hamlet* and *Pericles*. In *Hamlet*, there is a single scene in which a dumb show happens; and in *Pericles*, there are as many as three scenes where there are dumb shows. The dumb show is a "mimed dramatic performance whose purpose was to prepare the audience for the main action of the play to follow" (Cuddon, 243). In the dumb show a story or an idea is conveyed exclusively through gestures. Sometimes the dumb show acts as a symbol or an innuendo of what is going to happen next in the play. In most cases, the dumb show is directed either to a particular character, as to king Claudius in *Hamlet*, or to some idea. Another reason of the dumb show is to 'draw the audience's attention to the play and to stop them talking to one another'. Cuddon writes: "It may be that the Danish custom of the dumb show was a device to draw the audience's attention to the play to stop them talking to one another. So, with *Hamlet*" (Cuddon, 244). The music that invariably accompanies the dumb show is a powerful element to draw the attention of the aberrant members of the audience.

In all probability, the dumb show was brought into England from Italy perhaps around the 1550s, for in *Gorboduc* (1561) there is an imposing presence of this dramatic device—each one of the five acts of this play is preceded by a dumb show. The Tudor era was the heyday of the dumb show on the English stage. Some of the plays of that period where there are dumb shows are: Kyd's *The Spanish Tragedy* (1592), Peele's *The Old Wives' Tale* (1595) and *Battle of Alcazar* (1594), Greene's *Friar*

Bacon and Friar Bungay (1594), Webster's *The White Devil* (1612) and Middleton and Rowley's *The Changeling* (1623). After the Elizabethan age, the dumb show as such gradually fell into disuse, but did not altogether go into oblivion, for in the Jacobean period it was somewhat integrated in the masque—a device that was most popular then. Further, the dumb show continued to be on the stage in the form of the pantomime (or mime), which is a near cousin of the dumb show, or, in the form of harlequinade, as interludes in plays. Even in the 19th century the dumb show continued to be enjoyed by the audience. J.A. Cuddon writes: "Not a few 19th c. plays made use of dumb show in various ways (e.g. *The Dumb Boy,* 1821, *The Dumb Brigand,* 1832, *The Dumb Recruit,* 1840, *The Dumb Driver,* 1849, *The Dumb Sailor,* 1854)" (Cuddon, 244-45). And in the 20th c., playwrights did not absolutely forget this the age-old dramatic device of the dumb show, as may be apparent from Tom Stoppard's *Rosencrantz and Guildenstern are Dead* (1966) (Cuddon, 244-45).

Now, let us see Shakespeare's dumb shows in *Hamlet* and *Pericles*. The dumb show in *Hamlet* happens to be in the second scene of the third Act. To drive away all his lingering doubts about what the ghost of his father told him, i.e. about his belief that Claudius, his uncle, it was who murdered his father, Hamlet has engaged a travelling team of theatrical performers to enact the play "The Murder of Gonzago". As we have said, a dumb show always precedes the performance of a play which the dumb show foreshadows. All the players of the Gonzago play are ready to perform. Hamlet, Rosencrants, Guildenstern, Polonius, Ophelia, the King, the Queen, and Lords have taken seats. And then the dumb show begins. Let us follow the text of the play itself:

> *The trumpet sounds. Hautboys play. The Dumb Show enters.*
>
> *Enter a* King *and a* Queen, *very lovingly; the Queen embracing him and he her.*
>
> *She kneels, and makes show of protestation unto him. He takes her up, and declines his head upon her neck. He lies him down upon a bank of flowers; she, seeing*

him asleep, leaves him. Anon comes in a Fellow, *takes off his crown, kisses it, pours poison in the sleeper's ears, and leaves him. The Queen returns; find the King dead, and makes passionate action. The* Poisoner, *with some two or three* Mutes, *comes in again, seeming to condole with her. The dead body is carried away. The Poisoner woos the Queen with gifts: she seems harsh awhile, but in the end accepts his love.* [*Exeunt.*]

Almost immediately afterwards, the Prologue of the Gonzago play shows himself up on the stage. But just before his showing up, Ophelia, very perceptively comments on the dumb show: "Be like this show [the dumb show] imports the argument [the theme or meaning] of the play [the up-coming Gonzago play]."

Pericles has, as told before, three dumb shows, one each at the beginnings of the second and the third Acts, and one in the middle of the fourth Act. The first dumb show is in fact a demonstration of a part of the prologue-like speech of Gower. Gower says that in Tarsus Pericles was staying gloriously, and then, says he—

But tidings to the contrary
Are brought your eyes. What need speak I?

Here Gower pauses and the dumb show shows what he does not say—"What need speak I?"

Dumb Show

Enter, at one door, Pericles, *talking with* Cleon; *all the* Train *with them. Enter, at another door, a* Gentleman *with a letter to Pericles; Pericles shows the letter to Cleon. Pericles gives the Messenger a reward, and knights him. Exit Pericles at one doo and Cleon at another.*

Here the mute cinematographic dumb show shows us very realistically just one thing—a letter from Helicanus, who is in Tyre, comes to Pericles, who is now in Pentapolis. The content of the letter is revealed by Gower after the dumb show is over: Thaliard, a lord of Antioch is bent upon killing Pericles.

The delivery of the letter might have been possible by any other dramatic device but, perhaps, Shakespeare thought of embellishing the play with this lively and attention-drawing device of dumb show. Here we may notice that one peculiar feature about this first dumb show (just before II, i), and the other two latter dumb shows (just before III, i and within IV, iv), of *Pericles* is that they intervene each time the speech of Gower (the Prologue).

However, he second dumb show of *Pericles* occurs within Gower's speech at the beginning of the third Act. In the earlier dumb show Gower said that he needed not say anything because the dumb show would relate the matter, but here Gower tells the audience a quite different thing. He asks the audience to be attentive to the dumb show and use their "fine fancies", and tells them that he will explain the dumb show after it is over—

> With your fine fancies quaintly eche,
> What's dumb in show I'll plain with speech.
>
> *Dumb Show*
>
> *Enter* Pericles *and* Simonides *at one door, with* Attendants; *a* Messenger *meets them, kneels, and gives Pericles a letter. Pericles shows it Simonides; the Lords kneel to Pericles. Then enter* Thaisa, *with child, with* Lycordia, *a nurse. The King shows her the letter; she rejoices. She and Pericles take leave of her father, and depart with Lycordia and their Attendants. Then exeunt Simonides and the rest.*

As earlier given word by him, Gower then explains the dumb show. He says that tidings have come from Helicanus, a lord of Tyre, to the effect that Pericles must urgently leave Pentapolis for Tyre or of necessity lose the crown of Tyre, and that Pericles will bring with him his wife Thaisa, his daughter Marina, and Lycordia, and, lastly, that Pericles must be back to Tyre "in twice six moons".

The third dumb show in *Pericles* occurs within the fourth scene of the fourth Act, and not before the fourth Act, and in this sense this dumb show differs from the earlier two dumb shows; because they occur before the first scene of the first Act and before the first scene of the second act. All the same, this dumb show also, like the previous two, happens to be in the middle of Gower's speech.

Marina grew up till age 14 in Tharsus, under the protection of Cleon, governor of Tharsus. Cleon's wife, due to jealousy, asked her servants to kill her. The servants sold Marina to pirates and the pirates re-sold her to a brothel of Mytiline. Lysimachus, governor of Mytiline, rescues her, uncorrupted. Anxious and eager Pericles reaches Tharsus to meet his daughter Marina. Cleon's wicked wife Dionyza earlier publicised that Marina had died, and she erected a monument of her. After Pericles reaches Tharsus to see his daughter, he is given the false news of Marina's death and shown her fake monument. All this is deceptive, misleading, but the emotionally surcharged gullible Pericles believes all this as true, and sheds "biggest tears" unstoppable. The dumb show gives the audience a flash of all this.

Dumb Show

> *Enter* Pericles, *at one door, with all his* Train: Cleon *and* Dionyza *at the other. Cleon shows Pericles the tomb of Marina, whereat Pericles makes lamentation, puts on sackcloth, and in a mighty passion departs. Then exeunt Cleon and Dionyza.*

Earlier, Gower told the audience that he would make the event of this scene audio-visual: "Your ears unto your eyes I'll reconcile." This has been done. But he also promised that he would explain the dumb show. Accordingly, he now interprets this dumb show:

> See how belief may suffer by foul show!
> This borrowed passion stands for true old woe;
> And Pericles, in sorrow all devour'd,
> With sighs shot through and biggest tears o'ershower'd,
> Leaves Tharsus, and again embarks. He swears
> Never to wash his face nor cut his hairs;
> He puts on sackcloth, and to sea.

This dumb show aptly presents a Zeuxian picture of Pericles, broken down due to his belief in the loss of Marina, and also shows his deepest love of her.

There is also a succinct 'dumb show' that concludes the third scene of the final Act of *Cymbeline*, that is confined within the bound of the stage direction which is as follows:

> *Enter* Cymbeline, Belarius, Guiderius, Arviragus, Pisanio, *and* Roman Captives. *The Captains present Posthumus to Cymbeline, who delivers him over to a* Gaoler.
>
> *Exeunt omnes.*

This is not a legitimate dumb show in strict sense but rather just a stage direction for one. *The Wordsworth Dictionary of Shakespeare* has this about this 'dumb show': "This may not be a dumb show proper, but rather a survival in the printed play of notes for a scene that was never actually written" (Boyce, 165). To support this contention, *The Dictionary* has also this about *Cymbeline*: "The play was not published in Shakespeare's life-time, and appeared first in the First Folio (1623). The text was probably printed from a transcription of Shakespeare's Foul Papers, though some scholars believe it was taken from a Prompt-Book. As the only early version of the play, the Folio text has been the basis for all subsequent editions" (Boyce, 147).

However, the dumb show was in vogue in the theatre, as we have said, during Shakespeare's lifetime, and so perhaps the theatregoers, especially the groundlings, were expectant of the dumb show, and so Shakespeare prudently and sparingly utilized the device. However, it cannot be said that Shakespeare's dumb shows are unnecessary appendages of his plays. His dumb show, and for that matter any dramatist's dumb show, is not absolutely devoid of dramatic value. As a dramatic device, dumb show certainly has some value. What John Russell Taylor writes about the theatre of silence (and dumb show is a silent show) or of the theatre of the unspoken may justify to some extent the value of the dumb show. Taylor writes that Jean-Jacque Bernard evolved the theatre of silence "based on the belief that dialogue alone could not express the whole of what was going on stage; more important often was what the people on stage did not and could not express in words, and the dramatist's job was to arrange his dramas in such a way that this residue of the unexpressed could yet emerge and be understood by the audience" (Taylor,

251). Poet and dramatist Arthur Symons also believed that the stage actor always expresses what he is supposed to with the help of words, and when he cannot his only option was to express through the movement of his body. Svevolod Meyerhold, Antonin Arlaud, Nathalie Sarraut *et al.* knew this truth. Voicelessness may be vociferous, and Anton Chekhov demonstrated this in his plays with his eloquent pauses, Harold Pinter with his silences, Thornton Wilder with his mimes, and, above all, Samuel Beckett thought that silence (*dumbness*) is the most eloquent dramatic medium. The aesthetic value of the dumb show therefore should not be denied.

Lastly, two interesting facts may be mentioned about the dumb show. Firstly, a dumb show, like a prologue, may set a play in motion, for instance, John Marston's *Sophronisba* or *The Wonder of Women*. Secondly, the dumb show is also to be found, very rarely though, in the novel, for instance, in Thomas Hardy's epic drama *The Dynasts*.

However, after the Elizabethan age, new tastes emerged in the audience and around 1620 for a while the dumb shows completely petered out. Nevertheless, the effectuality of the device cannot be gainsaid, and so its allegorical nature silently continued to exist in plays. M.C. Bradbrook truly writes: "The early dumb shows were allegorical, and the later ones have a special atmosphere of portentousness which easily becomes allegorical. Silent movement is always doubly significant on the stage" (Bradbrook, 44).

Play-within-Play

Where this dramatic device of play-within-play originated we do not know for sure; may be this device was inspired by the epic, in which sometimes one story is embedded in another and the second story is nestled in yet another, and so forth, like Chinese boxes. In the *Mahabharata*, for instance, such arrangements of stories are to be found. In the classical Greek dramas this device is conspicuous for its absence. In the Elizabethan era, it was Shakespeare who resorted to this contrivance more often than most of his contemporary dramatists. Besides Shakespeare, some of the playwrights who have employed the device of play-within-play are: Thomas Kyd (*The Spanish Tragedy*), Richard Sheridan (*The Critic*), Jean Anouilh (*The Rehearsal*), Pierre Marivaux (*The Double Constancy*), Arthur Pinero (*Trelawny of the 'Wells'*), George Farquhar (*The Recruiting Officer*), Timberlake Wertenbaker (*Our Country's Good*), Ronald Harwood (*The Dresser*), Alan Ayckbourn (*A Chorus of Disapproval*), Michael Frayn (*Noises Off*), Tom Stoppard (*Rosencrantz and Guildenstern Are Dead, The Real Thing* and *The Real Inspector Hound*), *et al.*

In the history of plays, there has been no period, since the classical times, when the device of play-within-play had had a booming presence and, contrarily, there has been no era when it fell completely into disuse. However, the play-within-play is a sustainable technique in the sense that since its advent never has it been permanently relegated to the oblivion. The reasons are four. Firstly, it is an effective tool of the playwright to emphasize the fictionality of the main play. When the play-within-play is introduced, some of the principal characters of the main play metamorphose into a gang of spectators, i.e., they become at par with the original members of the audience. In Shakespeare's *The Taming of the Shrew*, for instance, the original characters—Christopher Sly and his huntsmen—are converted into spectators when the play-within-play is introduced. Earlier, Christopher and the huntsmen of the thin frame-story (or the Induction) were believed (by "willing suspension of disbelief") to be real persons but now, after their metamorphoses, they prove themselves to be fictional—illusory. But Christopher and the huntsmen were themselves fictional, in so far as they were playing the characters of the play *The Taming of the Shrew*. The characters of Christopher and the huntsmen actually were being enacted, say, for instance, by Tom, Harry, Dick, *et al.* So, in this case, the real becomes fictional and the fictional becomes real.

But what is the advantage of this technique? It is this. When Christopher and the huntsmen sit as 'spectators' or 'audience', then the fourth wall of the theatre collapses, and consequently the cooperation between the players (characters) and the original audience is enhanced, and thus the audience's suspension of disbelief is doubled, because the fake concentrated attention of the 'audience' of the play-within-play on the stage imparts a *suggestion* on the original audience to be as attentive as they are.

Secondly, through the device of the play-within-play the playwright can explicate to the audience a complex mystery of the story-line. Hamlet is in the balance as to whether to believe the ghost or not, whether his uncle is the culprit or not. The mouse-trap play—i.e. the play-within-play—discloses the mystery surrounding Hamlet's father's death to Hamlet, and also to the audience, thus helping the audience better follow the story-line.

Thirdly, the play-within-play at times provides self-reflexivity to the play, i.e. it comments on the structure of the original play. In *Hamlet*'s (III, ii) 'The Mouse-Trap' or the Gonzago play there is this self-reflexivity. Let us see 'The Mouse-Trap':

Enter Prologue.

Hamlet. We shall know by this fellow: the players cannot keep counsel; they'll tell all.

Ophelia. Will, 'a tell us what this show meant?

Hamlet. Ay, or any show that you will show him. Be not you asham'd to show, he'll not shame to tell you what it means.

Ophelia. You are naught, you are naught. I'll mark the play.

Prologue. For us, and for our tragedy,
Here stooping to your clemency,
We beg your hearing patiently. *[Exit.]*

Hamlet. Is this a prologue, or the poesy of a ring?

Ophelia. 'Tis brief, my lord.

Hamlet. As woman's love. [....]

And lastly, the play-within-play may sometimes be just a brief merriment for the audience. In *The Tempest* (IV, i), Prospero has ordered Ariel to arrange the presence of an audience ("Go bring the rabble") because he will present before all a play to be enacted by Iris, Ceres and Juno. The play will be enacted for the celebration of the betrothal of Ferdinand and Miranda. This play-within-play—this amusement, rather—does provide entertainment not only to those on the stage ("the rabble") but also to the audience.

Now let us have a quick survey of the plays-within-plays in the canon of Shakespeare. There are in all four plays in which there are plays-within-plays: *A Midsummer Night's Dream, The Taming of the Shrew, Hamlet* and *The Tempest.*

The play-within-play in *A Midsummer Night's Dream* occurs in the lone last scene of the fifth act. Theseus has sanctioned the marriages of two couples, Lysander and Hermia, and Demetrius and Helena, after avowing his own marriage with Hipolyta. The happy Theseus, the Duke of Athens, is now eager to witness the rehearsal of the play of Pyramus and Thisbe in his palace, before it is finally acted out in celebration of the three marriages. The play is to be enacted by the following cast:

Prologue	to be presented by	Quince
Pyramus	"	Bottom
Thisbe	"	Flute
Wall	"	Snout
Moonshine	"	Starveling
Lion	"	Snug

After the Prologue, the play [the play-within-play] begins and the catastrophe of the play happens in the deaths of Pyramus and Thisbe. The play-within-play closes with a Bargomask dance.

Other than the frame-story of *The Taming of the Shrew* (involving Christopher Sly's boozing), the rest of the whole play is virtually a play-within-play. The play is initiated by the Induction, which is the frame-story. The Induction comprises two scenes. In the first scene, the heavily drunk Christopher Sly is taken from the watering hole to the residence of the local Lord, where for a practical joke the Lord asks his servants to treat Christopher Sly very honourably and persuades him to believe that he has become insane for some years. The Lord also asks one of his servants, Page, to dress up like Christopher's wife. However, by now a travelling company of actors has arrived and the Lord asks them to perform the play of Pyramus and Thisbe for Christopher's entertainment. In the second scene of the Induction, everybody in the house of the Lord urges Christopher to believe that he is really out of his wits and Christopher accepts his mental derangement. Christopher further agrees that Page is his beautiful wife. At this moment the performance by the players is being readied, and Christopher readies himself to watch it along with his 'wife' Page, and the play-within-play or the main play begins.

The Taming of the Shrew is not a straight away or legitimate play-within-play, for the Petruchio-Katherina play is not actually contained within the Christopher Sly play, which is but an Induction. Nevertheless, it is also true that the Induction has the features of a play. So, if we conceive of the Induction as a play only then the Petruchio-Katherina play-part may be called a play-within-play.

The play-within-play in *Hamlet* is the most sharply featured and dramatically potential play-within-play. It happens to be in the second scene of the third Act. Hamlet is in the balance: to believe or not to believe in the words of the Ghost. As a radically moral being Hamlet must be above all doubts, and so he has thought of laying a trap in the way of his uncle Claudius—the trap that he calls 'The Mouse-Trap'. This trap is a play that will mirror the suspected crime of Claudius, and this play is the play-within-play of *Hamlet*. The story of the play-within-play is the murder of Gonzago by his nephew Lucianus by poisoning with the view to grab Gonzago's estate (and possibly also his wife Baptista). It is after this play that Hamlet is cocksure that Claudius killed his father with the connivance of his mother ("The lady doth protest too much, methinks"). Hamlet pronounces eureka to Horatio: "O good Horatio, I'll take the ghost's word for a thousand pound." Thus, this play-within-play takes the plot or story of the central play—*Hamlet*—out of the doldrums it had been in for some time and sets it in motion.

The play-within-play in *The Tempest* (IV, i) is an obligatory presentation, so to say, because, as Prospero tells Ariel, he promised to have it done on the betrothal of Ferdinand and Miranda and because the new couple expected it. Prospero orders Ariel:

> Go bring the rabble.
> O'er whom I give the power, here to this place.

Incite them to quick motion: for I must
Bestow upon the eyes of this young couple
Some vanity of mine art: it is my promise,
And they expect it from me.

This play-within-play is brief, and is enacted by three characters: Iris (messenger of the gods), Ceres (Greek Demeter) and Juno (Greek Hera). As this is a short play, to take a close look at it, it may be reproduced entire below.

Enter Iris

Iris. Ceres, most bounteous lady, thy rich leas
Of wheat, rye, barley, vetches, oats, and pease;
Thy turfy mountains, where live nibbling sheep,
And flat meads thatch'd with stover, them to keep;
Thy banks with pioned and twilled brims,
To make cold nymphs chaste crowns; and thy broom groves,
Whose shadow the dismissed bachelor loves,
Being lass-lorn; thy pole-clipt vineyard;
And thy sea-marge, sterile and rocky-hard,
Where thou thyself dost air—the Queen o' th' sky,
Whose wat'ry arch and messenger am I,
Bids thee leave these; and with her sovereign grace,
Here on this grass-plot, in this very place,
To come and sport. Her peacocks fly amain.
Juno *descends in her car*
Approach, rich Ceres, her to entertain.

Enter Ceres.

Ceres. Hail many-coloured messenger, that ne'er
Dost disobey the wife of Jupiter;
Who, with thy saffron wings, upon my flow'rs
Diffusest honey drops, refreshing show'rs;
And with each end of thy blue bow dost crown
My bosky acres and my unshrubb'd down,
Rich scarf to my proud earth—why hath thy Queen
Summon'd me hither to this short-grass'd green?

Iris. A contract of true love to celebrate,
And some donation freely to estate
On the blest lovers.

Ceres. Tell me, heavenly bow,
If Venus or her son, as thou dost know,
Do now attend the Queen? Since they did plot
The means that dusky Dis my daughter got,
Her and her blind boy's scandal'd company
I have forsworn.

Iris. Of her society
Be not afraid. I met her Deity
Cutting the clouds towards Paphos, and her son
Dove-drawn with her. Here thought they to have done
Some wanton charm upon this man and maid,
Whose vows are that no bed-rite shall be paid
Till Hymen's torch be lighted; but in vain.
Mars's hot minion is return'd again;
Her waspish-headed son has broke his arrows,
Swears he will shoot no more, but play with sparrows,
And be a boy right out.
[*Juno alights.*]

Ceres. Highest Queen of state,
Great Juno comes; I know her by her gait.

Juno. How does my bounteous sister? Go with me
To bless this twain, that they may prosperous be,
And honour'd in their issue.
They sing.

Juno. Honour, riches, marriage-blessing,
Long continuance, and increasing,
Hourly joys be still upon you!
Juno sings her blessings on you.

Ceres. Earth's increase, foison plenty,
Barns and garners never empty;

Vines with clust'ring bunches growing,
Plants with goodly burden bowing;
Spring come to you at the farthest,
In the very end of harvest!
Ceres' blessing so is on you.

....

[*Juno and Ceres whisper, and send Iris on employment.*]

....

Iris. You nymphs, call'd Naiads of the wind'ring brooks,
With your sedg'd crowns and ever harmless looks,
Leave your crisp channels, and on this green land
Answer your summons; Juno does command.
Come, temperate nymphs, and help to celebrate
A contract of true love; be not too late.
Enter certain Nymphs.
You sun-burnt sickle men, of August weary,
Come hither from the furrow, and be merry;
Make holiday; your rye-straw hats put on.
And fresh nymphs encounter everyone
In country footing.

Enter certain Reapers, *properly habited; they join with the* Nymphs *in a graceful dance; towards the end whereof* Prospero *starts suddenly, and speaks; after which, to a strange, hollow, and confused noise, they heavily vanish.*

This may not be a legitimate play-within-play, for it lacks a configured plot (plotless plays are not unimaginable, now) but certainly it may be called a deemed play-within-play, because there is dialogue in it. It is an exemplar of Shakespeare's unique play-within-play. Its wool-gathering imagination, bucolic setting, taffeta-like phraseology, airy characters, and "graceful dance" make it paradisial ("*Ferdinand.* Make this place Paradise"). It is surfeitingly delightful, required, and organically integrated into the play.

9
Ghosts and Apparitions

Shakespeare has utilized the phenomenon of ghost in his plays not very frugally, for, as the *Shakespeare Concordance* shows, the term 'ghost' occurs as many as 57 times in his plays and the term 'ghosts' 14 times. True, only the frequency of the terms 'ghost' and 'ghosts' in the plays does not prove the dramatic utility of the ghosts in them; nevertheless, it certainly points to an extent the functional efficacy of ghosts in his plays. However, we will try to understand the dramatic uses of ghosts in Shakespeare's plays, but later on.

Before that we should be clear about what is now generally meant by ghost and what Shakespeare actually meant by the term. Firstly, ghost must be differentiated from the Holy Ghost (or Holy Spirit) of Christianity which is the third person of the Trinity. Ghost is a spirit or soul of a man that can appear in this world after the death of that man. Ghost is not ghoul which is a demon that preys on the dead. E.B. Tylor, in his *Dictionary of Anthropology*, writes that in folklore ghost is "the soul of the deceased when it is believed to be perceptible to humans" (Tylor, 231). In the Elizabethan age, people had no doubt about the existence, or veracity, of ghosts. Henry Thew Stephenson, in his *The Elizabethan People*, writes: "To the average Elizabethan the ghost of his ancestor was a very real thing. Any ghost, in fact, might be met at almost any place, the time, however, usually being night. Perhaps no quality is so helpful to the would-be intelligent critic of Shakespeare as a genuine and vivid realization of how important this matter [of ghosts] was to the folk of that day. "Ghosts possessed not only the supernatural powers and qualities acquired by death, but also retained certain human qualities that were peculiar to them in life. Thus, when a ghost appeared he looked as he had looked in life, save for his pale and bloodless face, and, often, the expression of pain, sorrow, or remorse, dependent upon whatever way the fates were compelling him to work out his salvation in ghost-land. He retained his earthly voice, and generally appeared dressed as he was last seen in life, or in some characteristic garb, such as armour of a warrior, or the regal robes of a king" (Stephenson, 317-18). The ghosts of Shakespeare's plays agree with this.

The ghosts must be distinguished and differentiated from the 'ghost characters' in Shakespeare. The 'ghost characters' are actually no ghosts but are real people who are named, or referred to, in the texts of the plays but who never actually appear on the stage (or, as some critics say, who may be present on the stage but speak not a single word). It is generally assumed that the presence of ghost characters is due to the playwright's inadvertent mistake of forgetting to put words in their mouths or make them do something on the stage. Another assumption, less subscribed by critics, is that the ghost characters are due to the printers' mistake. And the third supposition is that the playwright introduced a character to develop it later on but he altogether forgot it afterwards. Whatever may be the reason of the existence of ghost characters, even Shakespeare has left a few of them in his plays.

In folklores, the term 'ghost' is used very loosely as synonymous with apparition, shade, spirit, spectre, spook, phanton, wraith, etc. Indeed, the meaning of the term 'ghost' is nebulous. Fernand Comte, in his *The Wordsworth Dictionary of Mythology*, tells us that "*Ghosts* are the manifestations of the dead to the living. They can take on very diverse appearances, from the exact form of the dead person, with his face and voice, to a shadow covered in white sheet. They cause very many phenomena: haunted houses, spirit-rapping, poltergeists, noises without apparent cause or showers of pebbles. Certain people, called mediums, say that they can communicate with them, make them appear and interpret their messages" (Comte,

229). Shakespeare does not seem either to be interested in the reality of ghosts or in the specificity of the term or in the differences between the term 'ghost' and such other terms as "apparition", "shade", etc. By 'ghost' Shakespeare seems to mean just a spirit or soul that survives death and appears in this world and communicate with humans. However, let us see the ghosts in Shakespeare's plays—

1. *Hamlet* (I, i). In this play, the ghost is that of Claudius or Hamlet senior, the murdered king of Denmark. The ghost of this play is so potent that, in fact, it kick-starts the whole play, and the play concludes when its command (of taking revenge) is somehow carried out by Hamlet. The ghost appears as many as four times in the play—to be specific, only in the first act (in the first scene twice, once in the fourth scene, and also once in the fifth).

In I, i, we see Francisco (a soldier) and Bernardo (an officer) guarding the castle of Elsinore in "bitter cold" at night. Horatio (friend to Hamlet) and Marcellus (an officer) appear there to take over the watch from them. Bernardo tells them that they saw the ghost at two previous nights. At this moment itself the Ghost appears—

Enter Ghost.

Marcellus. Peace, break off; look where it comes again.
Bernardo. In the same figure, like the King that's dead.
Marcellus. Thou art a scholar; speak to it, Horatio.
Horatio. Most like. It harrows me with fear and wonder.
Bernardo. It would be spoke to.
Marcellus. Question it Horatio.
Horatio. What art thou that usurp'st this time of night
Together with that fair and warlike form
In which the majesty of buried Denmark
Did sometimes march? By heaven I charge thee, speak!
Marcellus. It is offended.
Bernardo. See it stalks away.
Horatio. Stay! Speak, speak! I charge thee, speak! [*Exit Ghost*]

Marcellus. 'Tis gone, and will not answer.

After this, Bernardo, Marcellus and Horatio converse among themselves. Bernardo says the Ghost is "something more than fantasy", but Horatio is skeptical, and yet he says: "A mote it is to trouble the mind's eye." And then in the same scene (I, i) the Ghost reappears and spreads his arm, understandably to prove that he is no nothingness. Horatio continues to persuade the Ghost to speak, but the Ghost would not yield. The dawn is about to break out, for the cock crows. Marcellus is exasperated at the unresponsiveness of the Ghost and wants to strike at it but it is about to move away.

Marcellus. Shall I strike at it with my partisan?
Horatio. Do, if it will not stand.
Bernardo. 'Tis here! [*Exit Ghost*]
Marcellus. 'Tis gone!

The Ghost appear again in I, iv. and I, v. In the earlier two scenes, where the Ghost was present, Hamlet, the Prince of Denmark, was absent, but in these two scenes of the same first act, he is present. Not only this, in these two scenes there is communication between Hamlet and the spirit of his dead father (the Ghost)—the communication that is the prime moving power that goads Hamlet forward to action. In this sense, these two scenes are very vital. In the fourth scene of the first Act, at around twelve in the night, Hamlet, Horatio and Marcellus are lazily conversing. At this moment, there is a "*flourish of trumpets and two pieces go off*", which indicates that the king, Claudius, wakes up for an wassail. At this moment the same Ghost appears for the third time.

Enter Ghost.

Horatio. Look, my lord, it comes.
Hamlet. Angels and ministers of grace defend us!
Be thou a spirit of heath or goblin damn'd,
Bring with thee airs from heaven or blasts from hell,
Be thy intents wicked or charitable,
Thou com'st in such a questionable shape

That I will speak to thee. I'll call thee Hamlet,
King, father, royal Dane. O, answer me!...

But nothing will make the Ghost answer, it only beckons to Hamlet to move "to a more removed ground". Marcellus and Horatio dissuades Hamlet from following the Ghost but he will not listen:

Why, what should be the fear?
I do not set my life at a pin's fee;
And for my soul, what can it do to that,
Being a thing immortal as itself?
It waves me forth again; I'll follow it.

Horatio again persuades Hamlet but to no avail. The Ghost once again beckons Hamlet, and this time Hamlet is hell-bound to follow the Ghost, and for the first time directly addresses the Ghost itself: "Go on; I'll follow thee." Marcellus holds his hand to stop him; Horatio asks him to abide by their request; but every effort falls through. Hamlet is now a desperado:

Hamlet. My fate cries out,
And makes each petty arture in this body
As hardy as the Nemean lion's nerve. [*Ghost beckons*]
Still am I call'd. Unhand me, gentlemen.
By heaven, I'll make a ghost of him that lets me.
I say, away! Go on: I'll follow thee. [*Exeunt Ghost and Hamlet*

The last ever appearance of the Ghost occurs in the fifth scene of the same first act. It is the battlements of the Castle of Elsinore before which appear the Ghost and Hamlet, and they have a long conversation.

Hamlet. Whither wilt thou lead me? Speak. I'll go no further.
Ghost. Mark me.
Hamlet. I will.
Ghost. My hour is almost come
When I to sulph'rous and tormenting flames
Must render up myself.

Hamlet. Alas, poor ghost!
Ghost. Pity me not, but lend thy serious hearing.
To what I shall unfold.
Hamlet. Speak; I am bound to hear.
Ghost. So art thou to revenge, when thou shalt hear.
Hamlet. What?
Ghost. I am thy father's spirit,

....

Hamlet. O God!
Ghost. Revenge his foul and most unnatural murder.
Hamlet. Murder!

....

Hamlet. O my prophetic soul!
My uncle!
Ghost. Ay, that incestuous, that adulterate beast,

....

But soft! Methinks I scent the morning air.
Brief let me be.

....

O, horrible! O horrible! Most horrible!
If thou hast nature in thee, bear it not;
Let not the royal bed of Denmark be
A couch for luxury and damned incest.
But, howsoever thou pursuest this act,
Taint not thy mind, nor let thy soul contrive
Against thy mother aught; leave her to heaven,
And to those thorns that in her bosom lodge
To prick and sting her. Fare thee well at once.
The glowworm shows the matin to be near,
And gins to pale his uneffectual fire.
Adieu, adieu, adieu! Remember me. [*Exit*]

Briefly, the Ghost's charge to Hamlet—"Revenge his foul and most unnatural murder"—instantaneously sets the most dramatic part of the play in motion, only to come to the catastrophe in Hamlet's death and his final words: "the rest is silence."

2. ***Macbeth*** **(III, iv).** In *Macbeth*, the Ghost appears twice only in the fourth scene of the third act. Unlike the Ghost in *Hamlet*, this Ghost speaks not a single word in his two appearances. In *Hamlet*, the Ghost was the spirit of Hamlet's (murdered) dead father and in *Macbeth* the Ghost is the spirit of the dead (murdered) Banquo, a General of King Duncan.

Macbeth and Banquo, both generals of Duncan, the King of Scotland, are returning home after winning the battle against the rebels of Scotland and Norway. Three witches accost them on their way and prophesies that Macbeth will be (promoted by the king to the position of) the Thane of Cawdor, and Banquo's descendants will be kings. On his reaching the royal ambience, Duncan makes Macbeth the Thane of Cawdor. This materialization of the first prophecy of the witches doubles Macbeth's ambition, and he wishes to be the king himself and also that his descendants—and not Banquo's, as prophesied by the witches—will be kings in succession. Swiftly to materialize his dream, Macbeth by this time stabs Duncan to death, and himself puts on the crown. Next, to clear the path of his descendents to become kings, he has planned, foolproof, to get Banquo assassinated.

Now, free from all worries, Macbeth, presently the king, has thrown a banquet in the palace at Forres (III, iv). Guests have taken seats around the table, and only one seat is vacant—the seat that is reserved for Macbeth. The three hired assassins of Banquo come and report that Banquo has been dispatched "With twenty trenched gashes on his head". Macbeth, Lady Macbeth, Ross, Lennox, Lords and Attendants all are present in the feast. Lady Macbeth asks Macbeth to give the guests ceremonial welcome and cheer. Just at this moment Banquo's Ghost appears and sits on the seat reserved for Macbeth.

Enter the Ghost of Banquo *and sits in Macbeth's place.*

Macbeth. Sweet remembrance!
Now good digestion wait on appetite,
And health on both!

Lennox. May't please your Highness sit?

Macbeth.	Here had we now our country's honour roof'd, Were the grac'd person of our Banquo present; Who may I rather challenge for unkindness Than pity for mischance.
Ross.	His absence, sir, Lays blame upon his promise. Please 't your Highness To grace us with your royal company.
Macbeth.	The table's full.
Lennox.	Here is a place reserv'd sir.
Macbeth.	Where?
Lennox.	Here, my good lord. What is it that moves your Highness?
Macbeth.	Which of you have done this?
Lords.	What, my good lord?
Macbeth.	Thou canst not say I did it; never shake Thy gory locks at me.
Ross.	Gentlemen, rise; his Highness is not well.
Lady Macbeth.	Sit, worthy friends, My lord is often thus And hath been from his youth. .... Are you a man?
Macbeth.	Ay, and a bold one that dare look on that Which might appal the devil.
Lady Macbeth.	O proper stuff! .... Why do you make such faces? When all's done, You look but on a stool.
Macbeth.	Prithee see there. Behold! look! lo! how say you? Why, what care I? If thou canst nod, speak too. .... [*Exit Ghost.*]

Lady Macbeth. What, quite unmann'd in folly?
Macbeth. If I stand here, I saw him.

....

Lady Macbeth. My worthy lord,
Your noble friends do lack you.
Macbeth. I do forget.
Do not muse at me, my most worthy friends;
I have a strange infirmity, which is nothing
To those that know me. Come, love and health to all;
Then I'll sit down. Give me some wine fill full.

Enter Ghost.

I drink to the general joy o' th' whole table,
And to our dear friend Banquo, whom we miss,
Would he were here! To all and him, we thirst,
And all to all.
Lords. Our duties, and the pledge.
Macbeth. Avaunt, and quit my sight. Let the earth hide thee.
Thy bones are marrowless, thy blood is cold;
Thou hast no speculation in those eyes
Which thou dost glare with!
Lady Macbeth. Think of this good peers,
But as a thing of custom. 'Tis no other
Only it spoils the pleasure of the time.
Macbeth. What man dare, I dare.

....

Hence, horrible shadow!
Unreal mock'ry, hence! [*Exit Ghost.*]
Why, so; being gone,
I am man again. Pray you, sit still.

The Ghost of Banquo once again appears in the same scene (IV, i) along with "A Show of eight Kings" (Macbeth: "Thou art too like the spirit of Banquo") but for a trice.

In the case of the Ghost in *Macbeth*, two things need to be noticed. First, unlike the Ghost in *Hamlet*, the Ghost in *Macbeth* is seen only by Macbeth, and by none else. Second, also unlike the Ghost in *Hamlet*, the Ghost in *Macbeth* does not speak; it only moves its head. As soon as Macbeth notices the Ghost, he, unlike Hamlet, behaves like a patient of Parkinson's disease or like one in delirium tremens, and this is a manifestation of his unconscious guilt of getting Banquo murdered. Here Shakespeare's strategy is well apt. It is to be noticed here that by inducting the Ghost in *Macbeth*, he has accomplished a great dramatic feat; he has drawn the inside of Macbeth out. So in both *Hamlet* and *Macbeth*, the Ghosts have worked as great dramatic devices.

3. *Julius Caesar* (IV, iii and V, v). Triumphing over the Gauls and the army of Pompey, Caesar returns to Rome. Conspiracy is hatched by Cassius, Decius Brutus, and others to murder Caesar for fear of Caesar's suspected dictatorship in Rome. The conspirators murder Caesar. Antony (Marcus Antonius), a triumvir, reluctantly sides with the conspirators suspecting that Caesar would be a dictator, in spite of the fact that he loved Caesar. During the funeral of Caesar, Antony's high-falutin persuasive rhetoric incited the people of Rome against Brutus and Cassius, the key conspirators. For raising forces, Brutus and Cassius go to Sardis in Asia minor, and prepare for fighting against the forces of Antony. There in Sardis, Brutus is deeply broken, principally for two reasons. First, for fear of Brutus' life his wife Portia committed suicide by swallowing fire. Second, Antony is marching toward Philippi with a huge army to fight against his forces, and in the ensuing battle he fears he will be defeated and annihilated.

In IV, iii of *Julius Caesar*, Brutus is in his tent near Sardis. He is meditating on death, fearing he is near it ("We must die, Messala"). He is exhausted and feels sleepy, but his anxiety will not give him rest. So, he wants to read a book ("Look, Lucius, here's the book I sought for so;/ I put it in the pocket of my gown"). He asks Lucius to play on his instrument and Lucius plays and sings. Now he is most soporose and so dismisses Lucius who earlier slept but again is slumberous.

Brutus. It was well done; and thou shalt sleep again;
I will not hold thee long. If I do live,
I will be good to thee. [*Music and song. Lucius falls asleep.*]
This is a sleepy time. O murd'rous slumber!
Layest thou thy leaden mace upon my boy,
That plays the music? Gentle knave, good night.
....
Let me see, let me see; is not the leaf turn'd down
Where I left reading? Here it is, I think. [*Sits down*]

Enter the Ghost of Caesar

How ill this taper burns! Ha! Who comes here?
I think it is the weakness of mine eyes
That shapes this monstrous apparition.
It comes upon me. Art thou any thing?
Art thou some god, some angel, or some devil,
That make'st my blood cold and my hair to stare?
Speak to me what thou art.

Ghost. Thy evil spirit, Brutus.
Brutus. Why com'st thou?
Ghost. To tell thee thou shalt see me at Philippi.
Brutus. Well; then I shall see thee again?
Ghost. Ay, at Philippi.
Brutus. Why, I will see thee at Philippi, then. [*Exit Ghost*]
Now I have taken heart thou vanishest.

In V, v, the Ghost of Julius Caesar does not appear on the stage; its reappearance in Philippi (first appearance was in Sardis) we come to know from what Brutus tells Volumnius.

Brutus. Come hither, good Volumnius; list a word.
Volumnius. What says my lord?
Brutus. Why, this, Volumnius:

> The Ghost of Caesar hath appear'd to me
> Two several times by night—at Sardis once,
> And this last night here in Philippi fields.
> I know my hour is come.

The Ghost of Caesar, it seems from the above two cases of its appearing, is the moral agent for punishing Brutus for killing Caesar and restoring the moral order. Shakespeare, who believed in the universal moral order, has very effectively crafted the Ghost to establish this moral order.

4. *Richard III* (V, iii). This play covers an events-packed period of about three years (1483-85) between Richard's usurpation of the crown of England and his death in the battle field of Bosworth. Richard ran from his position of the Duke of Gloucester up to the royal throne through a serial killings of eleven persons who, he thought, stood, or might stand, on his way to the throne. However, we see ghosts only in the third scene of the fifth act of *Richard III*: Ghosts that are not two or three, but a bunch of eleven (Ghosts of the eleven persons Richard got killed).

Both Richard III and his most potential adversary and aspirant of the British crown, Richmond (Henry, Earl of Richmond and afterwards Henry VIII) have pitched tents on either side of the field of Bosworth, just before the ensuing battle next day. After conversing with Norfolk, Ralcliff, and others, Richard III waves them out and falls asleep. On the opposite side of the field (on the other side of the stage), Richmond, satisfied with his belligerent preparedness, says his prayer and falls asleep.

At this moment of the night, those eleven ghosts appear, one after another, before Richard III, in his dream, on one side of the field (stage) and before Richmond in his dream, on the other side of the field (stage), alternately. They all, one by one, curse Richard III and ask him to despair and die, and immediately afterwards enthuse Richmond with hope, and they retire. After the last ghost completes his censoring of Richard III and cheering of Richmond, Richard III starts out of his dream.

Enter the Ghost *of young* Prince Edward,
son to Henry the Sixth.

Ghost. [*To Richard*] Let me sit heavy on thy soul to-morrow!
Think how thou stabb'dst me in my prime of youth
At Tewksbury; despair, therefore, and die!
[*To Richmond*] Be cheerful, Richmond, for the wronged souls
Of butcher'd princes fight in thy behalf.
King Henry's issue, Richmond, comforts thee.
Enter the Ghost *of* Henry the Sixth.

Ghost. [*To Richard*] When I was mortal, my anointed body
By thee was punched full of deadly wholes.
Think on the Tower and me. Despair and die.
Henry the Sixth bids thee despair and die.
[*To Richmond*] Virtuous and holy, be thou conqueror!
Harry, that prophesied thou shouldst be King,
Dost comfort thee in thy sleep. Live and flourish!
Enter the Ghost *of* Clarence.

Ghost. [*To Richard*] Let me sit heavy in thy soul to-morrow!
I that was wash'd to death with fulsome wine,
Poor Clarence, by thy guile betray'd to death!
To-morrow in the battle think on me,
And fall thy edgeless sword. Despair and die!
[*To Richmond*] Thou offspring of the house of Lancaster,
The wronged heirs of York do pray for thee.
Good angels guard thy battle! Live and flourish!
Enter the Ghosts *of* Rivers, Grey, *and* Vaughan.

Rivers. [*To Richard*] Let me sit heavy in thy soul to-morrow,
Rivers that died at Pomfret! Despair and die!

Grey. [*To Richard*] Think upon Grey, and let thy soul despair!

Vaughan. [*To Richard*] Think upon Vaughan, and with guilty fear
Let fall thy lance. Despair and die!

All. [*To Richmond*] Awake, and think our wrongs in Richard's bosom
Will conquer him. Awake and win the day.
Enter the Ghost *of* Hastings.
Ghost. [*To Richard*] Bloody and guilty, guiltily awake,
And in a bloody battle end thy days!
Think on Lord Hastings. Despair and die.
[*To Richmond*] Quiet untroubled soul, awake, awake.
Arm, fight, and conquer, for fair England's sake!
Enter the Ghosts *of the two young* Princes.
Ghosts. [*To Richard*] Dream on thy cousins smothered in the Tower.
Let us be lead within thy bosom, Richard,
And weigh thee down to ruin, shame, and death
Thy nephews' souls bid thee despair and die.
[*To Richmond*] Sleep, Richmond, sleep in peace, and wake in joy;
Good angels guard thee from the boar's annoy!
Live, and beget a happy race of kings!
Edward's unhappy sons do bid thee flourish.
Enter the Ghost *of* Lady Anne, *his wife.*
Ghost. [*To Richard*] Richard, thy wife, that wretched Anne thy wife
That never slept a quiet hour with thee
Now fills thy sleep with perturbations.
To-morrow in the battle think on me,
And fall thy edgeless sword. Despair and die.
[*To Richard*] Thou quiet soul, sleep thou a quiet sleep;
Dream of success and happy victory.
Thy adversary's wife doth pray for thee.
Enter the Ghost *of* Buckingham.
Ghost. [*To Richard*] The first was I that help'd thee to the crown;
The last was I that felt thy tyranny.
O, in the battle think on Buckingham,

And die in terror of thy guiltiness!
Dream on, dream on of bloody deeds and death;
Fainting, despair; despairing, yield thy breath!
[*To Richmond*] I died for hope ere I could lend thee aid;
But cheer thy heart and be thou not dismay'd:
God and good angels fight on Richmond's side;
And Richard falls in fight of all his pride.
[*The Ghosts vanish. Richard starts out of his dream.*]

This long passage of all the eleven Ghosts' collocated speeches may seem rather tedious, but surely it very craftily and briefly narrates all the wrong doings of Richard III and the Ghosts' (or of the persons they represent) heart-felt wishes of punishments Richard III should receive.

Apparitions

Before we move further on, we should be careful about Shakespeare's use of the term 'apparition', for he does not always seem to use the term 'apparition' (plus 'ghost', 'spirit' and 'fiend') very consistently, specifically and definitively. For instance, in V, iv of *Cymbeline*, when Jupiter descends, Ghosts "fall on their knees". Here the Ghosts are not spirits of dead persons. Like the term 'ghost', Shakespeare also does not employ the term 'apparition' very specifically and definitively. Sometimes he uses the two terms interchangeably as well. However, the word 'apparition' derives from the Latin *apparere* which means 'to come forth' and so 'apparition' means 'that which appears', or a 'phantom'. The *Encyclopedia of Psychology*, edited by H.J. Eysenck, *et al.,* writes that apparition is a "Hallucinated figure.... A phantom or phantasm" (Eysenck, 73), Shakespeare seems to have this description for 'apparition' in his mind.

However, we may find four characteristics that may differentiate between the ghost and the apparition. The four characteristics that are present in the ghost but are absent in the apparition are: firstly, the ghost is the spirit of a dead person; secondly, the ghost seems to be a replica (with the same attire, armour, etc.) of the dead person at the moment he died; thirdly, the ghost appears to be a real person while the apparition appears shadow-like, or like an illusion or hallucination; and lastly, the ghost appears and sometimes talks with a living man while he is awake, but the apparition never talks with a living man; and unlike the ghost, may appear in a man's dream. Psychologists say that apparitions are mental projections of a man. Shakespeare perhaps knew this psychological explanation.

1. ***Macbeth*** **(IV, i).** Of all the plays of Shakespeare, *Macbeth* has the most dark and eerie atmosphere. It begins with the Witches and ends with the weird phenomenon of Birnam wood's coming to Dunsinane. And appropriately it is replete with apparitions and witches and a ghost. We come across apparitions in the first scene of the fifth act. Heretofore, Macbeth has committed two heinous crimes: he himself has stabbed king Duncan, his own well-wisher, to death; and he has dispatched Banquo, his competitor, for the royal lineage of the throne of Scotland, with the help of hired murderers. Though he is now the king of Scotland, his ambitions all are not materialized. He believes in the words of the third witch (I, iii) that told Banquo: "Thou shalt get kings, though thou be none." Macbeth fears that after him only Banquo's descendants, and not his, will be kings in tandem.

Macbeth so is impatient; he is in the jactitation of anxiety because his descendants will not be kings but Banquo's as per the prophecy of the third Witch. But he also doubts the Witch's prophecy. He cannot contain his anxiety; he must be above all doubts. Macbeth meets the prophetic Witches once more in the dark cave and charges them:

Macbeth. I conjure you by that which you profess –

....

....answer me

To what I ask you.

....

First Witch. Say, if thou'dst rather hear it from our mouths,

Or from our masters?

Macbeth. Call 'em; let me see 'em.

....

Thunder. First Apparition, *an Armed Head.*

Macbeth. Tell me thou unknown power—

First Witch. He knows thy thought.
Hear his speech, but say thou nought.
Apparition. Macbeth! Macbeth! Macbeth!
Beware Macduff;
Beware the Thane of Fife. Dismiss me.
Enough. [*He descends.*]
Macbeth. Whate'er thou art, for thy good caution, thanks;
Thou hast harp'd my fear aright. But one word more—
First Witch. He will not be commanded.
Here's another,
More potent than the first.
Thunder. Second Apparition, *a Bloody Child.*
Apparition. Macbeth! Macbeth! Macbeth!
Macbeth. Had I three ears, I'd hear thee.
Apparition. Be bloody, bold, and resolute; laugh to scorn
The pow'r of man, for none of woman born
Shall harm Macbeth. [*Descends.*]
Macbeth. Then live, Macduff; what need I fear of thee?
But yet I'll make assurance double sure
And take a bond of fate. Thou shalt not live;
That I may tell pale-hearted fear it lies,
And sleep in spite of thunder.
Thunder. Third Apparition, *a Child Crowned, with a tree in his hand.*
What is this
That rises like the issue of a king
And wears upon his baby brow the round
And top of sovereignty?
All. Listen, but speak not to't.
Apparition. Be lion-mettled, proud, and take no care
Who chafes, who frets, or where conspirers are;
Macbeth shall never vanquish'd be until

Great Birnam wood to high Dunsinane Hill
Shall come against him. [*Descends.*]

Macbeth. That will never be.

But though Macbeth plucks courage and says "That will never be", he is still dubious about Banquo's descendants to be kings of Scotland, and his apprehension comes out when he says:

Yet my heart
Throbs to know one thing;
..................................shall Banquo's issue ever
Reign in this Kingdom?

This time the Witches would not answer him in words but show him with the help of apparitions of eight kings and Banquo's ghost. The stage direction goes thus: "A Show of eight kings, *and* Banquo *last; the last king with a glass in his hand.*"

Macbeth. Thou art too like the spirit of Banquo; down!
Thy crown does sear mine eye-balls. And thy hair,
Thou other gold-bound brow, is like the first.
A third is like the former. Filthy hags!
Why do you show me this? A fourth! Start, eyes.
What, will the line stretch out to th' crack of doom?
Another yet? A seventh? I'll see no more.
And yet the eighth appears, who bears a glass
Which shows me many more; and some I see
That twofold balls and treble scepters carry.
Horrible sight! Now I see 'tis true;
For the blood-bolster'd Banquo smiles upon me,
And points at them for his. [*The show vanishes.*]

The apparitions of *Macbeth* have been drawn very craftily to show, as if in broad daylight, the most heinous crimes of Macbeth and consequent horrid psychological punishments he has to undergo and die at the end of all that.

2. *Cymbeline* (V, iv). Posthumus has been thrown into prison and there he is awaiting execution. Thinking about his wife Imogen for a while, he falls asleep, saying to himself: "O Imogen!/ I'll speak to thee in silence." And then, in his sleep, his dead father, mother and two brothers appear before him "*as in an apparition*". It should be noted here that the spirits of Posthumus' dead father, mother and two brothers that appear before him while he is *asleep* should be counted apparitions and not ghosts, for ghosts appear before one only when he is *awake*. In the "*Dramatis Personae*" of the text there is no mention of ghosts but only of "apparitions". In the stage direction in V, iv, it is given that Posthumus' father and others appear "*as in an apparition*". This is why we call them spirits or apparitions and not ghosts; but if we consider the fact that they are he spirits that escaped from their bodies when they died in the wars, then they may be called ghosts. Here is an instance of Shakespeare's using the two terms 'ghost' and 'apparition' interchangeably. However, following the stage-direction, let us call them apparitions.

The stage direction in fourth scene of the fifth act, before the appearance of the apparitions is this: "*Solemn* Music. *Enter, as in an apparition*, Sicilius Leonatus, *father to Posthumus, an old man attired like a warrior; leading in his hand an ancient matron, his* Wife, *and mother to Posthumus, with music before them. Then, after other music, follow the two young Leonati brothers to Posthumus, with wounds, as they died in the wars. They circle Posthumus round as he lies sleeping.*

Sicilius. No more thou thunder-master show
Thy spite on mortal flies.

....

Hath my poor boy done aught but well,
Whose face I never saw?
I died whilst in the womb he stay'd
Attending nature's law;
Whose father then, as men report
Thou orphan's father art,
Thou shouldst have been, and shielded him
From this earth-vexing smart.

Mother. Lucina lent not me her aid,
But took me in my throes,
That from me was Posthumus ripp'd,
Came crying 'mongst his foes,
A thing of pity.

Sicilius. Great Nature like his ancestry
Moulded the stuff so fair
That he deserv'd the praise o' th' world
As great Sicilius' heir.

First Brother. When once he was mature for man,
In Britain where was he
That could stand up his parallel,
Or fruitful object be
In eye of Imogen, that best
Could deem his dignity?

Mother. With marriage wherefore was he mock'd,
To be exil'd and thrown
From Leonati seat and cast
From her his dearest one,
Sweet Imogen?

....

Mother. Since, Jupiter, our son is good,
Take off his miseries.

Sicilius. Peep through thy marble mansion.
Help!
Or we poor ghosts will cry
To th' shinning synod of the rest
Against thy deity.

....

Jupiter *descends in thunder and lightning, sitting upon an eagle. He throws a thunderbolt. The Ghosts fall on their knees.*

Jupiter. No more, you petty spirits of region low,
Offend our hearing; hush! How dare you ghosts

Accuse the Thunderer whose bolt, you know,
Sky-planted, batters all rebelling coasts?

....

Be not with mortal accidents opprest:
No care of yours it is; you know 'tis ours.

....

Your low-laid son our godhead will uplift;
His comforts thrive, his trials well are spent.

....

He shall be lord of Lady Imogen,
And happier much by his affliction made.

....

Mount, eagle, to my palace crystalline. [*Ascends.*]

....

Sicilius. The marble pavement closes, he is enter'd
His radiant roof. Away! And, to be blest,
Let us with care perform his great behest. [*Ghosts vanish.*]

Posthumus. [*Waking*] Sleep, thou hast been a grandsire and begot
A father to me; and thou hast created
A mother and two brothers. But, O scorn,
Gone! They went hence so soon as they were born."

Shakespeare's ghost and apparition scenes are sensational displays as well as effective dramatic devices, in so far as they illustrate and enhance the story-lines. They are spectacles; and they reflect the inner workings of characters. Above all, they are organically integrated into the plots.

10
Witches, Fairies, Fiends, Spirits and Visions

Before we embark on a discussion on these dramatic contrivances of Shakespeare, let us see the frequencies of their uses in the plays of the bard as are given in the *Shakespeare Concordance*:

1. Witch (39), witches (13)
2. Spirit (259), spirits (128)
3. Fiend (66), fiends (15)
4. Fairy (40), fairies (36)
5. Vision (18), visions (03)

It is now hard to believe that the people of the Elizabethan era—an era that came on the heels of the English Renaissance—could be so gullible to the superstitions, but it is nothing else but true. A rendition of the superstitious people's mental geography may be found in Henry Thew Stephenson's *The Elizabethan People*. Stephenson writes: "It is difficult for us to imagine the sincere quality of the faith with which people then accepted the articles of folklore superstition that were in vogue. People not only believed in ghosts, witches, wise women, fortune tellers, palmists, astrologers, and fairies, with implicit faith; they also believed in omens by the score and score, connected with numberless plants and animals, with days of the week and hours of the day, with natural objects on the earth, the sun, the moon, and the stars. This was not a matter of faith with the common people alone; it was a part as well of the belief of the most educated, the most refined, the most intelligent of people" (Stephenson, 266). Shakespeare lived in the Elizabethan period, when people innocently believed in divers superstitions, strictly endorsed by the society. And, as a pro-people dramatist he endeavoured to mirror the superstitions-ridden society in his plays, with all exactitude.

Witches (in *Macbeth*)

In the Middle Age, Englanders believed that witches were numberless in Britannia. But the belief in witches did not go even when the Middle Age ended; the belief, though considerably weakened, existed as lately as the middle of the 18th century. Witches were haggard-looking women with tremendous power for evil-doings. People were afraid of evil influences and actions of the witches, and to ward off the evil doings of the witches harsh punishments were awarded to them. Acts were passed for punishing witches and witch-hunting was encouraged. A glimpse of the worried concern about witches may be had from the following entry on witches in L.W. Cowie's *The Wordsworth Dictionary of British Social History* where Cowie writes that (and we are quoting at some length) witches in England were punished as early as the Norman Conquest in the Ecclesiastical Courts by fines, penance or burning at the stake. After the Reformation in England, an Act made witchcraft a felony in 1543. Another Act made causing death by witchcraft a capital offence in 1563, and in that year an Act in Scotland imposed the death penalty for witchcraft and sorcery. "Trials for witchcraft were most numerous in England in the 17th century, but were never as frequent or harsh as in Scotland or on the Continent.... James I encouraged witch-hunting, and in 1603 an Act inflicted the death penalty for invoking evil spirits. In 1612 twelve witches were condemned at Lancaster and in 1634 seventeen witches at Pendle Forest (Lancs.) on the evidence of a boy who was found to be an impostor.... The last execution in England for witchcraft was in 1706 when a woman and her daughter, aged 11, were hanged at Huntingdon for having sold their souls to the devil and causing their neighbours to spit pins.... The laws against witchcraft were repeated in Britain in 1736, but superstitions about it lingered, especially in Northamptonshire and Huntingdon. As late as the 1760s in the country women were still being thrown into ponds, with their thumbs and toes tied together to undergo the ancient test to see whether they were witches or not. If they floated, they were pulled out to be punished as witches; if they sank, they often drowned" (Cowie, 319-20).

Above we have narrated the prejudices about witches and the inhumanely atrocious punishments meted out to them not as a passage of horror fiction but to show how far in the 16th and 17th centuries the people of England and neighbouring lands were bewitched with the malicious notions of witchery, witchcraft and witches. To "hold the mirror up to nature", therefore, Shakespeare was perhaps prudent enough to paint a few witches in his play *Macbeth*. In *Macbeth*, we come across witches in the first and the third scenes of the first act; in the fifth scene of the third act; and in the first scene of the fourth act. The prime moving force of the whole play of *Macbeth* may be said to be the Witches; and it is these three Witches in the short first scene that touch off the action of the play; and it is they that create the gloomy, eerie, suspenseful and ghostly atmosphere that the plot of the play passes through. The chorus of the three Witches, "Fair is foul, foul is fair" is the signature of the play. Let us discuss what dramatic functions these Witches perform in the four scenes of *Macbeth*.

(i) *Act I, scene i.* This very first, and very short, scene of *Macbeth* is exclusively occupied by three witches (without any name) who set the play in motion, create the mysterious atmosphere, and acts as a prologue to the whole play. It is a "desert place" now impacted by thunder and lightning. Enter three Witches.

First Witch. When shall we three meet again
In thunder, lightning, or in rain?
Second Witch. When the hurly-burly's done,
When the battle's lost and won.
Third Witch. That will be ere the set of sun.
First Witch. Where the place?
Second Witch. Upon the heath.
Third Witch. There to meet with Macbeth.

First Witch. I come, Graymalkin.
Second Witch. Paddock calls.
Third Witch. Anon!
All. Fair is foul, and foul is fair:
Hover through the fog and filthy air. [*Witches vanish.*]

Shakespeare here has very slyly employed the brief conversation of the Witches as the prologue to the "swelling action" of the play, particularly their "chorus": "Fair is foul, and foul is fair." The first part of the sentence innuendoes to Macbeth who is outwardly honest ("Fair") but under his skin is deceitful ("foul"). The second part of the sentence is merely a syllogistic transposition of the subject and the predicate without any impact on the meaning of the whole sentence. The "chorus" of the Witches is, in fact, almost the quintessential import of the play.

(ii) *Act III*, *scene v*: In this scene, we come across the three Witches meeting their "queen" Hecate, who first admonishes them for their alacrity in handling the case of Macbeth without her consultancy, and then advises them (in a long speech) as to what to do regarding Macbeth.

First Witch. Why, how now, Hecate! You look angrily.
Hecate. Have I not reason, bedlams as you are,
Saucy and overbold? How did you dare
To trade and traffic with Macbeth
In riddles and affairs of death;
And I, the mistress of your charms,
The close contriver of all harms,
Was never call'd to bear my part,
Or show the glory of our art?
....
Great business must be wrought ere noon:
Upon the corner of the moon
There hangs a vaporous drop profound;
I'll catch it ere it come to ground:
And that distill'd by magic sleights
Shall raise such artificial sprites

As by the strength of their illusion
Shall draw him on to this confusion:
He shall spurn fate, scorn death, and bear
His hopes 'bove wisdom, grace and fear: And you all know, security
Is mortals' chiefest enemy.
[*Music and song within: "Come away, come away" &c.*]
Hark! I am call'd: my little spirit see,
Sits in a foggy cloud, and stays for me. [*Exit.*]

First Witch. Come, let's make haste: she'll soon be back again. [*Exeunt*]

(iii) *Act IV, scene i*: We meet with the Witches for the last time in the first scene of the fourth Act. Macbeth has come to the "cavern" where the three Witches are preparing a charm or magical potion (a broth) with the power of which they will answer the impending questions of Macbeth. In this scene, the witches themselves do not answer Macbeth's questions but through the mouths of three Apparitions, who are the three Witches' masters, as per Macbeth's desire. First Witch asks Macbeth—

First Witch. Say, if thou'dst rather hear it from our mouths,
Or from our masters?

Macbeth. Call 'em; let me see 'em.

....

Thunder. First Apparition, *an Armed Head.*

Macbeth. Tell me, thou unknown power—

First Witch. He knows your thought.
Hear his speech, but say thou nought.

Apparition. Macbeth! Macbeth! Macbeth!
Beware Macduff;
Beware the Thane of Fife. Dismiss me.
Enough [*He descends.*]

Macbeth. Whate'er thou art, for thy good caution, thanks;

Thou hast harp'd my fear aright. But one word more—

First Witch. He will not be commanded.
Here's another,
More potent than the first.

Thunder. Second Apparition, *a bloody Child.*

Apparition. Macbeth! Macbeth! Macbeth!

Macbeth. Had I three ears, I'd hear thee.

Apparition. Be bloody, bold, and resolute, love to scorn
The pow'r of man, for none of woman born
Shall harm Macbeth. [*Descends.*]

Macbeth. Then live Macduff; what need I fear of thee?
But yet I'll make assurance double sure
And take a bond of fate. Thou shalt not live:
That I may tell pale-hearted fear it lies,
And sleep in spite of thunder.

Thunder. Third Apparition, *a Child Crowned with a tree in his hand.*

What is this
That rises like the issue of a king,
And wears upon his baby brow the round
And top of sovereignty?

All. Listen, but speak not to 't.

Apparition. Be lion-mettled, proud, and take no care
Who chafes, who frets, or where conspirers are;
Macbeth shall never vanquish'd be until
Great Birnam wood to high Dunsinane Hill
Shall come against him. [*Descends.*]

Macbeth. That will never be.

....

Can tell so much—shall Banquo's issue ever
Reign in this kingdom?

All. Seek to know no more.

Macbeth. I will be satisfied....

A Show of eight Kings, *and* Banquo *last;*
the last king with a glass in his hand.

Macbeth. Thou art too like the spirit of Banquo; down!
Thy crown does sear mine eye-balls. And thy hair,
Thou other gold-bound brow, is like the first.
A third is like the former. Filthy hags!
Why do you show me this? A fourth? Start, eyes.
What, will the line stretch out to th' crack of doom?
Another yet? A seventh? I'll see no more.
And yet the eighth appears, who bears a glass
Which shows me many more; and some I see
That twofold balls and treble sceptres carry.
Horrible sight! Now I see 'tis true;
For the blood-bolter'd Banquo smiles upon me,
And points at them for his. [*The show vanishes.*]

Notice that all the Witches are prophetic both in the first scene of the first act and in the first scene of the fourth act. These two scenes foreshadow what is going to happen to Macbeth. In this sense, these two scenes of the Witches are dramatically very efficacious.

Fairies

Fairies are frequenter than witches in Shakespeare *Chambers Twentieth Century Dictionary* tells us that a fairy is "an imaginary being, generally of diminutive and graceful human form, capable of kindly or unkindly acts towards man". Our socially conscious Shakespeare has not utilized fairies in multiple plays, though, but his *A Midsummer Night's Dream* has been abundantly peopled with fairies: Peaseblossom, Cobweb, Moth, Mustardseed and their king Oberon and queen Titania. "Shakespeare was not the first Elizabethan dramatist to introduce fairies into his plays, though he was the first to use them on the scale of *A Midsummer Night's Dream*. There are fairies in Lyly's delicate comedies *Galathea* and *Endymion*, written for the Children of the Chapel about 1588, and Robert Green's

James IV is 'presented by Oboron, King of Fayeries'. The fairies were also popular ingredients in the 'entertainments' given to Elizabeth on her progresses; for example at Woodstock in 1575 'the Queen of the Fayry drawen with six children in a wagon of state' presented her with an embroidered gown; at Norwich in 1578 she was met by fairies and the Fairy Queen, and at Elvetham in 1591 there were dancing fairies and their Queen Aureola. From childhood Shakespeare must have been acquainted with the fairies of Warwickshire folk-lore, and Puck, or Robin Goodfellow, is one of these" (Halliday, 1969, 160-61).

1. *A Midsummer Night's Dream*. In *A Midsummer Night's Dream*, as per the *dramatis personae*, there are as many as seven named fairies—Peaseblossom, Cobweb, etc., as told above. Besides, there are a number of other fairies to attend to Oberon and Titania. The importance of the functions of the fairies in this play may be guessed from the fact that the fairies occupy it from the beginning of the first scene of the second act to the end of the first scene of the fourth act.

What is a fairy? A fairy is but a spirit. In the first scene of the second act of *A Midsummer Night's Dream*, a Fairy very beautifully introduces himself/herself to Puck (or Robin Goodfellow) thus:

> Over hill, over dale,
> Through bush, through brier,
> Over park, over pale,
> Through flood, through fire,
> I do wander every where,
> Swifter than the moon's sphere;
> And I serve the Fairy Queen,
> To dew her orbs upon the green.
> The cowslips tall her pensioner be;
> In their gold coats spots you see;
> Those be rubies, fairy favours.
> In those freckles live their savours,
> I must go seek some dewdrops here,
> And hang a pearl in every cowslip's ear.

It will take a long space to narrate in some details the actions of the seven fairies in the five scenes of the play from

II, i to IV, i. So we are here giving merely sketchy summaries of those five scenes.

The first scene of the second act is set in a wood near Athens. Puck, the Robin Goodfellow, a fairy apt in mischief-mongering, tells the Fairy nearby that King Theseus and Queen Hippolyta are coming to the wood "to-night" for witnessing the performance of the play "Pyramus and Thisbe" and thus celebrate their wedding. Meantime, Oberon, the King of the fairies, and his Queen Titania quarrel there over the changeling boy which Titania will not part with. Oberon plots a vengeance on her.

In the next scene (II, ii), Titania's retinue sings her to sleep. Oberon puts the juice of the flower called love-in-idleness into Titania's eyes so that she falls in love with the first creature she sees on waking. On Oberon's order Puck also drops the juice into Lysander's eye (so that he falls in love with Hermia). In the next scene (III, i) we see Bottom is given a mask of ass's head to wear. Here Bottom sings a song:

> The ousel cock, so black of hue,
> With orange-tawny bill,
> The throstle with his note so true,
> The wren with little quill.

Titania awakes with the sound of the song and, as expected, falls in love with Bottom. She prays to Bottom:

> I pray thee, gentle mortal, sing again:
> Mine ear is much enamour'd of thy note;
> So is mine eye enthralled to thy shape;
> And thy fair virtue's force perforce doth move me
> On the first view to say, to swear, I love thee.

In the next scene (III, ii) Puck reports to Oberon that after waking from sleep Titania has ludicrously fallen in deep infatuation of a monster, which is actually Bottom, whose head has been changed to that of an ass: "My mistress with a monster is in love." Oberon orders Puck to squeeze the magic juice of the flower love-in-idleness into Demetrius' eyes, but Puck mistakenly does that into the eyes of Lysander, as a result of which Lysander falls in love of Hermia.

Lastly, in the first scene of the fourth act, we see Titania lying with the changed Bottom, who is in the shape of an ass. And this Bottom (ass) requests Titania for "a handful or two of dried peas" (as fodder) and asks all the other fairies to depart, for he is feeling sleepy. And then Bottom (ass) and Titania sleep in a loving embrace. Now Puck (Robin) comes in and Oberon shows him this risible romantic sight. Then Oberon asks Titania to hand over the "changeling child"—their bone of contention—to him and she obeys in her soporific orientation in the fairy land. Now, Oberon wakes her up by touching her eyes and the King of the fairies and the Queen of the fairies are happily reconciled.

2. *The Merry Wives of Windsor.* We also come across fairies in the fifth scene of the fifth act of this play, of course not in an outlandish *A Midsummer Night's Dream*'s dreamy land but in the realistic setting of *The Merry Wives of Windsor*. However, these are not real fairies but human beings dressed like fairies. Sir John Falstaff's immoral plot of seducing honest Mistress Ford and Mistress Page is divulged to them, and to punish him, who is dressed like Herne, Mistress Ford and Mistress Page device a trick in the fourth scene of the fourth act, which includes humans dressed like fairies.

Mistress Ford. Marry, this is our device—
That Falstaff at that oak shall meet with us,
Disguis'd like Herne, with huge horns on his head.

Mistress Page. Well let it not be doubted but he'll come,
And in this shape. When you have brought him thither,
What shall be done with him? What is your plot?

Mistress Ford. That likewise have we thought upon, and thus:
Nun Page my daughter, and my little son,
And three or four more of their growth, *we'll dress*

Like urchins, ouphes, and fairies, green and white,
With rounds of waxen tapers on their heads,
And rattles in their hands; upon a sudden,
As Falstaff, she, and I, are newly met,
Let them from forth a sawpit rush at once
With some diffused song; upon their sight
We two in great amazedness will fly.
Then let them all encircle him about,
And *fairy-like*, to pinch the unclean knight;
And ask him why, that hour of *fairy revel*,
In their so sacred paths he dares to tread
In shape profane. (*italics mine*)

Again we see fashioned fairies, i.e. humans dressed like fairies, in the fifth scene of the fifth act. Here Falstaff once more and more than before and for the last time is tormented by humans camouflaged as fairies. Stage direction: "*Enter* Sir Hugh Evans *like a satyr*, Anne Page *as a fairy*, *and* Others *as the Fairy Queen, fairies, and Hobgoblin; all with tapers.*" Falstaff is affrighted of these supernatural beings from his past experience (he is still dressed like Herne):

Falstaff. They are *fairies*; he that speaks to them shall die.
I'll wink and couch: no man their works must eye.
[*Lies down upon his face.*]
....

The Fairy Queen asks the fairies to persecute Falstaff with their burning tapers.

Fairy Queen. With trial-fire touch me his finger-end;
If he be chaste, the flame will back descend,
And turn him to no pain; but if he start,
It is the flesh of a corrupted heart.
Puck. A trial, come.
Evans. Come, will this wood take fire?

	They put the tapers to the fingers, and he starts.
Falstaff.	Oh, oh, oh!
Fairy Queen.	Corrupt, corrupt, and tainted in desire! About him, *fairies*; sing a scornful rhyme; And, as you trip, still pinch him to your time. .... Pinch him, *fairies*, mutually; Pinch him for his villainy; Pinch him and burn him and turn him about, Till candles and star-light and moonshine be out. (*italics mine*)

During this song they pinch Falstaff. Doctor Caius *comes one way, and steals away a fairy in green;* Slender *another way, and takes off a fairy in white; and* Fenton *steals away* Anne Page. *A noise of hunting is heard within. All the fairies run away.* Falstaff *pulls off his buck's head, and rises.*

Fiends

A fiend is a spirit or supernatural being whose chief trait is that it is brimful of hatred and mischief. Shakespeare has utilized the myth of fiend only in *King Henry IV, Part I.* In the third scene of the final act of this play, when the French army is about to be vanquished, Joan la Pucelle (Joan of Arc: 1412-31) stands firm to back the French legion and save her country. F.E. Halliday writes about Joan: "In *1 Henry VI*, she [Joan of Arc or Joan la Pucelle] is introduced to the Dauphin as 'a holy maid', rejects his offer of love, raises the siege of Orleans, and persuades Burgandy to desert the English cause for the French. In V, iii she conjures up fiends and offers them her soul and body for a French victory, but is captured by the Duke of York" (Halliday, 254) and then tortured and burned. Let us look at the text of the play:

	Alarum; excursion. Enter La Pucelle.
Pucelle.	The Regent concurs and the French men fly. Now help, ye charming spells and periapts; And ye choice spirits that admonish me

And give me signs of future accidents;
[*Thunder.*]
You speedy helpers that are substitutes
Under the lordly monarch of the north,
Appear and aid me in this enterprise!
[*Enter Fiends*]
This speedy and quick appearance argues proof
Of your accustom'd diligence to me.
Now, ye familiar spirits that are cull'd
Out of the powerful regions under earth,
Help me this once, that French may get the field.
[*They walk and speak not.*]
O, hold me not with silence over-long!
Where I was wont to feed you with my blood,
I'll lop a member off and give it you
In earnest of a further benefit,
So you do condescend to help me now.
[*They hang their heads.*]
No hope to have redress? My body shall
Pay recompense, if you will grant my suit.
[*They shake their heads.*]
Cannot my body nor blood sacrifice
Entreat you to your wonted furtherance?
Then take my soul—my body, soul, and all,
Before that England give the French the foil.
[*They depart.*]

Spirit

Of all the terms for all the categories of supernatural beings, Shakespeare has used the term "spirit" most frequently, as we have shown at the beginning of this chapter. He has employed the term "spirit" 259 times and the term "spirits" 128 times. Why so? Because by the term "spirit" he has meant many divers things at various places in his plays—witch, fairy, fiend, ghost as well as spirit itself. Spirit in Shakespeare is, therefore, a portmanteau word, originating from Latin "*spiritus*" which simply means "breathe". But now it denotes many things—"vital principle: the principle of thought: the soul: a disembodied soul: a ghost: an incorporeal being" (*Chambers Twentieth Century Dictionary*), etc. So Shakespeare had the freedom to employ the word with different denotations and connotations.

However, we find a spirit *per se* in the fourth scene of the first act of *Henry VI, Part II.* This is a named spirit, his name being Asnath, another name of Satan. He is conjured up from under the earth by the witch Mergery Jourdain. *The Wordsworth Dictionary of Shakespeare* writes about the name of Asnath: "It is thought that Shakespeare intended his name as an anagram of 'Sathan', a common 16th-century spelling of 'Satan'" (Boyce, 42). Now, in order to know the fates of the Duke of Suffolk, the Duke of Somerset and King Henry VI, arrangement has been done for consulting a spirit in the garden of the Duke of Gloucester. Roger Bolinbroke will conjure up the spirit Asnath from under the earth and Mergery Jourdain, the witch, will control the activities of the spirit Asnath so that Bolinbroke may question Asnath. Two priests—Southwell and Hume will assist in the ceremonies.

The ceremonies begin (*we are repeating here, because in this scene there are both the Witch, which is La Pucelle, and the Spirits*). The magic circle is drawn. Bolinbroke or Southwell reads the charm: "*Conjuro te*", etc. "It thunders and lightens terribly; then the Spirit riseth."

Spirit. Adsum.

Mergery Jourdain. Asnath,

By the eternal God, whose name and power
Thou temblest at, answer that I shall ask;
For till thou speak thou shalt not pass from hence.

Spirit. Ask what thou wilt; that I had said and done.

Bolinbroke. [*Reads*] "First of the king: what shall of him become?"

Spirit.	The Duke yet lives that Henry shall depose; But him outlive, and die a violent death. [*As the spirit speaks, Southwell writes the answer.*]
Bolinbroke.	"What fates await the Duke of Suffolk?"
Spirit.	By water shall he die and take his end.
Bolinbroke.	"What shall befall the Duke of Somerset?"
Spirit.	Let him shun castles: Safer shall he be upon the sandy plains Than where castles mounted stand. Have done, for more I hardly can endure.
Bolinbroke.	Descend to darkness and the burning lake; False fiend, avoid! [*Thunder and lightning. Exit spirit.*]

Shakespeare here may have followed the contemporary social belief in the prognosticating power of spirits, or the vogue of consulting Apollo at Delphi in classical plays, or he may have kept in mind Marlowe's *Doctor Faustus*, in which Faustus enters into a contact with the spirit Mephistophilis, if, of course, *Doctor Faustus* is elder to *Henry VI, Part II*. Dramatically, the prophesy of the Spirits in *Henry VI, Part II* well prepares the audience, as does the chorus, for succeeding dramatic events.

Visions

Shakespeare also has employed the term "vision" in divers senses—apparition, ghost and imaginative perception. "Vision" comes from Latin *visio*, meaning "to see". But ordinary seeing is no vision. Vision is "seeing the invisible", having belief or faith in the real existence of the "visible" (the "seen") invisible thing. In Shakespeare, we come across visions in *Henry VI, Part I, Cymbeline, A Midsummer Night's Dream* and *Henry VIII*. Visions always come either in sleep or in sleep-like state.

1. In *Henry VI, Part I.* In the second scene of the first act of this play, the vision occurs to Joan La Pucelle (Joan of Arc). The French army is routed by the English in the field, and Charles, the Dauphin and the future king of France, is despondent. The

Bastard of Orleans brings before Charles and Reigner, the Duke of Anjou and titular king of Naples, Joan La Pucelle who, the Bastard believes, is divinely inspired and might help the demurring French with her supernatural power. Pucelle tells Charles, the Dauphin:

> Dauphin, I am by birth a shepherd's daughter,
> My wit untrain'd in any kind of art.
> Heaven and our lady gracious hath it pleased
> To shine on my contemptible estate:
> Lo, whilst I waited on my tender lambs,
> And the sun's parching hear display'd my cheeks,
> God's mother deigned to appear to me
> *And in a vision full of majesty*
> *Will'd me to leave my base vocation*
> *And free my country from calamity:*
> *Her aid she promised and assured success:*
> *In complete glory she reveal'd herself*
> *And whereas I was black and swart before,*
> *With those clear rays which she infused on me*
> *That beauty am I bless'd with which you see.* (*italics mine*)

2. ***Cymbeline.*** In *Cymbeline*, there are two scenes where we see vision: IV, ii and V, iv. In the second scene of the fourth act, the drug-administered insensate Imogen comes back to consciousness, and finding the headless body of Cloten mistakes it as that of Posthumus and cries: "O, my lord, my lord!" On the other side, the Roman army is hell-bent to pounch upon England. Lucius, a Captain, other officers and a Soothsayer are waiting at Mitford-Haven for the coming in of that army. To have a fore-knowledge of the war, Lucius asks the Soothsayer: "Now, sir,/ What have you dream'd of late this war's purpose?" The Soothsayer replies:

> Last night the very gods show'd me a *vision*—
> I fast and pray'd for their intelligence—thus
> I saw Jove's bird, the Roman eagle wing'd
> From the spongy south to this part of the west,

There vanish'd in the sunbeams: which portends—
Unless my sins abuse my divination—
Success to the Roman host. (*italics mine*)

And in the fourth scene of the fifth act, Posthumus, while in the British prison, has a vision which falsifies the Soothsayer's earlier vision. And the falsity of the Soothsayer's vision was innuendoed to in his own above narrative: "*Unless my sins abuse my divination—*". However, in the prison Posthumus, after some rambling about his loss of liberty, falls asleep with this belief of his: "O Imogen!/ I'll speak to thee in silence." Now solemn music is played, and "*as in an apparition*" or as "ghosts", Posthumus' father Sicilius, his mother, and his two young brothers appear, and all of them "*circle Posthumus round as he lies sleeping.*" Then they all lament for Posthumus and recall his valour and virtues. Lastly, Posthumus' father, mother, and his two young brothers invoke the aid of Jupiter.

Mother. Since Jupiter, our son is good, Take off his miseries.

Sicilius. Peep through thy marble mansion. Help!
Or we poor *ghosts* will cry
To th' shining synod of the rest
Against thy deity.

Brothers. Help, Jupiter! Or we appeal, And from thy justice fly.

Jupiter *descends in thunder and lightning, sitting upon an eagle. He throws a thunderbolt. The ghosts fall on their knees.*

Jupiter. No more, you petty spirits of region low,
Offend our hearing; hush! How dare you *ghosts*
Accuse the Thunderer whose bolt, you know,
Sky-planted, batters all rebelling coasts?

....

Be content;
Your low-laid son our godhead will uplift;
His comforts thrive, his trials well are spent.

....

He shall be lord of Lady Imogen,
And happier much by his affliction made.
This tablet lay upon his breast, wherein
Our pleasure his full fortune doth confine;
And so away; no farther with your din
Express impatience, lest you stir up mine.
Mount, eagle, to my palace crystalline. [*Ascends.*]

....

Sicilius. The marble pavement closes, he is enter'd
His radiant roof. Away! And, to be blest,
Let us with care perform his great behest. [*Ghosts vanish.*]

Posthumus. [*Waking*] Sleep, thou hast been a grandsire and begot
A father to me; and thou hast created
A mother and two brothers. But, O scorn,
Gone! They went hence so soon as they were born. (*italics mine*)

3. ***A Midsummer Night's Dream.*** In the first scene of the fourth act of *A Midsummer Night's Dream*, both Titania and Bottom experience visions, one after the other. First, Titania. Oberon, the King of the fairies and Titania, his wife and the Queen of the fairies, quarreled over the possession of their changeling—a boy. To assuage her he devices a humorous trick—he asks Puck to squeeze the juice of the magic plant love-in-idleness in the eyes of Titania. Puck carries out the order, and Titania falls asleep. When she awakes up, she falls in love with Bottom, the weaver, who was donning a mask of an ass's head (or a swain's head). By now their quarrel is compromised, and Oberon dispels the magic-juice-induced spell from Titania's eyes. She wakes and in her wonderment tells Oberon:

Titania. My Oberon! What *visions* have I seen!
Methought I was enamour'd of an ass.

Oberon. There lies your love.

Titania. How came these things to pass?
O, how mine eyes do loathe his visage now!
(*italics mine*)

At the end of the same scene (IV, i), we hear Bottom boasting of having had a vision. He was sleeping. Awaking he delivers his soliloquy:

> *Bottom.* [Awaking] When my cue comes, call me, and I will answer. My next is "Most fair Pyramus". Heigh-ho! Peter Quince! Flute, the bellows-mender! Snout, the tinker! Starveling! God's my life, stol'n hence, and left me asleep! I have had a most rare *vision.* I have had a dream, past the wit of man to say what dream it was. Man is but an ass if he go about to expound the dream...I will get Peter Quince to write a ballad of this dream. It shall be call'd "Bottom's Dream", because it hath no bottom; and I will sing it in the latter end of a play, before the Duke. Peradventure, to make it the more gracious, I shall sing it at her death. [*Exit.*]
>
> (*italics mine*)

Though Bottom tell us that he has had "visions", we may not take his words at face value, because in his soliloquy he is merely jabbering nonsensically about his "vision". Further, Bottom's "vision" is actually "dream".

4. In *Pericles*, Diana appears to Pericles, the Prince of Tyre, in a vision in the first scene of the fifth act. Grief-stricken Pericles has reached the shore of Mytilene and the officials there believe that his grief will be lessened at the sight of his lost-and-found daughter Marina. They, therefore, present Marina to Pericles overboard. Recognition follows, and Pericles is drowned in his excitement from over joy. All leave him alone and he slips into deep sleep. Now Diana, goddess of light (or moon) appears before him in his dream as a *vision.*

Diana appears to Pericles as in a vision.

Diana. My temple stands in Ephesus. Hie thee thither,
And do upon mine alter sacrifice.
There, when my maiden priests are met together,

Before the people all,
Reveal how thou at sea didst lose thy wife.
To mourn thy crosses, with thy daughter's call,
And give them repetition to the life.
Or perform my bidding or thou liv'st in woe;
Do it, and happy—by my silver bow!
Awake and tell thy dream. [*Disappears.*]

Pericles. Celestial Dian, goddess argentine, I will obey thee. Helicanus!

5. ***Henry VIII*** has a *vision* in the second scene of the fourth act. Queen Katherine is divorced by Henry VIII, and she is now on death-bed. In her grief she hears from Griffith one happy news—treacherous Wolsey is dead. Katherine's ultimate moment arrives, and she is quite exhausted and drooping. She tells Griffith:

Good Griffith,
Cause the musicians play me that sad note
I nam'd my knell, whilst I sit meditating
On that celestial harmony I go to. [*Sad and solemn music.*]

Griffith. She is asleep. Good wench, let's sit down quiet.
For fear we wake her. Softly, gentle Patience.
The Vision.

Enter, solemnly tripping one after another, six personages *clad in white robes, wearing on their heads garlands of bays, and golden vizards on their faces; branches of bays or palm in their hands. They first congee unto her,* then dance; and, at certain *changes, the first two hold a spare garland over her head, at which the other four make reverent curtsies. Then the two that held the garland deliver the same to the other next two, who observe the same order in their changes, and holding the garland over her; which done, they deliver the same garland to the last two, who likewise observe the same order; at which, as it were by inspiration, she makes in her sleep signs of rejoicing, and holdeth up her hands to heaven. And so in their dancing vanish, carrying the garland with them. The music continues.*

Katherine. Spirits of peace, where are ye?
Are ye all gone?
And leave me here in wretchedness behind ye?
Griffith. Madam, we are here.
Katherine. It is not you I call for.
Saw you none enter since I slept?
Griffith. None, madam.
Katherine. No? Saw you not, even now, a blessed troop
Invite me to a banquet; whose bright faces
Cast thousand beams upon me, like the sun?
They promis'd me eternal happiness,
And brought me garlands, Griffith, which I feel
I am not worth yet to wear. I shall assuredly.
Griffith. I am most joyful, madam, such good dreams
Possess your fancy.
Katherine. Bid the music leave,
They are harsh and heavy to me. [*music ceases.*]

Shakespeare lived in the cusp between the medieval and modern worlds, and so it was not the least unnatural for him to be influenced by the blend of the belief systems of his contemporary society, or, for that matter, to employ some of them in his plays as dramatic devices. Andre Nataf, in his *The Wordsworth Dictionary of the Occult*, gives us a few instances of Shakespeare's use of popular beliefs:

> "*A Midsummer Night's Dream* is deeply marked with popular cosmology; *Love's Labour's Lost* carries an Orphic love theme with the lovers setting one another tests. *The Merchant of Venice* contains Pythagorean ideas:
> There's not the smallest orb that you behold'st
> But in his motion like an angel sings...
> But, whilst this muddy vesture of
> decay Doth grossly close it in, we
> cannot hear it.

In *The Tempest*, we see a magician fighting against the forces of evil and putting young lovers through an initiation. However, alchemy has pride of place, especially in *The Winter's Tale*. The play is saturated with alchemical philosophy and symbolism, as Paul Arnold points out. For example, the striking scene of Hernione's 'resurrection' must surely be based on the alchemical description of the King and queen going down into the tomb and rising again" (Nataf, 220).

Besides popular cosmology, alchemy, magic, Pythagorianism and hermeticism of the medieval world, Shakespeare has in his plays also well-appropriated contemporary society's belief in ghosts, witches, fairies, fiends and visions for his applause-evoking and illuminating dramatic devices. Perhaps among the above-mentioned pseudo-sciences he was particularly an ardent believer in alchemy—seemingly a magical process of converting base metal into gold and also transforming the structure of human consciousness. Andre Nataf goes on to say that "Shakespeare stands on the threshold of the medieval and modern worlds. It is not surprising that, like Hieronymus Bosch in the artistic sphere, his work should be filled with mythology, magic and esotery. Shakespeare was also undoubtedly affected by illuminism and Cabalism which were at that time enormously influential in intellectual circles" (Nataf, 220). Nataf even goes further and makes the stunning comment that "alchamy has an even intimate function in Shakespeare's works; it may even be his real heart" (*ibid.*).

11
Masque and Pageant

The performance of the masque is now almost a thing of the bygone days, but in the 14th, 15th and 16th centuries in England it was in welcome vogue. *The Oxford Companion to the English Language* writes about masque: "A usually short dramatic entertainment with music and spectacle. It developed in Renaissance Italy and became a pastime of the English court and aristocracy in the late 16c and early 17c. It was usually presented by amateurs in disguise; at the end, the actors would reveal themselves and join the spectators in a dance. Plots were slight, often classical, or allegorical. The dramatic element came to be increasingly subordinated to the musical and visual effects, which could be costly. The form attracted poets rather than dramatists, though Jonson wrote court masques. Shakespeare introduced masque-like interlude in *The Tempest* and there is a wordless masque in *Henry VIII*" (McArthur, 646). The term 'masque' is also spelled as 'mask' and 'maske'. To avoid the confusion between 'masque', meaning the theatrical 'masque', with 'mask', meaning a covering of the face or disguise, modern critics prefer the spelling 'masque' (of course the face-covering mask is often used in the performance of masque). The masque probably originated in Italy and came to England via France in the 14th century. In England, it was perhaps informed by the autochthonous genre of 'mummery' or 'disguising'. The special features of the masque are lavish use of gorgeous clothes, spectacles and poetic speeches. Anti-masque is a later development and is a show contrary to the masque, and is a comic-grotesque appendage to it. Generally, the anti-masque's theme is evil or suffering while the theme of the masque is good or peace.

The Oxford Companion to the Theatre gives a brief history of the popularity of masque in England: "In Elizabethan times the masque provided an excellent means of complimenting the queen in her own palace, or entertaining her on her summer progress through England. The speeches were written by poets and scholars, often anonymously, and the main interest centered on the costumes, scenery, songs, and dances. The masque reached its height under the Stuarts, and became a literary rather than a social force in the hands of Ben Jonson, who in 1603 succeeded Samuel Daniel as Court poet" (Hartnoll, 624). The masque may be called a dramatic entertainment, entertainment being the principal objective. If we choose to search for the meagre similarity between drama proper and masque, we will find that like in drama in masque also there is dialogue, and as sometimes the drama is preceded by a prologue, so also in most cases the prologue's prolegomena precedes the main masque. However, we may learn more about the masque from Henry Thew Stephenson. In his *The Elizabethan People*, Stephenson writes (we are quoting at some length): "The masque, which reached its greatest glory during the reign of King James, had a very meagre beginning long before in England. In the beginning, it was nothing more than a form of disguising indulged in by some of the regular guests who took part in a festive occasion where dancing was a part of the ceremony. These details must be constantly borne in mind. The masquers were of the regular and expected guests, there was always a dance to give rise to the masque, and there was a disguise. Bacon, in his essay *Of Masques and Triumphs*, says, "Let the suits of the masquers be graceful and such as become the person when the vizers are off; not after examples of known attires—Turks, soldiers, mariners; and the next step in the development of the masque, namely the assumption of some costume that was so unusual as to require a word of explanation. It was customary to have this explanation of what the masquers represented spoken by a page, and it is such a speech that is referred to in *Romeo and Juliet* under the name 'without-book prologue'. When the page had spoken his piece, he withdrew and left the masquers to choose their partners for the dance from among the ladies present.

"Out of this prologue grew the habit of prefacing the dancing by more or less elaborate conversation, written for the masquers beforehand and committed by them to memory. As soon as it was done with, they [the masquers], as usual, chose their partners, and the dance which gave occasion for the masque began. This dramatic dialogue in turn developed to such an extent that it became more than an easy task for amateurs, and professional actors, often of the comic and vaudeville type, were called in to assist. They and their parts constituted the anti-mask. As was the case with the prologue, as soon as the anti-masque was over, or the whole dramatic entertainment which contained the anti-masque, was over, the professional actors withdrew, leaving the masquers proper to go on with their dancing. "Let the anti-masquers not be long," says Bacon; "they have been commonly of fools, satyrs, baboons, wild men, antiques, beasts, spirits, witches, Ethiopes, pigmies, turquets [Turkish dwarfs], nymphs, rustics, Cupids, statues moving, and the like" (Stephenson, 253).

The masque comprises music, singing, dancing, and acting. It has a prologue, a story or plot, characters, and a theme. The masque is an ordered, organized composition, unlike the anti-masque which is merely a medley of music and dance. The anti-masque precedes the masque and so it is also called ante-masque; and as, unlike the ordered composition of the masque it is wild and disorderly, it is called anti-masque. Milton's *Camus* is a perfect illustration of the masque. The masque has been denoted by different names at different times: "What is probably the first use of the term occurs in Hall's Chronicle for 1512 where 'maske' applies to a dance of masked figures. According to Ben Jonson, masques were formerly called 'disguisings'. John Lydgate, in the period 1427-35, composed seven of these entertainments which he called 'mummings' or 'mummings by way of disguisings'" (Cuddon, 497). In the Tudor period, interest in the masque as an entertainment was growing up, and at the end of Elizabeth's reign poetic element was added to it, making masque a literary genre as well and making it a formative influence on the main-stream drama, especially on the instance of Inigo Jones. But the masque lost its popularity and influence around the forties of the 16th century due to the English Civil War (1642-51) and the recalcitrant opposition of the Puritans. However, before the genre went into perennial oblivion, the English people saw a few dozens of popular masques, such as Sidney's *The Lady of May*, Daniel's *The Vision of Twelve Goddesses*, Jonson's *The Masque of Beauty*, Chapman's *The Masque of the Middle Temple and Lincoln's Inn*, Congreve's *The Judgment of Paris*, Shirley's *The Triumph of Peace*, Beaumont's *The Masque of the Inner Temple and Gray's Inn*, etc. However, it must be granted that Jonson was the greatest writer of the genre and a prolific writer at that. Besides his *The Masque of Beauty*, he has about a dozen other popular masques: *The Masque of Lord Haddinton's Marriage, The Masque of Queens, The Golden Age Restored, Lovers Made Men, The Masque of Augurs, Pan's Anniversary, (or The Shepherd's Holiday), Neptune's Triumph for the Return of Albion, The Fortunate Isles, and their Union,* etc.

Shakespeare has no stand-alone masques, but he has employed half a dozen masques in the bodies of his six plays—*Much Ado About Nothing, Timon of Athens, Romeo and Juliet, Love's Labour's Lost, Henry VIII* and *The Tempest.* Besides, in *The Merchant of Venice* and *The Taming of the Shrew* he has made passing references to the masque, and in a few plays of his there are masque-like scenes as well.

1. *Much Ado About Nothing* (II, i, 71-135)

In a hall in Leonato's house are assembled Leonato, the Governor of Messina; Antonio, Hero, Beatrice, Margaret, Ursula and others, for a festivity. As there was a conversation among them, Leonato suddenly announces: "The revelers are ent'ring, brother; make good room." Antonio hurriedly puts on his mask. And then enter Don Pedro, the Prince of Arragon; Claudio, lover of Hero; Benedick, Balthasar, Don John and Borachio, all wearing masks, along with a drum. The masque is soon to begin, and so Don Pedro chooses Hero as his partner; Balthasar, attendant on Don Pedro, takes away Margaret, attendant on Hero; Antonio, brother to Leonato, chooses Ursula, another attendant on Hero; and Benedick, a young lord of Padua, takes the hand of Beatrice, niece to Leonato. This done, music begins to play and all of them dance, and after the masque is over, all leave but Don John, Borachio and Claudio.

So far, the masque seems plain and simple, but it is not so, for Shakespeare seldom employs events in his plays for one purpose only—for only entertainment. The dramatic value of this masque, besides its amusement value, lies hidden as a ploy to "bridge" the hiatus between Claudio and hero. The masque here is but an occasion for making that "bridge". To understand this we have to go back to the first scene of the first act (lines, 268-90), where Claudio cannot be hopeful about going the way of love of Hero, and Don Pedro assures him of his yeoman's service to that end:

Don Pedro. Thou wilt be like lover presently,
And tire the hearer with a book of words.
If thou dost love fair Hero, cherish it;
And I will break with her, and with her father,
And thou shalt have her.

....

Claudio. How sweetly you do minister to love,

....

Don Pedro. What need the *bridge* much broader than the *flood*?
The fairest grant is the necessity.
Look what will serve is fit. Tis once, thou lovest;
And I will fit thee with the remedy.
I know we shall have revelling to-night;
I will assume thy part in some disguise,
And tell fair Hero I am Claudio;
And in her bosom I'll unclasp my heart,
And take her hearing prisoner with the force
And strong encounter of my amorous tale.
Then, after, to her father I will break;
And the conclusion is she shall be thine.
In practice let us put it presently.

(*italics mine*)

2. *Timon of Athens* (I, ii, 111-51)

To show his disproportionate magnanimity and open-handedness, Timon has arranged an elaborate banquet in his house. Guests have flowed into the banqueting room. Stage direction: "Hautboys *playing loud music. A great banquet serv'd in*; Flavius *and* Others *attending; and then enter* Lord Timon, *the States, the Athenian Lords*, Ventidius, *which Timon redeem'd from prison. Then comes, dropping after all,* Apemantus discontentedly, like himself." Ventidius offers to repay the money as per his promise, with which Timon got him released from prison, but Timon now emphatically declines.

Timon. O, by no means,
Honest Ventidiu! You mistake my love;
I gave it freely ever; and there's none
Can truly say he gives, if he receives.

....

Ventidius. A noble spirit!

Apemantus says the Grace and eats and drinks. He knows the assembled guests all are cold flatterers, and wishes Timon could kill them, but Timon says all of them are his "good friends".

At this moment, a servant announces that a bevy of ladies, led by Cupid, wants admittance. On Timon's nod, they enter the banquet room. Here the stage direction is: "*Music*. Re-enter Cupid, with a Masque of Ladies as Amazons, with lutes in their hands, dancing and playing." Then after a philosophical speech by Apemantus, "*The Lords rise from the table, with much adoring of Timon; and to show their loves, each single out an Amazon, and all dance, men with women, a lofty strain or two to the hautboys, and cease.*" Timon thanks the masquers for their entertainment, and they thank him and depart.

The masque has served two dramatic purposes: one, it is appropriate for Timon's great and rich banquet; and secondly, it shows his prodigality and unwise magnanimity in inviting guests without discrimination.

3. *Romeo and Juliet* (I, iv and I, v)

The Old Capulate has arranged a banquet with a masque. Romeo, Mercutio and Benvolio are ready on the street to participate in that banquet, uninvited and disguising themselves with masks, for Romeo must see his lady-love Rosaline who is invited there. The stage direction at the beginning of the fourth scene of the first act runs thus: "*Enter* Romeo, Mercutio, Benvolio, with five or six Maskers; Torch-bearers." The three conversing among themselves about their doings in the masque. Benvolio says that there will be no "without-book prologue" (the prologue of a masque, without a text, is so-called) and no Cupid "hoodwink'd with a scarf,/ Bearing a Tartar's painted bow of lath,/ Scaring the ladies like a crow-keeper;..." Mercutio wants Romeo to dance, but he will not, for he has "a soul of lead". Benvolio knows that the Old Capulate has invited one and all around, and so he asks everybody to enter the banquet hall without hesitation, and begin to dance:

Benvolio. Come, knock, and enter; and no sooner in
But every man betake him to his legs.

Benvolio commands: "Strike, drum." And they move towards Capulate's house.

In the immediately following scene (I, v), we see the "Maskers", invited by the Old Capulate, ready for the masque. Banquet over, servants clear the tables. Then "*Enter* Capulate, *with all the* Guests *and* Gentlewomen *to the Maskers*."

Capulate. Welcome, gentlemen! Ladies that have their toes
Unplagued with corns will have a bout with you.
Ah ha, my mistress! Which of you all
Will now deny to dance?
....
You are welcome, gentlemen. Come, musicians, play.
A hall, a hall! Give room; and foot it, girls.
[*Music plays, and they dance.*]

4. *Love's Labour's Lost* (V, ii, 120-65)

This is a peculiar play that has all the elements of a masque—masks, prologue, music, dance, dialogues, and pairing of men and women—all programmed but the masque is not actually performed. Boyet tells the Princess of France that Ferdinand, the King of Navarre, along with his Lords, all masked and in Russian guises, will meet her, with music by blackamoors. The Princess construes it as a plot, and she devises a counter-plot: she and her women, too, will be in masks so that the King and the Lords cannot find their several true ladies of choice.

Princess. ....
There's no such sport as sport by sport o'erthrown,
To make theirs ours, and ours none but our own;
So shall we stay, mocking intended game,
And they well mock'd depart away with shame.
[*Trumpet sounds within.*]

Boyet. The trumpet sounds; be mask'd; the maskers come.
[*The Ladies mask.*]

Enter Blackamoors *with music.* Moth *as Prologue, the* King *with his* Lords *as maskers, in the guise of Russians.*

There is a reason behind the Princess' declining the King's proposal of a masque with her and her entourage. The King (Ferdinand), Berowne, Longaville and Dumaine had vowed to lead the life of celibacy for three years and so when the Princess arrived in Navarre along with her ladies, the King ordered them to keep themselves one mile away from the court. This order hurt the sentiment of the Princess and the ladies so much that they decided to fail the King's proposal of a masque. In spite of their vows, the four celibates fell in love with four of the travelling ladies, viewing them from afar, the King falling in love of the Princess. But as the King plotted to meet the party of the Princess, so the hurt Princess counter plotted to fail the King's design. Both the parties were in masks, and, as plotted by the Princess, the known right pairings were disrupted and a medley followed. Now, as the dancing was declined by the Princess, the King proposed chatting in pairs—in random pairs: the King with Rosaline, Dumaine with Maria, Longaville with Katherine, and Berowne with the Princess. Accordingly, the four pairs mutually conversed, apart from each other. At the end, the King thanked the Princess and her ladies, and the King, the lords, and Blackamoors departed. And then the Princess thanked the King and Lords ridiculously.

King. Farewell, mad wenches; you have simple wits.
[*Exeunt King, Lords, Blackamoors.*]

Princess. Twenty adieus, my frozen Muscovits.

This (failed) masque provides interesting comic climax of the play. Like most other masques of Shakespeare, this one is absolutely integral, organic to the plot.

5. *Henry VIII* (I, iv, 57-108):

The masque in this play happens to be at the end of the first act. Like in *Love's Labour's Lost*, this masque is integral to the structure of the plot of the play, and here lies its dramatic importance. The simple episodic plot of the play hinges on the conflict between Cardinal Wolsey and Henry VIII. Henry, with his fiery passion for Anne Bullen, is desperate to marry her, divorcing Katherine, the present Queen, and Wolsey opposes it tooth and nail. The fourth scene of the first act is the episode where Henry's impassioned love of Anne is exposed, giving momentum to the whole play. And Henry's secret love is revealed through the masque of this scene.

Cardinal Wolsey has arranged a banquet in which a masque will be presented. Guests from the Kingdom and also from France have arrived. Wolsey welcomes all. Then—

> *Hautboys. Enter the* King, *and* Others, *as maskers, habited like shepherds, usher'd by the* Lord Chamberlain. *They pass directly before the Cardinal, and gracefully salute him.*

Wolsey enquires of Lord Chamberlain: "A noble company! What are their pleasures?" Chamberlain tells him that the guests to-night "under your fair conduct,/ Crave leave to view these ladies and entreat/ An hour of revels with 'em." The gentlemen choose their ladies. The King chooses Anne Bullen and tells her:

King. The fairest hand I ever touch'd!
O beauty,
Till now I never knew thee!

Music plays and all, including the King, are in masks and dance. The masque over, King Henry VIII, asks the Chamberlain: about the lady with whom he danced: "What fair lady's that?" The Chamberlain replies: "An't please your Grace, Sir Thomas Bullen's daughter—."

6. *The Tempest* (IV, i, 39-142)

Prospero gives Miranda in marriage to Ferdinand—"take my daughter." But before Ferdinand breaks her "virgin-knot", Prospero is going to celebrate the wedding with his "another trick"—a masque:

Prospero ....
for I must
Bestow upon the eyes of this young couple
Some vanity of my art; it is my promise,
And they expect it from me.

This "vanity" or empty ostentation of Prospero's "art" is the masque in *The Tempest*. Prospero himself illustrates the "vanity" or empty ostentation of the masque, after it is presented in his cell, to Ferdinand.

Prospero. You do look, my son, in a mov'd sort,
As if you were dismay'd; be cheerful, sir.
Our revels now are ended. These our actors,
As I foretold you, were all spirits, and
Are melted into air, into thin air;...

The masquers being ostentatiously attired, their presentation seems real but actually it is nothing more than a "baseless fabric" of a "vision".

However, this present masque follows the anti-masque of the earlier banquet scene in which banquet, that Ariel arranged, everything on the tables vanished on the magical order of Prospero, who wanted to punish the wrong-doer Antonio. To enjoy this present masque, Prospero asks Ferdinand to be attentive and silent: "No tongue! All eyes! Be silent." And now soft music is played and the pastoral masque begins. Iris, the rainbow goddess and messenger of the gods, comes down from the skies, and then comes down from there Juno, the Queen of the heaven, in her car. Lastly descends Ceres (Greek Demeter), the goddess of agriculture and horticulture.

Iris then calls the Naiads to come and celebrate the marriage of Ferdinand and Miranda:

> You nymphs, call'd Naiads, of the wind, ring brooks,
> With your sedg'd crowns and harmless looks,
> Leave your crisp channels, and on this green land
> Answer your summons.

Iris now calls up the sicklemen or reapers to come and mingle with the nymphs:

> You sun-burnt sicklemen, of August weary,
> Come hither from the furrow, and be merry;
> Make holiday; your rye-straw-hats put on,
> And these fresh nymphs encounter every one,
> In country footing [dancing].

Accordingly, certain reapers, in their appropriate dress, approach and mingle with the nymphs, and present a "*graceful dance*" with them. Before the dance or the masque is nearly over, Prospero involuntarily recalls that Caliban and his followers had attempted to kill him, and suddenly becomes anguished at the grave ingratitude of the half-beast Caliban. Swiftly he thanks the dancers and orders them to stop. Unlike the masque of *Love's Labour's Lost,* this present masque of *The Tempest* is fully actualized.

As told earlier, there are two plays of Shakespeare where there are no masques performed but there are obvious references to masque: *The Merchant of Venice* and *The Taming of the Shrew*. In the fifth scene of the second Act of *The Merchant of Venice*, Shylock, the Jew, warns his daughter Jessica not to open the window to see the vulgar Christian procession of masque going along the high road.

> *Shylock.* What, are there masques? Hear you me, Jessica:
> Lock up my doors, and when you hear the drum,
> And the vile squealing of the wry-neck'd fife,
> Clamber not you up to the casements then,

Nor thrust your head into the public street
To gaze on Christian fools with varnish'd faces;
But stop my house's ears—I mean my casements;
Let not the sound of shallow fopp'ry enter
My sober house. By Jacob's staff, I swear I
have no mind of feasting forth to-night
But I will go.

In the very next scene (II, vi), we hear that masquers have arrived before Shylock's house, understandably for the performance of a masque in the dinner thrown by Bassanio, who will soon sail abroad. Gratiano and Salerio take out Jessica, who is in boy's clothes, from Shylock's house so she can participate in that performance where Lorenzo will be present. It is nine o'clock at night and so lest Bassanio is late for the board, Antonio *cancels the masque*—

Fie, fie, Gratiano, where are all the rest?
'Tis nine o'clock; our friends all stay for you;
No masque to-night; the wind is come about;
Bassanio presently will go aboard;
I have sent twenty out to seek for you.

In the fifth scene of the second act of *The Merchant of Venice*, Shylock's stern warning against Jessica's looking at the passing masque—quoted above—is a graphic portrayal of the hatred Shylock nurses in his heart against the Christians. In the immediately next scene, Antonio stops the masque because Bassanio is in a hurry to set sail for the wind is blowing. In the sixth scene of the second act, the masquers have arrived but the masque is not performed. Here Shakespeare has very cunningly presented a spectacle on the stage with the help of the dressed-up masquers.

In *The Taming of the Shrew*, Petruchio has married the Amazonian Katherina, the Shrew, and taken her away to his country house to tame her by denying her food, sleep, and even clothes and caps of her choice, calling them trash. In the third scene of the fourth act of the play, a haberdasher has brought a cap of her choice but Petruchio pooh-poohs the cap off and the haberdasher departs. Immediately before the haberdasher, a tailor had came with a gown which was to the choice of Katherina, but in order to deprive her of clothes, Petruchio that time also sniggered at the gown. He compares the gaudy gown with the clothes of *masquers* and means to say that *masquers' attires are* humorous, sarcastic. Petruchio tells Katherina:

> Thy gown? Why, ay, Come tailor, let us see't.
> O merry, God! What masquing stuff is here?

As we have seen, Shakespeare has used the masque in a variety of ways, and in most cases his masquerades are perceptibly embedded in the plays, and sometimes incognito. He has also used a whole play as a semblance of masque. *A Midsummer Night's Dream* is such a masque-like play. *The Wordsworth Dictionary of Shakespeare* says about this masque-like play: "Like many masques, this comedy presents a world of magic and metamorphosis in brilliant spectacles involving picturesque supernatural beings. It also makes much use of music and dance, and its finale is itself masque-like. It is given over to celebration, with further dancing and a comical performance (*Pyramus and Thisbe*) similar to an anti-masque—the realistic farce that was commonly part of a masque itself. Like a masque again, Acts I to IV are very symmetrically plotted, moving from the court of Theseus to the woods and back again.... There are internal symmetries also. For example, two songs are used—one to put Titania to sleep in II, ii, and the other to wake her in III, i—and Quince and his cast appear four times, twice on either side of Bottom's adventure" (Boyce, 1996, 434).

The anti-masque, as we have said is a contradiction of the masque in that the masque is orderly or harmonious while the anti-masque is disorderly, and while the masque ends in peace or happiness, the anti-masque ends in discord or sadness. However, as we have seen a while ago, the celebration of the wedding of Theseus and Hippolyta in the lone scene of the fifth act of *A Midsummer Night's Dream*, will be done with a performance of the play "Pyramus and Thisby", a play that is, as Theseus tells us, a "very tragical mirth". In this sense, the play "Pyramus and Thisby" is an anti-masque.

But how is this very fantastical play "Pyramus and Thisby" a "very tragical mirth"? Philostrate, Theseus' Master of the Revels, explains to Theseus:

> A play there is, my lord, some ten words long,
> Which is brief as I have known a play:
> But by ten words, my lord, it is too long,
> Which makes it tedious; for in all the play
> There is not one word apt, one player fitted.
> And tragical, my noble lord, it is:
> For Pyramus therein doth kill himself.
> Which when I saw rehears'd, I must confess,
> Made mine eyes water; but more merry tears
> The passion of loud laughter never shed.

Such comic, silly, risible effect upon the audience is a major feature of the anti-masque, a sort of farcical tragedy that evokes loud laughter and "merry tears".

Let us see a bit closely the play "Pyramus and Thisby" which is the anti-masque in *A Midsummer Night's Dream*.

Quince, the carpenter, speaks the Prologue, in which he tells that the play (the anti-masque or the play-within-play) is a (humorous) tragedy, and then introduces the *dramatis personae*: Pyramus and Thisby (the lovers), Wall (Snout, a tinker, holding up his finger), Moonshine (Snug, a joiner, holding a 'lanthorn', i.e. lantern, and a dog) and a Lion (a man dressed like a lion). The Prologue then briefly narrates the story of the play.

> *if you will know,*
> *By moonshine did these lovers think no scorn*
> *To meet at Ninus' tomb, there, there to woo.*
> *This grisly beast, which Lion hight by name,*
> *The trusty Thisby, coming first by night,*
> *Did scare away, or rather did affright;*
> *And as she fled, her mantle she did fall;*
> *Which Lion vile with bloody mouth did stain.*
> *Anon comes Pyramus, sweet youth and tall;*
> *And finds his trusty Thisby's mantle slain;*

Whereat with blade, with bloody blameful blade,
He bravely broach'd his boiling bloody breast;
And Thisby, tarrying in mulberry shade,
His dagger drew, and died.

Quince's Prologue over, the players begin the play. Pyramus and Thisby mutually profess their love to each other—

Pyramus. *Not Shafalus to Procrus, was so true.*
Thisby. *As Shafalus to Procrus, I to you.*

[Shafalus is a miscalling of Cephalus, and Procrus is a miscalling of Procris or Procne.]

After this, the play is enacted up to the point where Pyramus kills himself as Quince, the Prologue, narrated. Then Thisby comes out of the "mulberry shade", grieves of Pyramus' suicide, and stabs herself and dies. And then, the play "Pyramus and Thisby" being over, Bottom, a weaver, asks Theseus: "Will it please you to see the Epilogue, or to hear a Bergomask dance between two of our company?"

Theseus. No epilogue, I pray you;... But come, your Bergomask; let your epilogue alone.

And then a Bergomask—a peasant country dance—ensues and ends. And Theseus says goodbye to all—

This palpable-gross play hath well beguil'd
The heavy gait of night. Sweet friends, to bed.

A superficial look at this play of "Pyramus and Thisby" may not show it as an anti-masque but a close look will do. For one thing, the play is enacted by "Hard-handed men that work in Athens here" as Philostrate tells Theseus, and the anti-masque is generally done by such people, i.e., people devoid of finery. Secondly, the play is accompanied by music and dance, like the anti-masque, the dance being with heavy gaits, and being a low country dance. Thirdly, the play is a "palpable-gross play" as Theseus tells us, wild to be precise, which is appropriate for an anti-masque. Fourthly, the play is rather a confusion like the anti-masque, for it is, as Theseus says, a "tragical mirth"—a jumble of tragedy and comedy. And lastly, before the enactment of the play of "Pyramus and Thisby", Theseus expected from Philostrate an 'abridgment' (pastime) of a masque, and this play is just that an anti-masque. This anti-masque by its contrariety to masque highlights the masque of sorts that is *A Midsummer Night's Dream*. And here lies the dramatic value of this anti-masque.

The anti-masque of The Tempest is nestled in the third scene of the third act. Prospero has ordered Ariel to arrange a banquet for Alonso, Sebastian, Antonio, Ganzalo, Adrian, Francisco and others in "another part of the island" away from Prospero's Cell. The stage direction says: "*Solemn and strange music; and Prospero on the top, invisible. Enter several strange Shapes, bringing in a banquet; and dance about it with gentle actions of salutations; and inviting the King, &c., to eat, they depart.*" This is a magical or illusory banquet, intended to punish Alonso, Sebastian and Antonio who dethroned Prospero. The strange Shapes bring in the banquet and vanishes strangely. Sebastian is hungry and is not concerned with the strange behaviour of the strange Shapes, but is eager to partake of the feast.

Francisco. They vanish'd strangely.
Sebastian. No matter, since.
They left their viands behind; for we have stomachs.

But sooner than Sebastian and others can partake of the food, strangely enough the banquet vanishes, as we may learn from the following stage direction: "*Thunder and lightning. Enter* Ariel, *like a harpy; claps his wings upon the table; and, with a quaint device, the banquet vanishes*". The bird-like Ariel then explains to the three—Antonio, Sebastian and Alonso—the reason behind the vanishing of the banquet:

Ariel. You are three men of sin, whom Destiny,
That hath to instrument this lower world
And what is in't, the never surfeited sea
Hath caus'd to belch up you; and on this island
Where man doth not inhabit—you 'mongst men
Being most unfit to live. I have made you mad;
....
And a clear life ensuing.

Thus, Ariel tells them that they are "men of sin" (for dethroning the rightful Prospero) and so he has punished them by vanishing the banquet. But he also assures them of "a clear life ensuing" (Alonso's son Ferdinand to marry Miranda, and all that). Then Ariel melts into thunder; soft music is played; those strange Shapes return; and dance with grimaces and mimics; and, lastly departs with the empty dinner table. The stage direction clearly contrives all these: "*He vanishes in thunder; then, to soft music enter the Shapes again, and dance, with mocks and mows, and carrying out the table*".

This episode's being an anti-masque may also be obvious from the above stage direction where it is enjoined that music is to play and the strange Shapes are to return to the stage and dance with "mocks" or mimicry and "mows" or grimaces and then retire very humorously along with the empty dinner table.

Pageant

Pageant is a series of dramatic performances, or a scene of pompous display. In the medieval England, 'pageant' meant a wheeled car or a movable car on the top board of which mystery or morality plays (also called cycle plays) were performed. The car was called "pageant wagon". It had four or six wheels and was drawn by horses. The term "pageant" may have derived from Latin *pagina* meaning 'page', 'slab' or 'board'. The "pageant wagon" used to be paraded around for multiple dramatic performances at various places before the public. In the early modern time, this conception of the pageant changed, and then by pageant was meant gorgeous annual processions of the King or the Queen or of the Lord Mayor of London. *The Oxford Companion to the Theatre* tells us that "A further extension of the medieval meaning [of the term pageant] is found in the pageants, or stationary stages, set up out of doors or inside to welcome royal or distinguished visitors or to celebrate a marriage or an embassy. These were popular in Tudor and Elizabethan times, and on them were enacted entertainments of songs and speeches, with a dramatic interlude, usually allegorical, specially written for the occasion" (Hartnoll, 713). Today, in dramaturgy, the term pageant means any show of strange, gorgeous or pompous spectacle on the stage. It is in this sense that we will use the term pageant here.

And it is also in this sense that Orie Latham Hatcher has used the term pageant in his *A Book for Shakespeare Plays and Pageants*. In this book Hatcher says that he has found pageants in twenty-one (or twenty-two? *vide infra*) out of thirty-seven plays of Shakespeare. We are giving below those twenty-one plays, including their respective scenes where there are pageants (Hatcher, 235-39):

1. *Love's Labour's Lost*: I, i; II, i; IV, i; IV, ii; V (entire).
2. *The Comedy of Errors*: I (entire); II (entire).
3. *The Two Gentlemen of Verona*: I, i; I, ii; II, vii; IV, ii; IV, iv; and II, i; II, iv; IV, iv.
4. *Richard III*: I, ii; I, iv; II, ii; V, iii.
5. *Romeo and Juliet*: I, v; II, i; II, i-ii; II, iii; II, vi; III, v; V (entire).
6. *A Midsummer Night's Dream*: I, i; I, ii; III, i; IV, ii; V (entire).
7. *The Merchant of Venice*: I (entire), III, i; III, ii; IV, i.
8. *I and II Henry IV*:

   I Henry IV: I, iii; II, iv; III, ii; IV, ii.

   II Henry IV: V, i-iii; V, v.
9. *Henry V*: III, iv; V, ii.
10. *The Taming of the Shrew: Induction*; III, i; IV, iii; IV, iv; V, ii.
11. *The Merry Wives of Windsor:* II, i; II, ii; IV, vi; V (entire).
12. *As You Like It*: II, iv; III, ii; III, iii; III, v; V, i; V, iv.
13. *Twelfth Night*: I, v; II, v; III, iv; IV, ii; V, i.
14. *Julius Caesar*: I, i; II, i; III, ii; IV, iii.
15. *Hamlet*: Hamlet, the Ghost, the King and Queen, Polonius;

    Ophelia and Laertes; the players at their first appearance; the grave diggers.

16. *Othello*: I, iii; V, ii.
17. *King Lear*: I, i; II, iv; III, ii; III, iii; IV, vi.
18. *Macbeth*: I, iii; I, v; I, vi; I, vii; II, ii; II, iii; III, i; IV, i; V, i.
19. *Antony and Cleopatra*: III, x; III, ii; III, xii; III, xiii; IV, i (in that order).
20. *The Tempest*: I, ii; III, i; III, ii; IV, i.
21. *The Winter's Tale*: Perdita and Florizel, the old shepherd, two shepherdesses—Mopsa and Dorcas; three carters, three neat herds, three swineherds, Autolycus; many country maidens and youths.

Orie Latham Hatcher, in making his inventory of the pageants in Shakespeare's plays, has overlooked *Henry VIII*, in which play there are three very conspicuous pageants, as revealed in the stage directions in three respective scenes (II, iv; IV, i; and V, v) of the play. In the fourth scene of the second act, King Henry VIII's divorcing of Queen Katherine is going to be ratified in a hall in Blackfriars, where the King, cardinal Wolsey, and several royal dignitaries have assembled. The elaborate stage direction of this scene itself describes the pageant: "*Trumpets, sennet, and cornets. Enter two* Vergers, *with short silver wands; next them, two* Scribes *in the habit of doctors; after them, the* Archbishop of Canterbury *alone; after him, the* Bishop of Lincoln, Ely Rochester, *and* Saint Asaph; *next them with some small distance, follows a* Gentleman *bearing the purse, with the great seal, and a* Cardinal's *hat; then two* Priests, *bearing each a silver cross; then a* Gentleman Usher *bareheaded, accompanied with a* Sergeant-at-Arms *bearing a silver mace; then two* Gentlemen *bearing two great silver pillars; after them, side by side, the two* Cardinals, Wolsey *and* Campeius; *two* Noblemen *with sword and mace. Then enter the* King *and* Queen *and their* Trains. *The King takes place under the cloth of state; the two Cardinals sit under him as judges. The Queen takes place some distance from the King. The Bishops place themselves on each side the court, in manner of a consistory; below them the Scribes. The Lords sit next the*

Bishops. The rest of the Attendants stand in convenient order about the stage."

The next pageant happens to be in the first scene of the fourth act. The scene is in a street in which two Gentlemen meet and witness the celebration of Queen Anne's Coronation. The second Gentleman tells the first Gentleman about the up-coming pageant of the celebration: "In celebration of this day with shows,/ Pageants, and sights of honour." In the performance of the play, the royal Train passes over the stage. Trumpets and hautboys sound.

"The Order of the Coronation

1. *A lively flourish of trumpets.*
2. *Then two Judges.*
3. Lord Chancellor, *with purse and mace before him.*
4. Choristers singing. [*Music.*]
5. Mayor of London, *bearing the mace.*

   Then Garter, *in his coat of arms, and on his head he wore a gilt copper crown.*
6. Marquis Dorset, *bearing a sceptre of gold, on his head a demi-coronal of gold. With him, the* Earl of Surrey, *bearing the rod of silver with the dove, crowned with an earl's coronet. Collars of Esses.*
7. Duke of Suffolk, *in his robe of estate, his coronet on his head, bearing a long white wand, as High Steward. With him, the* Duke of Norfolk, *with the rod of marshalship, a coronet on his head. Collars of Esses.*
8. *A canopy borne by four of the* Cinqueports; *under it the* Queen *in her robe; in her hair richly adorned with pearl, crowned. On each side her, the* Bishop of London *and* Winchester.
9. *The old* Duchess of Norfolk, *in a coronet of gold, wrought with flowers, bearing the Queen's train.*
10. Certain Ladies *or* Countesses, *with plain circlets of gold flower without.*

> [*Exeunt, first passing over the stage in order and state, and then a great flourish of trumpets.*]"

The last pageant, like the first one, is at the beginning of the fifth scene of the fifth act. The occasion of the pageant is the christening of the child Princess Elizabeth of England in the royal palace. The stage direction runs thus:

> "*Enter* Trumpets *sounding; then two Aldermen*, Lord Mayor, Garter, Cranmer, Duke of Norfolk, *with his marshal's staff*, Duke of Suffolk, *two* Noblemen *bearing great standing-bowls for the christening gifts; then four* Noblemen *bearing a canopy, under which the* Duchess of Norfolk, *godmother, bearing the child richly habited in a mantle, etc., train borne by a* Lady; *then follows the* Marchioness Dorset, *the other godmother, and* Ladies. The troop pass once about the stage, and Garter speaks."

Of all the pageants in Shakespeare's plays, these three of *Henry VIII* are the most rich and magisterial, and quite integral to the play. Shakespeare has nowhere used the device of masque in his plays merely for entertainment but also to serve his dramatic purposes.

12
Conspectus and Conclusion

Let us now look at the distribution of Shakespeare's dramatic devices, that we have discussed, in each of his 37 plays in order to see—

1. if there is any pattern in the distributions;
2. if there is any impact of the devices on the popularity (or excellence) of the plays; and
3. if the distributions are linked with the time-line of their compositions.

We will survey, below, the distributions under only nine heads: Song, Dance, Music, Masque, Play-within-play, Spirits (including Witches, Fiends, Visions, Faeries and Satyr), Ghosts (including Apparitions), Dumb Shows, and Clowns (including Fools and Jesters).

1. *The Tempest* (1611-12: Popular)

   Act I: scene i (nil), scene ii (song)

   Act II: scene i (song), scene ii (song)

   Act III: scene i (nil), scene ii (song), scene iii (music, dance)

   Act IV: scene i (spirits, play-within-play, dance, song)

   Act V: scene i (music, song)

   *Song (6), Music (2), Dance (2), Spirits (1) and Play-within-play (1)

2. *The Two Gentlemen of Verona* (1594-95: Unpopular)

   Act I: scene i (clown), scene ii (nil), scene iii (nil)

Act II: scene i (clown), scene ii (nil), scene iii (clown), scene iv (clown), scene v (clown), scene vi (nil), scene vii (nil)

Act III: scene i (clown), scene ii (nil)

Act IV: scene i (clown), scene ii (music, song), scene iii (nil), scene iv (clown)

Act V: scene i (nil), scene ii (nil), scene iii (nil), scene iv (nil)

*Clown (8), Song (1), Music (1)

3. *The Merry Wives of Windsor* (1599: Popular)

Act I: scene i (clown), scene ii (nil), scene iii (clown), scene iv (song)

Act II: scene i (clown), scene ii (clown), scene iii (nil)

Act III: scene i (song), scene ii (nil), scene iii (clown), scene iv (nil), scene v (clown)

Act IV: scene i (nil), scene ii (clown), scene iii (nil), scene iv (nil), scene v (clown), scene vi (nil)

Act V: scene i (nil), scene ii (nil), scene iii (nil), scene iv (spirits), scene v (spirits, song)

*Clown (8), Song (3), Spirit (2)

4. *Measure for Measure* (1603-04: Unpopular)

Act I: scene i (nil), scene ii (clown), scene iii (nil), scene iv (clown)

Act II: scene i (nil), scene ii (clown), scene iii (nil), scene iv (clown)

Act III: scene i (nil), scene ii (clown)

Act IV: scene i (song), scene ii (nil), scene iii (clown), scene iv (nil), scene v (nil), scene vi (nil)

Act V: scene i (clown)

*Clown (7), Song (1)

5. *Comedy of Errors* (1593-94: Popular)

Act I: scene i (nil), scene ii (nil)

Act II: scene i (nil), scene ii (nil)

Act III: scene i (nil), scene ii (nil)

Act IV: scene i (nil), scene ii (nil), scene iii (nil), scene iv (nil)

Act V: scene i (nil)

*No embellishments. The plot itself is risible enough for comedic effect.

6. ***Much Ado About Nothing*** (1598-9: Popular)

   Act I: scene i (nil), scene ii (nil), scene iii (nil)

   Act II: scene i (masque, music, dance), scene ii (nil), scene iii (music, song)

   Act III: scene i (nil), scene ii (nil), scene iii (clown), scene iv (nil), scene v (clown)

   Act IV: scene i (nil), scene ii (clown)

   Act V: scene i (clown), scene ii (song), scene iii (music, song), scene iv (masque, music, dance)

   *Clown (4), Music (4), Song (3), Masque (2), Dance (2)

7. ***Love's Labour's Lost*** (1594-5: Unpopular)

   Act I: scene i (clown), scene ii (nil)

   Act II: scene i (nil)

   Act III: scene i (song, clown)

   Act IV: scene i (clown, song), scene ii (clown), scene iii (nil)

   Act V: scene i (clown), scene ii (masque, clown, play-within-play)

   *Clown (5), Song (2), Masque (1), Play-within-play (1)

8. ***A Midsummer Night's Dream*** (1595-6: Popular)

   Act I: scene i (nil), scene ii (clown)

   Act II: scene i (nil), scene ii (song)

   Act III: scene i (clown, song), scene ii (nil)

   Act IV: scene i (spirit, music), scene ii (clown)

   Act V: scene i (play-within-play, spirit, song, dance)

*Clown (3), Song (3), Spirit (2), Music (1), Dance (1), Play-within-play (1)

9. *The Merchant of Venice* (1596-7: Popular)

Act I: scene i (nil), scene ii (nil), scene iii (nil)

Act II: scene i (nil), scene ii (clown), scene iii (clown), scene iv (nil), scene v (clown), scene vi (nil), scene vii (nil), scene viii (nil), scene ix (nil)

Act III: scene i (nil), scene ii (music, song), scene iii (nil), scene iv (nil), scene v (clown)

Act IV: scene i (nil), scene ii (nil)

Act V: scene i (clown, music)

*Clown (5), Music (2), Song (1)

10. *As You Like It* (1599-1600: Popular)

Act I: scene i (nil), scene ii (clown), scene iii (nil)

Act II: scene i (nil), scene ii (nil), scene iii (nil), scene iv (clown), scene v (song, clown, song, song), scene vi (nil), scene vii (clown, music, song)

Act III: scene i (nil), scene ii (clown), scene iii (clown), scene iv (nil), scene v (nil)

Act IV: scene i (clown), scene ii (clown, song), scene iii (nil)

Act V: scene i (clown), scene ii (nil), scene iii (clown, song), scene iv (clown, song, clown, dance)

*Clown (12), Song (7), Music (1), Dance (1)

11. *The Taming of the Shrew* (1593-4: Popular)

Induction: scene i (nil), scene ii (nil)

Act I: scene i (nil), scene ii (nil)

Act II: scene i (nil)

Act III: scene i (nil), scene ii (music)

Act IV: scene i (song), scene ii (nil), scene iii (nil), scene iv (nil), scene v (nil)

Act V: scene i (nil), scene ii (nil)

*Music (1), Song (1)

12. *All's Well That Ends Well* (1602-3: Unpopular)

    Act I: scene i (nil), scene ii (nil), scene iii (clown, song)

    Act II: scene i (nil), scene ii (clown), scene iii (nil), scene iv (clown), scene v (nil)

    Act III: scene i (nil), scene ii (clown), scene iii (nil), scene iv (nil), scene v (nil), scene vi (nil), scene vii (nil)

    Act IV: scene i (nil), scene ii (nil), scene iii (nil), scene iv (nil), scene v (clown)

    Act V: scene i (nil), scene ii (clown), scene iii (nil)

    *Clown (6), Song (1)

13. *Twelfth Night* (1599-1600: Popular)

    Act I: scene i (music), scene ii (nil), scene iii (nil), scene iv (nil), scene v (clown)

    Act II: scene i (nil), scene ii (nil), scene iii (clown, song, song, song), scene iv (music, song, clown), scene v (nil)

    Act III: scene i (music, clown), scene ii (nil), scene iii (nil), scene iv (nil)

    Act IV: scene i (clown), scene ii (clown, song), scene iii (nil)

    Act V: scene i (clown, song)

    *Clown (7), Song (6), Music (3)

14. *The Winter's Tale* (1610-11: Unpopular)

    Act I: scene i (nil), scene ii (nil)

    Act II: scene i (nil), scene ii (nil), scene iii (nil)

    Act III: scene i (nil) scene ii (nil), scene iii (clown)

    Act IV: scene i (nil), scene ii (nil), scene iii (song, clown, song), scene iv (music, dance, clown, song, song, dance, clown)

    Act V: scene i (nil), scene ii (clown), scene iii (nil)

    *Clown (5), Song (4), Dance (2), Music (1)

15. *King John* (1596-7: Unpopular)

    Act I: scene i (nil)

    Act II: scene i (nil)

Act III: scene i (nil), scene ii (nil), scene iii (nil), scene iv (nil)

Act IV: scene i (nil), scene ii (nil), scene iii (nil)

Act V: scene i (nil), scene ii (nil), scene iii (nil)

*No dramatic embellishments.

16. ***King Richard the Second*** (1595-6: Unpopular)

Act I: scene i (nil), scene ii (nil), scene iii (nil), scene iv (nil)

Act II: scene i (nil), scene ii (nil), scene iii (nil), scene iv (nil)

Act III: scene i (nil), scene ii (nil), scene iii (nil)

Act IV: scene i (nil)

Act V: scene i (nil), scene ii (nil), scene iii (nil), scene iv (nil), scene v (music), scene vi (nil)

*Music (1)

17. ***1 Henry IV*** (1597-8: Popular)

Act I: scene i (nil), scene ii (clown), scene iii (nil)

Act II: scene i (clown), scene ii (clown), scene iii (nil), scene iv (clown)

Act III: scene i (nil), scene ii (nil), scene iii (clown)

Act IV: scene i (nil), scene ii (clown), scene iii (nil), scene iv (nil)

Act V: scene i (clown), scene ii (nil), scene iii (clown), scene iv (clown), scene v (nil)

*Clown (9)

18. ***2 Henry IV*** (1597-8: Unpopular)

Induction: (nil)

Act I: scene i (nil), scene ii (clown), scene iii (nil)

Act II: scene i (clown), scene ii (clown), scene iii (nil), scene iv (clown, song, music)

Act III: scene i (nil), scene ii (clown)

Act IV: scene i (nil), scene ii (nil), scene iii (clown), scene iv (nil), scene v (nil)

Act V: scene i (clown), scene ii (nil), scene iii (clown, song, song), scene iv (nil), scene v (clown)

Epilogue: (dance)

*Clown (9), Song (3), Music (1), Dance (1)

19. *Henry V* (1598-9: Popular)

Prologue: (nil)

Act I: scene i (nil), scene ii (nil)

Act II: Prologue (nil), scene i (clown), scene ii (nil), scene iii (clown), scene iv (nil)

Act III: Prologue (nil), scene i (nil), scene ii (clown), scene iii (nil), scene iv (nil), scene v (nil), scene vi (clown), scene vii (nil)

Act IV: Prologue (nil), scene i (clown), scene ii (nil), scene iii (nil), scene iv (clown), scene v (nil), scene vi (nil), scene vii (nil), scene viii (nil)

Act V: Prologue (nil), scene i (clown), scene ii (nil)

*Clown (7)

20. *1 Henry VI* (1589-90: Unpopular)

Act I: scenes i through v (nil)

Act II: scenes i through v (nil)

Act III: scenes i through iv (nil)

Act IV: scenes i through vii (nil)

Act V: scene i (nil), scene ii (nil), scene iii (spirit), scene iv (nil), scene v (nil)

*Spirit (1)

21. *2 Henry VI* (1590-1: Unpopular)

Act I: scenes i through iii (nil), scene iv (spirit)

Act II: scene i (clown), scene ii through scene iv (nil)
Act III: scene i through scene iii (nil)

Act IV: scene i (nil), scene ii (clown), scene iii (clown), scene iv (nil), scene v (nil), scene vi (clown), scene vii (clown), scene viii (clown), scene ix (nil), scene x (clown)

Act V: scene i (nil), scene ii (nil)

*Clown (7), Spirit (1)

22. *3 Henry VI* (1590-1: Unpopular)

Act I: scenes i through iii (nil)

Act II: scenes i through vi (nil)

Act III: scenes i through iii (nil)

Act IV: scenes i through viii (nil)

Act V: scenes i through vii (nil)

*No dramatic embellishments.

23. *King Richard III* (1592-3: Popular)

Act I: scenes i through iv (nil)

Act II: scenes i through iii (nil)

Act III: scenes i through vii (nil)

Act IV: scenes i through v (nil)

Act V: scene i (nil), scene ii (nil), scene iii (spirit), scene iv (nil), scene v (nil)

*Spirit (1)

24. *King Henry VIII* (1612: Unpopular)

Prologue: (nil)

Act I: scenes i through iii (nil), scene iv (music, dance)

Act II: scenes i through iv (nil)

Act III: scene i (song), scene ii (nil)

Act IV: scene i (music), scene ii (music, spirit, dance, music)

Act V: scenes i through v (nil)

Epilogue: (nil)

*Music (4), Dance (2), Song (1), Spirit (1)

25. *Troilus and Cressida* (1601-1602: Unpopular)

Prologue: (nil)

Act I: scenes i through iii (nil)

Act II: scene i (clown), scene ii (nil), scene iii (clown)

Act III: scene i (music, song), scene ii (nil), scene iii (clown)

Act IV: scenes i through v (nil)

Act V: scene i (clown), scene ii (clown), scene iii (nil), scene iv (clown), scenes v through x (nil)

*Clown (6), Music (1), Song (1)

26. *Coriolanus* (1607-8: Unpopular)

Act I: scenes i through x (nil)

Act II: scenes i through iii (nil)

Act III: scenes i through iii (nil)

Act IV: scenes i through iv (nil), scene v (music), scene vi (nil), scene vii (nil)

Act V: scenes i through vi (nil)

*Music (1)

27. *Titus Andronicus* (1592-3: Unpopular)

Act I: scene i (nil)

Act II: scenes i through iv (nil)

Act III: scene i (nil), scene ii (nil)

Act IV: scene i (nil), scene ii (nil), scene iii (clown), scene iv (clown)

Act V: scenes i through iii (nil)

*Clown (2)

28. *Romeo and Juliet* (1595-6: Popular)

Prologue: (nil)

Act I: scene i (nil), scene ii (clown), scene iii (nil), scene iv (masque), scene v (masque, music, dance)

Act II: Prologue (nil), scenes i through iii (nil), scene iv (song), scene v (nil)

Act III: scenes i through v (nil)

Act IV: scenes i through iii (nil), scene iv (music), scene v (nil)

Act V: scenes i through iii (nil)

*Masque (2), Music (2), Clown (1), Song (1), Dance (1)

29. ***Timon of Athens*** (1604-5: Unpopular)

Act I: scene i (nil), scene ii (music, music, masque, dance)

Act II: scene i (nil), scene ii (clown)

Act III: scenes i through v (nil), scene vi (music)

Act IV: scenes i through iii (nil)

Act V: scenes i through iv (nil)

*Music (3), Clown (1), Masque (1), Dance (1)

30. ***Julius Caesar*** (1599-1600: Popular)

Act I: scene i (nil), scene ii (music), scene iii (nil)

Act II: scenes i through iii (nil)

Act III: scenes i through iii (nil)

Act IV: scene i (nil), scene ii (nil), scene iii (music, song, spirit)

Act V: scenes i through iv (nil), scene v (spirit)

*Music (2), Spirit (2), Song (1)

31. ***Macbeth*** (1605-6: Popular)

Act I: scene i (spirit), scene ii (nil), scene iii (spirit), scene iv through scene vi (nil)

Act II: scenes i through iv (nil)

Act III: scenes i through iii (nil), scene iv (spirit), scene v (spirit)

Act IV: scene i (spirit, music, song, music, spirit, dance), scene ii (nil), scene iii (nil)

Act V: scenes i through viii (nil)

*Spirit (6), Music (2), Song (1), Dance (1)

32. ***Hamlet, Prince of Denmark*** (1600-1: Popular)

Act I: scene i (ghost), scene ii (nil), scene iii (nil), scene iv (ghost), scene v (ghost)

Act II: scene i (nil), scene ii (nil)

Act III: scene i (nil), scene ii (play-within-play, dumb show, music), scene iii (nil), scene iv (ghost)

Act IV: scenes i through iv (nil), scene v (song, song, song, song, song), scene vi (nil), scene vii (nil)

Act V: scene i (clown, song, song, song, song), scene ii (music)

*Song (9), Ghost (4), Music (2), Clown (1), Play-within-Play (1), Dumb Show (1)

33. ***King Lear*** (1605-6: Popular)

Act I: scenes i through iii (nil), scene iv (clown), scene v (clown)

Act II: scenes i through iii (nil), scene iv (clown)

Act III: scene i (nil), scene ii (clown, song), scene iii (nil), scene iv (clown), scene v (nil), scene vi (clown, play-within-play), scene vii (nil)

Act IV: scenes i through vi (nil), scene vii (music)

Act V: scenes i through iii (nil)

*Clown (6), Music (1), Song (1), Play-within-play (1)

34. ***Othello*** (1602-3: Popular)

Act I: scenes i through iii (nil)

Act II: scene i (nil), scene ii (nil), scene iii (song, song)

Act III: scene i (music, clown), scene ii (nil), scene iii (nil), scene iv (clown)

Act IV: scene i (nil), scene ii (nil), scene iii (song, song)
Act V: scene i (nil), scene ii (nil)

*Song (4), Music (1), Clown (2)

35. ***Antony and Cleopatra*** (1606-7: Popular)

Act I: scenes i through v (nil)

Act II: scenes i through iv (nil), scene v (music), scene vi (nil), scene vii (music, music, dance, song)

Act III: scenes i through xiii (nil)

Act IV: scenes i through ii (nil), scene iii (music), scenes iv through xv (nil)

Act V: scene i (nil), scene ii (clown)

*Music (4), Dance (1), Song (1), Clown (1)

36. ***Cymbeline*** (1609-10: Unpopular)

Act I: scenes i through vi (nil)

Act II: scene i (nil), scene ii (nil), scene iii (music, song), scene iv (nil), scene v (nil)

Act III: scenes i through vi (nil)

Act IV: scene i (nil), scene ii (song), scene iii (nil), scene iv (nil)

Act V: scenes i through iii (nil), scene iv (music, ghost), scene v (nil)

*Music (2), Song (2), Ghost (1)

37. ***Pericles, Prince of Tyre*** (1608-9: Unpopular)

Act I: Chorus: (nil)

scenes i through iv (nil)

Act II:

Chorus: (nil) Dumb Show

scenes i through v (nil)

Act III: Chorus: (nil) Dumb Show

scenes i through iv (nil)

Act IV:

Chorus: (nil)

scenes i through iii (nil), scene iv (dumb show)

Act V:

Chorus: (nil)

scene i (song, music, spirit), scene ii (nil)

*Dumb Show (3), Song (1), Music (1), Spirit (1)

Now, first, let us see if there is any pattern in the distribution of the embellishments in the plays of Shakespeare, meaning if certain embellishments occur more, or less, in a particular genre or genres of his plays—tragedy, comedy, history, and romance. But, before that it must be made clear that the counting of frequencies of the embellishments (shown in the parentheses) in each of the plays are not fool proof, owing, sometimes, to their lack of clear contours, or to their amorphousness (it is really hard to quantify Shakespeare). The popularity (P) and unpopularity (UP) indicated above and below are from general opinion.

Tragedy

1. *Coriolanus* (UP): Music (1)
2. *Titus Andronicus* (UP): Clown (2)
3. *Romeo and Juliet* (P): Masque (2), Music (2), Clown (1), Song (1), Dance (1)
4. *Julius Caesar* (P): Music (3), Spirit (2), Song (1)
5. *Macbeth* (P): Spirit (6), Music (2), Song (1), Dance (1)
6. *Hamlet* (P): Song (9), Ghost (4), Music (2), Clown (1), Play-within-Play (1), Dumb Show (1)
7. *Othello* (P): Song (4), Music (1), Clown (1)
8. *Antony and Cleopatra* (P): Music (5), Dance (1), Song (1), Clown (1)
9. *Timon of Athens* (UP): Music (3), Clown (1), Masque (1), Dance (1)
10. *Lear* (P): Clown (5), Music (1), Play-within-Play (1), Song (1)

   *Music (20), Clown (12), Song (18), Masque (3), Dance (4), Spirit (8), Ghost (4), Play-within-Play (2), Dumb Show (1)

   *9 embellishments; total frequency 72; per play average 7.2% approx.

Comedy

1. *Two Gentlemen of Verona* (UP): Clown (8), Song (1), Music (1)
2. *Merry Wives* (P): Clown (8), Song (3), Spirit (2)
3. *Measure for Measure* (UP): Clown (7), Song (1)
4. *Comedy of Errors* (P): No embellishment
5. *Much Ado* (P): Clown (4), Music (4), Song (3), Masque (2), Dance (2)

6. *Love's Labour* (UP): Clown (5), Song (2), Masque (1), Play-within-Play (1)
7. *A Midsummer Night's Dream* (P): Clown (3), Song (3), Spirit (2), Music (1), Dance (1), Play-within-Play (1)
8. *The Merchant of Venice* (P): Clown (5), Music (2), Song (1)
9. *As You Like It* (P): Clown (12), Song (7), Music (1), Dance (1)
10. *Taming of the Shrew* (P): Music (1), Song (1)
11. *All's Well* (UP): Clown (6), Song (1)
12. *Twelfth Night* (P): Clown (7), Song (6), Music (3)
13. *Troilus and Cressida* (UP): Clown (6), Music (1), Song (1)

    *Clown (69), Song (30), Music (14), Spirit (4), Masque (3), Dance (4), Play-within-Play (2)

    *7 embellishments; total frequency 126; per play average 9.7% approx.

History

1. *King John* (UP): No embellishments
2. *Richard II* (UP): Music (1)
3. *1 Henry IV* (P): Clown (9)
4. *2 Henry IV* (UP): Clown (9), Song (3), Music (1)
5. *Henry V* (P): Clown (7)
6. *1 Henry VI* (UP): Spirit (1)
7. *2 Henry VI* (UP): Clown (7), Spirit (1)
8. *3 Henry VI* (UP): No embellishments
9. *Richard III* (P): Spirit (1)
10. *Henry VIII* (UP): Music (4), Dance (2), Song (1), Spirit (1)

    *Clown (32), Music (6), Song (4), Spirit (4), Dance (2)

    *5 embellishments; total frequency 48; per play average 4.8% approx.

Romance

1. *Pericles* (UP): Dumb Show (3), Song (1), Spirit (1)
2. *Cymbeline* (UP): Music (2), Song (2), Ghost (1)
3. *Winter's tale* (UP): Clown (5), Song (4), Dance (2), Music (1)
4. *Tempest* (P): Song (6), Music (2), Dance (2), Spirit (1), Play-within-Play (1)

   *Song (13), Music (5), Clown (5), Spirit (2), Ghost (1), Dance (4), Dumb Show (3), Play-within-Play (1)

   *8 embellishments; total frequency 34; per play average 8.6% approx.

Is there any pattern in the distributions of the embellishments in the four genres of the plays shown above? The answer is very difficult to make, the playwright being Shakespeare. However, we may come across some findings in the distributions, as shown below.

1. Clowning is generously employed in the plays: in 23 plays, out of 37, there are clowning (including foolery and jesting). Of the 13 comedies only 3 are empty of clowning; of the 10 tragedies—and this is to be specially noted—only 2 are vacant of clowning; of the 10 histories 6 are lacking in clowning; and—and this, too, is to be noted—only in one of the 4 romances, there is clowning. Shakespeare's comedies and tragedies are flushed with clowning, and this was the reason that Voltaire disrespectfully once called him a "buffoon" (Ralli, 46).
2. Violating Aristotle's dictum, Shakespeare was bold enough to employ clowning liberally, even in his tragedies, besides the other embellishments.
3. Interestingly, in the cluster of his tragedies Shakespeare has used all the nine embellishments, we are discussing about, while the cluster of comedies is devoid of ghosts and dumb shows, that of the histories lacks in the use of dumb show, masque and play-within-play, and

the cluster of romances is wanting in the use of the masque.

Our second enquiry was: if there is any impact of the embellishments on the popularity or excellence of the plays. This is an enormous question, any answer to which must require true knowledge of the composition and nature of the audience, down the ages, and the inner or native force of the plays.

Shakespeare was both of his age as well as of all ages to follow. He wrote the plays keeping in mind the motley audience before the Elizabethan stage, and he was rewarded enough. From this we may assume that these embellishments went a long way in aiding the plays to achieve an added appeal. But are these embellishments on our modern stage unwelcome baggage? Perhaps no, if the performances are carried out appropriately. Sitting among to-day's audience and watching Shakespeare's plays presented on the modern stage without changing even an iota of their original shapes, we can, with our imagination well appreciate and enjoy them. Those who deny this, deny the immense power of the 'necessary angel', the imagination. Remember we can still enjoy the remote *Ramayana* and *Mahabharata* (recall Peter Brook's 9-hour-long stage presentation of *Mahabharata* in Paris that ran for about 1,400 nights) and *Iliad* and *Odyssey* with all their obsolete trappings and hoary fabrications. This is no hyperbole. Goethe was wonder-struck with the dramatic beauty of Kalidas' (4 A.D.) *Sakuntala* (Production of *Sakuntala* by Grotowsky was simply astounding).

But, there must be a caution: these embellishments are no guarantee that a play will win the applause of the audience, for there are plays of Shakespeare, packed with these embellishments, that failed to do so (see above), and there is *The Comedy of Errors,* that having none of these, has become popular. And, again, being bereft of them all is no guarantee of success, as *King John* and *Henry VI, Part 3* have pathetically demonstrated (see above).

Our last query was: if the distributions of the embellishments are linked anyway with the time-line of the compositions of the plays. Shakespeare's literary life ranged from 1589/90 to 1612, covering around 22 years. To see when, during these 22 years did Shakespeare employ these nine embellishments the most frequently and when the least—when liberally and when sparingly—let us divide the whole time-span of 22 years into five sections or periods: 1589 to 1595; 1596 to 1600; 1601 to 1605; 1606 to 1610; and 1611 to 1612. And then see the distributions of the embellishments in the plays of the particular periods. (For the chronology of the plays here adopted see F.E. Halliday's *A Shakespeare Companion*, Penguin Books, 1969.)

1589/90-1595

1. ***1 Henry VI*** (UP): Spirit (1)
2. ***2 Henry VI*** (UP): Spirit (1), Clown (7)
3. ***3 Henry VI*** (UP): No embellishments
4. ***Taming of the Shrew*** (P): Music (1), Song (1)
5. ***Richard III*** (P): Spirit (1)
6. ***Titus Andronicus*** (UP): Clown (2)
7. ***The Two Gentlemen of Verona*** (UP): Clown (8), Music (1), Song (1)
8. ***Comedy of Errors*** (P): No embellishments
9. ***Love's Labour's Lost*** (UP): Clown (5), Song (2), Masque (1), Play-within-Play (1)
10. ***Richard II*** (UP): Music (1)

    *Spirit (3), Clown (22), Music (3), Song (4), Masque (1), Play-within-Play (1)

    *6 embellishments; total frequency 34, per play average 3.4.

1596-1600

1. ***Merry Wives*** (P): Clown (8), Song (3), Spirit (2)
2. ***Much Ado*** (P): Clown (4), Music (4), Song (3), Masque (2), Dance (2)
3. ***Midsummer Night's Dream*** (P): Clown (3), Song (3), Spirit (2), Music (1), Dance (1), Play-within-Play (1)

4. *The Merchant of Venice* (P): Clown (5), Music (2), Song (1)
5. *As You Like It* (P): Clown (12), Song (7), Music (1), Dance (1)
6. *Twelfth Night* (P): Clown (7), Song (6), Music (3)
7. *King John* (UP): No embellishments
8. *Romeo and Juliet* (P): Masque (2), Music (2), Clown (1), Song (1), Dance (1)
9. *Julius Caesar* (P): Music (3), Spirit (2), Song (1)
10. *Hamlet* (P): Song (9), Ghost (4), Music (2), Clown (1), Play-within-Play (1), Dumb Show (1)
11. *1 Henry IV* (P): Clown (9)
12. *2 Henry IV* (UP): Clown (9), Song (3), Music (1)
13. *Henry V* (P): Clown (7)

    *Clown (66), Song (37), Spirit (6), Music (16), Masque (4), Dance (5), Play-within-Play (2), Ghost (4), Dumb Show (1)

    *9 embellishments; total frequency 141; per play average 10.8% approx.

1601-1605

1. *Measure for Measure* (UP): Clown (7), Song (1)
2. *All's Well That Ends Well* (UP): Clown (6), Song (1)
3. *Troilus and Cressida* (UP): Clown (6), Music (1), Song (1)
4. *Othello* (P): Song (4), Music (1), Clown (1)
5. *Timon of Athens* (UP): Music (3), Clown (1), Masque (1), Dance (1)

    *Clown (21), Song (7), Music (5), Masque (1), Dance (1)

    *5 embellishments; total frequency 35; per play average 7%.

1606-1610

1. *Coriolanus* (UP): Music (1)
2. *Macbeth* (P): Spirit (6), Music (2), Song (1), Dance (1)
3. *Lear* (P): Clown (5), Music (1), Play-within-Play (1), Song (1)
4. *Antony and Cleopatra* (P): Music (5), Dance (1), Song (1), Clown (1)
5. *Pericles* (UP): Dumb Show (3), Song (1), Spirit (1)
6. *Cymbeline* (UP): Music (2), Song (2), Ghost (1)

   *Music (11), Spirit (7), Song (6), Dance (2), Clown (6), Dumb Show (3), Ghost (1), Play-within-Play (1)

   *8 embellishments; total frequency 37; per play average 6.2% approx.

1611-1612

1. *The Winter's Tale* (UP): Clown (5), Song (4), Dance (2), Music (1)
2. *The Tempest* (P): Song (6), Music (2), Dance (2), Spirit (1), Play-within-Play (1)
3. *Henry VIII* (UP): Music (4), Dance (2), Song (1), Spirit (1)

   *Clown (5), Song (11), Dance (6), Music (7), Spirit (2), Play-within-Play (1)

   *6 embellishments; total frequency 32; per play average 10.7% approx.

To repeat, our last question was: whether the distributions of the embellishments are in any way linked with the time-line of the compositions of the plays. Let us see.

1589/90 to 1595

In this period, as we see from the above-mentioned analysis of the distributions of the embellishments, Shakespeare utilized the embellishments the least in his 10 plays (historical 5, comedy 4, tragedy 1), of which only three have been popular: *The Taming of the Shrew* (comedy), *Richard III* (historical), and *Comedy of Errors* (comedy).

1596 to 1600

It was this period when Shakespeare employed the embellishments the most in his 13 plays (comedy 7, historical 4, and tragedy 2) of which 11 were popular and only two have been unpopular: *King John* and 2 *Henry VI* (both historical). This period was Shakespeare's brightest.

1601 to 1605

In this period, Shakespeare moderately resorted to the embellishments in his 5 plays (3 comedies and 2 tragedies) of which only one has become popular: *Othello* (tragedy).

1606 to 1610

Like the immediately preceding period, this one was also not so bright for Shakespeare in terms of the number of popular plays. He turned out 6 plays (4 tragedies and 2 romances) of which only two have proved popular: *Macbeth* and *Lear* (both tragedies). This was also the period when he employed the embellishments rather sparingly.

1611 to 1612

In this last creative period, Shakespeare once again turned to utilizing liberally the dramatic embellishments. He composed only 3 plays in these nearly 2 years. (2 romances and 1 historical play) and of them only one proved to be popular—*The Tempest* which is packed with song and music.

One thing about Shakespeare has perhaps eluded the attention of critics so far and that is that no Elizabethan or Jacobean dramatist, other than Shakespeare, employed so much dramatic embellishments in his plays as did Shakespeare: song, dance, music, masque, play-within-play, spirits, witch, fiend, vision, fairy satyr, ghosts, dumb show, and clown, fool and jester. These are not the only dramatic embellishments that are there in Shakespeare, but we have chosen to deal only with these seventeen.

Why was Shakespeare rather so lavish as to these dramatic devices or embellishments? The answer lies in the nature of the Elizabethan and Jacobean audience or theatre-goers that was a medley of the social high-ups and the lumpen work-force or the outcastes, and those between. Some from around the court—the lords and ladies—would go to the theatre mostly to show their taste or to display themselves, some down below would go to the theatre chiefly to refresh themselves in the altered ambience, casually attending to a turn of the play, and the party of nuisance would complement themselves if they could make some disruptions with cat-calls, hollering or jeering. We may imagine the bizarre complexion of the audience from what Margaret Jane Kidnie wrote in her essay "Shakespeare's Audience": "Gosson claims in *The School of Abuse* that in the theatre 'you shall see such heaving and shoving, such itching, such winking, and such manning them home when the sports are ended that it is a right comedy to mark behaviour'...." The author of *A Second and Third Blast of Retreat from Plays and Theatres* (1580), probably Anthony Munday, asserts that 'harlots' who are past all shame make themselves at the playhouses the object of men's eyes. If we are to believe this author, sexual intercourse actually took place during performance [of plays]" (Wells, 38). And Hamlet's carping quip at Polonius briefly but boldly suggests the same thing about Shakespeare's audience: "He's for a jig, or a tale of bawdry, or he sleeps" (*Hamlet*, III, ii, 495). Of course, there certainly were in the audience souls refined, however small their number be, otherwise plays by none other than Shakespeare with high poetry and theatrical brilliance would not endure.

However, how to draw the attention of such an assembly of Polonius-like people to the goings-on on the stage? This is not a silly question, and this is not a question obsolete to-day. For if the dramatist fail here, the very play will abort. Granville-Barker here has a counsel to offer not to the dramaturg but to the audience as a whole: "Leave your armchair throne of judgment, says Granville-barker, submit for the while to be tossed to and fro in the action of the play: drama's first aim is to subdue us" (Styan, 5). The Theatre will *subdue* us? Yes, but how? The audience, or for that matter we, will not willingly hold our disbelief in suspension unless we are *subdued*. But how to *subdue* us, the audience? This is a crucial point in the theatre.

In our time, there are at least three contrivances for that: one, "violence", advocated by Antonin Artaud's theatre of cruelty; two, engaging the audience in a "dialectic", maintained by Bertolt Brecht in his theory of epic theatre; and the third, showing the audience, immured in life, the absurdity of it advanced by Thomas Beckett. In each of the three there is a sort of shock with which to whip up the audience's heed to the stage. Artaud said that theatrical performances must first whiff off the thousand bits of fleeting thoughts and moods from the heads of the spectators with images of violence and then tether in their attention to the stage. Take, for instance, Artaud's staging of P.B. Shelley's *Cenci*. The play itself contains themes of violence and murder, but Artaud accentuated the violence to a higher degree. For instance, Artaud's stage direction in the very first scene of *Cenci* provides for suggestions of maximum disorder, disturbance and agitation with the help of wind-blown drapes, amplified sounds, figure engaged in orgy, etc. This was apropos of Artaud's concept of the 'theatre of cruelty', whose objective is to wake up the spectators' spirituality by liberating their subconscious from the restrictive ethos. This concept of visual violence Artaud learned from the Balinese dance (which may remind one of the flamenco dances or the whirling dance of certain fakirs or dervishes) performed in 1931 at the Parish Colonial Exposition. The violent Balinese dance, with its dazzling and elaborate costumes and loud rhythms, aims, for one thing, to hold in grip the attention of the aggregate spectators. Artaud was inspired by the magnetic attraction of this dance and learned from it that the attention of the audience has to be per force summoned to the stage for successful theatrical effect. Vsevolod Meyerhold and Eugenio Barba followed in the footsteps of Artaud; Samuel Beckett got the same necessary effect producing absurdity on the stage as did Alfred Jarry with his pataphysical extreme absurdity.

That image of violence is a prime (but not only) means of capturing the focus of the audience's attention was not unknown to the playwrights of the Elizabethan era. Kyd's *Spanish Tragedy* and Shakespeare's *Titus Andronicus* are, for instance, drenched with blood so. But there are some other attention-drawing theatrical devices than violence: spectacles, emotion-charged harangues, critical plots, sudden turn in the course of an action, etc. Shakespeare has all these in his plays, but he has much more in them: music, dance, clowning, song, dream, supernatural beings, etc. Why? Unlike his contemporary playwrights who were after the perfection of their dramatic art, while almost oblivious of the audiences, Shakespeare was, as Johnson wrote in his *Preface to Shakespeare*, "so much careful to please" his audience for material success, and so added embellishments all the more. But the additions do not, and will never, devalue his dramatic oeuvres for they are inalienably integrated with their spirit and vitality.

References

Aristotle, *The Poetics of Aristotle*, translated by S.H. Butcher, [downloaded from Project Gutenberg], 2013.

Baker, George Pierce, *Dramatic Technique*, no date, The Riverside Press, Cambridge, Massachusetts, USA. [downloaded from Project Gutenberg]

Boas, Frederick S., *An Introduction to the Reading of Shakespeare*, 1947, Oxford University Press, Great Britain.

Boyce, Charles, *The Wordsworth Dictionary of Shakespeare*, 1996, Wordsworth Reference, Great Britain (first published in 1990 as *Shakespeare A-Z* by Facts on File, New York).

Bradbrook, M.C., *Themes and Conventions of Elizabethan Tragedy*, 1979, Cambridge University Press and Vikas Students' Edition, Delhi.

Capra, Fritjof, *The Tao of Physics*, 1984, A Bantam New Age Book, Bantam Books, USA and Canada.

Cecil, David, *Hardy, the Novelist: An Essay in Criticism*, 1997 (Indian reprint), Kalyani Publishers, Ludhiana, New Delhi, Calcutta, etc. India.

Comte, Fernand, *The Wordsworth Dictionary of Mythology*, Wordsworth Reference, 1991, Edinburgh.

Cook, Nicholas, *Music: A Very Short Introduction*, 2000, Oxford Univ. Press, Oxford, New York.

Cowie, L.W., *The Wordsworth Dictionary of British Social History*, 1973, Wordsworth Reference, London.

Cuddon, J.A., *The Penguin Dictionary of Literary Terms and Literary Theory*, 1999, Penguin Books, England, USA, New Zealand and Canada.

Cunliffe, Richard John, *A New Shakespearean Dictionary*, 1910, Blackie and Son Ltd, London, Glasgow, Bombay.

Douce, France, *Illustrations of Shakespeare, and Ancient Manners*, 1839, R. Griffin & Co., etc., London. [downloaded from Project Gutenberg]

Dryden, John, *An Essay of Dramatic Poetry*, edited by Thomas Arnold, 1918, Clarendon Press, Oxford.

Eliot, S.T., *The Sacred Wood; Essays on Poetry and Criticism*, 1920, Melhuen & Co., London.

Eysenck, H.J., *et al.* (eds.), *Encyclopedia of Psychology*, 1975, Fontana/Collins, Great Britain.

Fox, Levi, *The Shakespeare Handbook*, 1987, Mobius International, London.

Fripp, Edgar I., *Shakespeare: Man and Artist*, Vol. I, 1964, Oxford University Press, London, New York, Toronto.

Goad, Harold, *Language in History*, 1958, Penguin Books, Great Britain and Australia.

Gwynn, Stephen, *The Masters of English Literature*, Indian reprint 1989, Surjeet Publications, Delhi.

Halliday, F.E., *A Shakespeare Companion*, 1964, Penguin Books, England.

Hamilton, Edith and Cairns, Huntington, *The Collected Dialogues of Plato*, 1973, Princeton University Press, USA (New Jersey).

Hartnoll, Phyllis (ed.), *The Oxford Companion to the Theatre*, 1972, Oxford University Press, London.

Hatcher, Orie Latham, *A Book for Shakespeare's Plays and Pageants*, 1916, E.P. Dutton & Company, New York.

Knight, Charles, *William Shakespeare: A Biography*, Originally published in 1860, published by Forgotten Books in 2013.

Knight, G. Wilson, *The Crown of Life*, 1969, Methuen & Co., London.

Long, John H., *Shakespeare's Use of Music*, 1955, Univ. of Florida Press, Gainesville, Florida.

McArthur, Tom (ed.), *The Oxford Companion to the English Language*, 1992, Oxford University Press, Oxford and New York.

Mobley, Jonnie Patricia, *NTC's Dictionary of Theatre and Drama Terms*, 1998, National Textbook Company (NTC), Daryaganj, New Delhi-110 002.

Moncur-Sime, A.H., *Shakespeare: His Music and Song*, 1936, Kegan Paul, Trench, Truber & Co., Great Britain.

Nataf, Andre, *The Wordsworth Dictionary of the Occult*, 1994, Wordsworth Editions Ltd., Hertfordshire, England.

Naylor, Edward W., *Shakespeare and Music*, 1896, J.M. Dent, London.

Nicoll, Allardyce, *World Drama: From Aeschylus to Anouilh*, 1952, George G. Harrap & Co., London.

Potter, Simeon, *Language in the Modern World*, 1966, A Pelican Book, England.

Preminger, Alex (ed.), *Princeton Encyclopedia of Poetry*, 1975, The Macmillan Press, Ltd., USA.

Progress Publishers, Moscow, *Shakespeare in the Soviet Union: A Collection of Essays*, Complied by Roman Samarin and Alexander Nikolyukin, translated from the Russian by Avril Pyman, 1966.

Raleigh, Walter, *Shakespeare*, 1953, MacMillan & Co., London.

Ralli, Augustus, *A History of Shakespeare Criticism*, Vol. I, 1965, The Humanities Press, New York, p. 46.

Russian Academy of Sciences, *26th Shakespeare Readings 2016: 400 Years of Immortality*, Paper Abstracts, 2016, Moscow.

Sarker, Sunil Kumar, *T.S. Eliot: Poetry, Plays and Prose*, 1995, Atlantic Publishers, New Delhi.

Smith, Nichol (ed.), *Eighteenth Century Essays on Shakespeare*, 1903, James MacLehose and Sons [uploaded by Guntenberg Project in 2009].

Smith, Sir William, *A Smaller Dictionary of the Bible*, 1927, John Murray, Albemarle Street, W., London.

Speaight, George, *The History of the English Puppet Theatre*, 1853, John de Graff, New York.

Spencer, T.J.B., *Shakespeare: A Celebration*, 1964, Penguin Books, Great Britain.

Stephenson, Henry Thew, *The Elizabethan People*, 1912, Henry Holt and Company, New York.

Stern, J.P., *Nietzsche*, 1981, Fontana/Collins, Great Britain.

Styan, J.L., *The Elements of Drama*, 1979 (First Cambridge University Press 1960), CUP-Vikas Publishing House, New Delhi, Bombay, Calcutta.

Taylor, John Russell, *The Penguin Dictionary of the Theatre*, 1966, Penguin Books, England, Australia, USA.

Thiselton-Dyer, Rev. T.F., *Folk-Lore of Shakespeare*, 1884, Harper & Brothers, Franklin Square, New York.

Tylor, E.B., *Dictionary of Anthropology*, 1988 (Indian edition), Goyal Saab, New Delhi.

Warde, Frederick, *The Fools of Shakespeare*, 1913, McBride, Nast & Company, New York.

Wells, Stanley and Orlin, Lena Cowen, *Shakespeare: An Oxford Guide*, first Indian edition 2007, Oxford University Press, New Delhi.

Index